Christian Kühn

Capital Structure Decisions in Institutional Buyouts

GABLER EDITION WISSENSCHAFT

Entrepreneurship

Herausgegeben von
Professor Dr. Malte Brettel, RWTH Aachen,
Professor Dr. Lambert T. Koch, Universität Wuppertal,
Professor Dr. Tobias Kollmann, Universität Duisburg-Essen,
Campus Essen,
Professor Dr. Peter Witt, Wissenschaftliche Hochschule für
Unternehmensführung (WHU), Vallendar

„Entrepreneurship" ist ein noch relativ junger Forschungszweig, der jedoch in Wissenschaft und Praxis stetig an Bedeutung gewinnt. Denn Unternehmensgründungen und deren Promotoren nehmen für die wirtschaftliche Entwicklung einen zentralen Stellenwert ein, so dass es nur folgerichtig ist, dem auch in Forschung und Lehre Rechnung zu tragen.

Die Schriftenreihe bietet ein Forum für wissenschaftliche Beiträge zur Entrepreneurship-Thematik. Ziel ist der Transfer von aktuellen Forschungsergebnissen und deren Diskussion aus der Wissenschaft in die Unternehmenspraxis.

Christian Kühn

Capital Structure Decisions in Institutional Buyouts

With a foreword by Prof. Dr. Malte Brettel

Deutscher Universitäts-Verlag

Bibliografische Information Der Deutschen Bibliothek
Die Deutsche Bibliothek verzeichnet diese Publikation in der Deutschen Nationalbibliografie; detaillierte bibliografische Daten sind im Internet über <http://dnb.ddb.de> abrufbar.

Dissertation RWTH Aachen, 2005

1. Auflage Februar 2006

Lektorat: Brigitte Siegel / Nicole Schweitzer

Der Deutsche Universitäts-Verlag ist ein Unternehmen von Springer Science+Business Media.
www.duv.de

Umschlaggestaltung: Regine Zimmer, Dipl.-Designerin, Frankfurt/Main
Druck und Buchbinder: Rosch-Buch, Scheßlitz
Gedruckt auf säurefreiem und chlorfrei gebleichtem Papier

ISBN 978-3-8350-0229-6

Foreword

Years before private equity and buyouts became subject to political discussions, academics covered that type M&A transaction already in the 1980s and 90s. Prominent examples like the takeover of Dynamit Nobel, Celanese or Pro7Sat1 have triggered controversial debates on the economic impact of buyouts. However, finance scholars have realised quite early that the structure and financing of buyouts impose efficiency gains. Beyond operational levers the financial structure has a substantial impact on the return on investment as well as the likelihood of a deal's failure. However, while theory pinpoints a clear understanding how buyouts function, empirical research has hardly delivered satisfactory answers.

Given the large body of empirical studies covering "usual" corporate finance decisions the fairly small number of empirical buyout financing study is surprising. More importantly, the few existing studies lack homogenous samples and a stringent theoretical framework. Therefore, the results published to date appear to be somewhat muddied and too focussed on specific aspects such as the agency cost of free cash flow.

The present thesis by Christian Kühn attempts to overcome these deficits. It analyzes whether the financial structuring follows theoretical patterns addressed in other corporate finance studies. Given the specific nature with substantial capital market frictions, one would assume established patterns to show up more powerfully than in earlier empirical studies. To fully grasp these patterns, he investigated a homogenous group of almost 100 institutional buyouts carried out in Europe over the last seven years by means of multinomial logistic regressions. The results are highly robust and provide a basis for interesting conclusions.

With his thesis, Christian Kühn makes a valuable research contribution to both buyout and corporate finance literature. The analysis not only helps to better understand an economically important and controversially debated type of transaction but also allows challenging corporate finance theories within an extreme setting. In this context, it treats aspects that have not been fully addressed hitherto.

The thesis draws its special value for the reader from the author's ability to work theoretically well founded on the basis of excellent empirical data. Researchers benefit from the theoretical implications for the agency and trade-off theory. Practitioners can capitalize on the identified financing mechanism as regards a financial structure's appropriateness for a specific deal.

I wish that this thesis attracts the broad readership that it deserves.

Prof. Dr. Malte Brettel

Acknowledgement

This dissertation would not have been possible without the help of many people to whom I wish to extend my gratitude.

First, I am greatly indebted to Professor Dr. Malte Brettel, my thesis advisor. He has helped form my thinking in fundamental ways, and I would have not completed this thesis without his support. I also owe much gratitude to Professor Dr. Wolfgang Breuer, my second thesis advisor, for comments on corporate finance issues that have substantially improved the dissertation.

I would like to thank L.E.K. Consulting for financial support during my doctoral studies, and in particular Dr. Paul M. Jowett who provided me with valuable contacts in the European buyout industry. I owe much gratitude to my interview partners from various buyout firms and acquisition finance banks. Their input helped substantially to structure my ideas and reflect the practitioner's perspective.

Moreover, I would like to thank a considerable number of fellow doctoral students, colleagues and friends, especially Nils Hoffmann and Jörg Reichert. They were not only open for valuable discussions but also made my doctoral studies a highly enjoyable time.

In addition, I am very grateful to my partner Inna Krohmer, whose love and comprehension was an essential requisite for the successful completion of such an endeavour. Finally, but very important, I am greatly indebted to my parents for endowing me with the right values and education, and for supporting me in everything I did. Their backing has always been the basis for my development. Therefore, I dedicate this dissertation to them.

Christian Kühn

Table of contents

List of abbreviations

a.M. .... am Main

APV.................................. Adjusted Present Value

BIMBO.............................. Buy-in Management Buyout

bn...................................... billion

bps .... basis points

BFuP.................................. Betriebswirtschaftliche Forschung und Praxis

BörsG .... Börsengesetz

CAGR................................ Compound annual growth rate

CMBOR .... Centre for Management Buy-Out Research

Co. .... Company

COC .... Controller of the Currency

c.p. .... ceteris paribus

DBW .... Die Betriebswirtschaft

DC .... Debt Capital

DCF .... Discounted Cash Flow

DD .... Due Diligence

Dipl-Kfm. .... Diplom-Kaufmann

Diss.................................. Dissertation

Dr. .... Doktor

Dt...................................... Deutsche(r)

EBIT .... Earnings before interest and taxes

EBITDA .... Earnings before interest, taxes, depreciation, and amortization

EBITDAC .... Earnings before interest, taxes, depreciation, amortization, and after capex

EBO.................................. Employee Buyout

EC..................................... Equity Capital

Ed. .... Editor

Eds.................................... Editors

e.g. .... exempli gratia

et al. .... et alii

etc. .... et cetera

EU .... European Union

EURIBOR .... Euro Interbank Offered Rate

e.V. .... eingetragener Verein

EV .... Entreprise Value

EVCA .... European Venture Capital Association

FCF .... Free Cash Flow

FDIC .... Federal Deposit Insurance Corporation

FN .... Footnote

FU .... Freie Universität

IAS .... International Accounting Standards

IBO .... Institutional Buyout

i.e. .... id est

IFRS .... International Financial Reporting Standards

IPO .... Initial Public Offering

IRR .... Internal Rate of Return

IT .... Information Technology

GAAP .... Generally Accepted Accounting Principles

GBP .... Great Britain Pound

GmbH .... Gesellschaft mit beschränkter Haftung

GmbHG .... GmbH-Gesetz

Habil. .... Habilitation

HGB .... Handelsgesetzbuch

HLT .... Highly Leveraged Transaction

HoldCo. .... Holding Company

HYB .... High-yield bonds

i.B. .... im Breisgau

KKR .... Kohlberg, Kravis & Roberts

KMU .... Kleine und mittlere Unternehmen

KPMG .... Klynveld Peat Marvick Goerdeler

LBO................................. Leveraged Buyout

LISREL .... Linear structural relations

LL.................................... Loglikelihood

Logit .... Logistic regression

LP .... Limited Partnership

LR.................................... Likelihood Ratio

Ltd. .... Limited

M&A .... Mergers & Acquisitions

MBI .... Management Buyin

MBO................................ Management Buyout

Mio. .... Million

MIT .... Massachusetts Institute of Technology

MM.................................. Modigliani / Miller

MW .... Mann-Whitney

NFL .... Net financial liabilities

NDTS .... Non-debt tax shield

NewCo. .... New Company

NFL .... Net financial liabilities

No.................................... Number

NPV................................. Net Present Value

NVCA .... National Venture Capital Association

OBO .... Owner Buyout

OECD.............................. Organization of Economic Cooperation and Development

OLS .... Ordinary least squares

opt.................................... optimal

p....................................... page

p.a. .... per annum

PE.................................... Private Equity

PIK .... Pay-in-kind

PIYC .... Pay-if-you-can

PLS .... Partial least squares

pp. .... pages

Prof. .... Professor

R&D .... Research & Development

RWTH .... Rheinisch-Westfälische Technische Hochschule

SARL .... Société à responsabilité limitée

SME .... Small- and medium-sized entreprise

SPSS .... Statistical Product and Service Solutions

SPV .... Special-Purpose Vehicle

SSRN .... Social Science Research Network

StÄndG .... Steueränderungsgesetz

Stdev .... Standard deviation

StSenkErgG .... Steuersenkungsergänzungsgesetz

StSenkG .... Steuersenkungsgesetz

StVBG .... Steuerverkürzungsbekämpfungsgesetz

StVerAbG .... Steuervergünstigungsabbaugesetz

UK .... United Kingdom

US .... United States

USD .... United States Dollar

VC .... Venture Capital

VIMBO .... Vendor-initiated management buyout

Vol. .... Volume

vs. .... versus

WACC .... Weighted Average Cost of Capital

WISU .... Das Wirtschaftsstudium

WpHG .... Wertpapierhandelsgesetz

ZfB .... Zeitschrift für Betriebswirtschaft

ZfbF .... Zeitschrift für betriebswirtschaftliche Forschung

List of figures

List of tables

1. Introduction

Within the area of corporate financial management few topics have been as intensely researched as the question of how firms choose their capital structure. Since the seminal work of MODIGLIANI / MILLER (MM)[1] in 1958, a large body of theoretical and empirical literature has pointed to the existence of capital market imperfections and has gradually relaxed the strict preconditions under which MM's irrelevance theorem holds.[2] Substantial progress has been made in understanding how market frictions affect financing patterns, and the picture no longer looks as gloomy as that drawn by MYERS some twenty years ago when he considered the capital structure question to be still unanswered.[3]

However, despite the extensive research of almost five decades, the theory of capital structure remains one of the most controversial issues in modern corporate finance. A surprising lack of consensus even on fundamental issues has prompted researchers to continue to refine and test existing capital structure theories in different settings.[4]

This thesis attempts to add to the research by empirically testing major capital structure theories in the context of institutional buyouts (IBO), a special type of buyout[5] driven by financial investors, who generally take majority shares in established companies. The specific characteristics of IBOs will allow us to examine the robustness of established theories in a context which deviates substantially from most empirical studies hitherto.

1.1. Background

Over the last 30 years, the world buyout market has experienced impressive growth rates reaching a global volume of USD115bn in 2003, a year-on-year increase of 33%.[6] Kohlberg Kravis Roberts (KKR), a private equity (PE) firm that started in 1976, was the pioneer among the professional and

---

[1] Modigliani, F./ Miller, M.H. (1958).

[2] Important milestones in the development of capital structure theories after MM (1958) are Modigliani, F./ Miller, M.H. (1963); Kraus, A/ Litzenberger, R.H. (1973); Jensen, M.C./ Meckling, W.H. (1976); Myers, S.C. (1977); Ross, S.A. (1977); Leland, H.E./ Pyle, D.H. (1977); Myers, S.C. (1984); Myers, S.C./ Majluf, N.S. (1984); Jensen, M.C. (1986); Brander, J.A./ Lewis, T.R. (1986); Stulz, R.M. (1990); Aghion, P./ Bolton (1992); Hart, O./ Moore, J. (1994); Zingales, L. (2000).

[3] Myers, S.C. (1984), p. 575.

[4] Frank, M. Z. / Goyal, V.K. (2003), p. 1.

[5] Buyout transactions are variously labeled in the literature (e.g. leveraged buyouts, management buyouts, management buyins, etc.). In general, this thesis uses the term buyout. However, when a reference is made to buyouts which are subject to our empirical study, the term institutional buyout (IBO) will be applied. See chapter 2.1.1 for the rationale and exact definitions of the terms used.

specialised non-venture private equity investors to acquire companies by means of the buyout concept as we know it today.[7] Until the late 1980s buyout activity soared both in terms of number of transactions and average transaction size, culminating in the USD 25bn buyout of RJR Nabisco by KKR in 1989.[8] However, the collapse of the high-yield debt[9] market triggered by increased pressure from regulators, rating agencies and stock market authorities on banks to reduce their exposure to high-yield debt led to a downturn in buyout activity in the early 90s.[10] Despite the recessionary dip between 2000 and 2002 the global buyout market has continued to grow substantially and averaged annual growth rates of 10.4 per cent between 1998 and 2003.[11] On the European level, only 436 IBOs were registered between 1998 and 2004, a minor share of all buyouts[12] in terms of numbers of transactions. However, in value terms they accounted for 56 per cent of the market in 2003 and have thus become the most important buyout transaction type in Europe.

Figure 1: Number and value of IBOs in Europe (1998-2004)

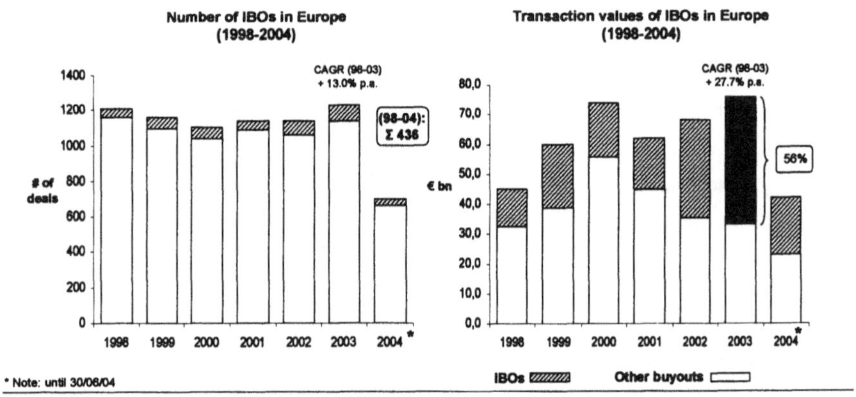

Source: Bureau van Dijk (Zephyr), CMBOR European Management Review 2003, Deloitte & Touche 2003, PriceWaterhouseCoopers 2004.

[6] 3i / PriceWaterhouseCoopers (2003), p. 4.

[7] In the 1960s, "bootstrap" financing, a form of company acquisition similar to the buyout concept emerged, see Baker, G.P./Smith, G.D. (1998), p.1 and Schmid, H. (1994), pp. 49-50. A second similar form in the 1970s was the phenomenon of going-private transactions of small listed companies through a share buyback by the company owners, see Schmid, H. (1994), p. 51.

[8] For detailed information see Michel, A./Shaked, I. (1991).

[9] High-yield debt (or "junk bonds") represents below investment grade debt (see Chapter 4.3.2.2) and fueled the buyout market, making ever larger buyouts feasible. The collapse of the high-yield market brought about the bankruptcy of its front-runner investment bank Drexel Burnham Lambert in 1990.

[10] Jensen, M.C. (1991), pp. 27-29; Kaufman, A./ Englander, E.J. (1993), p. 89.

[11] 3i / PriceWaterhouseCoopers (2004), p. 6.

[12] See chapter 2.1.2.1 for an overview of the different buyout types.

The relevance of buyouts for the transformation and development of economies has led researchers to increasingly shed light on their functioning. Since the mid-80s the financial structure of buyouts has been at the center of interest. Understanding buyout financing patterns is motivated by two aspects. First, the financial structure itself represents a lever for value creation, and second, the specific nature of buyouts makes them a fruitful field of research in which to test established capital structure theories:

1.) The way a buyout is financed has both a direct and indirect impact on the value of the bought-out company and the internal rate of return (IRR)[13] to the equity investors. A range of empirical contributions has pointed to the critical role of the capital structure in creating shareholder value. In a prominent study, for example, LONG / RAVENSCRAFT have identified a significant positive relation between the performance of going-private transactions and their degree of leverage.[14] The various hypotheses as to how the financial structure affects a company's value have already helped us to better understand the buyout phenomenon and LBOs[15] in particular.

JENSEN'S disciplination hypothesis represents a key contribution in this area. He argues that problems related to managerial incentives are reduced in LBOs due to the high proportions of equity held by managers and the disciplinary effect of debt.[16] A second important finance-related source of value creation is the reduction of the corporate tax burden, which is determined by the amount of interest-bearing debt capital. Chapter 3.1 outlines the different theories for how the financial structure affects the value of a company.

In the case of buyouts, value creation through the financial structure relates to the acquisition phase of the transaction, which represents the first of the three phases a deal undergoes.[17] Given that the buyout market has matured with increasing competitive pressure on buyout firms, they have realised the need to focus on other operational and strategic levers beyond financial engineering.[18]

[13] For a definition and critical discussion of the IRR concept, see e.g. Ross, S.A./ Westerfield, R.W./ Jaffee, J.F.(2005), pp. 152-163.
[14] Long, W.F. / Ravenscraft, D.J. (1993a), p.24.
[15] For a definition of LBOs refer to chapter 2.1.1.
[16] Jensen, M.C. (1986). See also 3.4.2.2.
[17] Berg, A. / Gottschalg, O. (2003), pp. 5-6. The other phases are the holding period and the exit phase. These are treated in chapters 2.3.3 and 2.3.4.
[18] Baker, G.P. / Smith, G.D. (1998), pp. 2-3; Wright. M., et al. (2000), p. 15.

Accordingly, over the last few years non-financial value drivers, particularly from the holding period, have attracted the attention of academics.[19] However, financial structuring remains a key step in the buyout transaction, as an unbalanced capital structure might contribute to business failure regardless of the operational performance.[20] Particularly the use of differentiated financial instruments allows a firm to maintain the necessary financial flexibility.[21]

2.) In addition to financial structure as a value lever, a second rationale for studying buyout capital structures arises which represents the main motivation for this thesis. Given their specific nature, IBOs represent an ideal field in which to study traditional capital structure theories and to test their robustness in a special setting. Among these characteristics the following five are of particular relevance:[22]

- Private transaction with substantial information asymmetries between the parties involved
- Discrete nature of the event
- Partial separation of ownership and control
- Simultaneous decision on the financing layers
- Cash-flow based lending[23]

Many of the issues that capital structure theories tackle may be intensified by the characteristics of buyouts.[24] Over the last twenty years, most empirical tests have been carried out for large publicly quoted companies.[25] However, starting with MM (1958), capital structure theories do not make an explicit distinction between types of companies but rather claim universal validity in theoretical terms.[26]

Hence, researching buyout capital structures adds to the literature of researching private companies and should allow us to test the validity of capital structure theories in an extreme environment.

---

[19] See chapter 2.3.3.

[20] Golland, F. (2003a), p. 179; Wujtowicz, R.P. (1994), p. 81; Wright, M. et al. (1994), pp. 21-40.

[21] Golland, F. (2003a), p. 179.

[22] Chapter 2 discusses buyout characteristics in detail.

[23] Of course, these characteristics do not apply exclusively to buyouts. The last two characteristics, for example, also relate to corporate spin-offs. For a delineation of buyouts from spin-offs refer to chapter 2.1.2.2.

[24] Roden, D.M./ Lewellen, W.G. (1995), p. 76.

[25] For an overview of important empirical work up to 1999 refer to Schwenhold, F. (2001). Frequently cited empirical tests from the recent past are Frank, M. Z. / Goyal, V.K. (2003); Lemmon, M.L. / Zender, J.F. (2002); Fama, E.F./ French, K.R. (2002) and Shyam-Sunder, L./ Myers, S.C. (1999).

[26] Neus, W. (1995), S. 2.

Since the majority of tests have been performed in the US, investigating IBOs in the European marketplace shall further increase the marginal benefit of the empirical test presented in this thesis. Following the argumentation of RAJAN / ZINGALES (1995), an examination of capital structure theories outside the usual environment helps to better evaluate the robustness of capital structure theories and should provide a basis to further support or reject traditional thinking.[27]

Besides the specific nature of IBOs in terms of information asymmetries, the simultaneous decision on the different financing layers represents a very appealing feature to corporate finance research.[28] If firms choose a financial structure, then firm characteristics will determine the actual financing mix. The relations between firm characteristics and leverage are more easily detectable in a sample of buyouts because the financial structure does not evolve from prior operating histories.[29] This motivation is similar to the examinations by GILSON (1997) and ALDERSON / BETKER (1995) studying the role of transaction and liquidation cost in the leverage choice of firms emerging from financial distress.[30]

At the same time, the validity of traditional theories is also tested for a set of non-giant firms, as buyouts usually affect small and medium-sized businesses. In 2002, only 14 per cent of the total number of transactions involved values of more than €100m.[31] Deals below this threshold are clearly considered by practitioners as small transactions.[32] Therefore, this thesis also covers small company finance, a relatively young research field, which the scientific community only began to discover 10 to 15 years ago and which has not yet received the attention it deserves.[33] Or as ZINGALES (2000) put it: "Empirically, the emphasis on large companies has led us to ignore (or study less than necessary) the rest of the universe: the young and small firms, which do not have access to public markets".[34]

[27] Rajan, R./ Zingales, L. (1995), p. 1421.
[28] Diamond, D.W. (1993), p. 361.
[29] In fact, much of the existing research claims that firms will tend to move back towards historical debt levels to the extent that these deviate from optimum. See e.g. Fama, E./ French, K. (2002); Hovakimian, A./ Opler, T./ Titman, S. (2001) or Taggart, R.A. (1977).
[30] Gilson, S. (1997); Alderson, M.J./ Betker, B.L. (1995).
[31] CMBOR (2003), p. 42.
[32] Source: interviews; official limits (OECD/EU) do not define company size on the basis of company value. In contrast, the number of employees (<250) and total turnover (<€40m) constitute a SME. See OECD (2002), p. 7.
[33] See Neus, W. (1995) for a good theoretical account. Examples of empirical works are Berger, A.N./ Udell, G.F. (1998); Jordan, J. et al. (1998); Michaelas, N., et al. (1999), and Scherr, F.C./ Hulbert, H.M. (2001).
[34] Zingales, L. (2000), p. 1629.

1.2. State of research

Due to the relevance of buyouts within the corporate landscape, researchers have increasingly turned their attention towards this phenomenon. Buyout financing has been the subject of various articles both of theoretical and practical nature. They fall into four categories: studies examining the impact of leverage on the performance of firms, articles that focus on selected determinants of buyout financing, theoretical models, and articles for and by practitioners.

1.) Most of the articles published in prominent journals focus on the consequences of buyouts and, accordingly, on the consequences of a new capital structure.[35] Some articles emphasize how increased leverage impacts the performance of buyouts.[36] Others discuss how leverage serves as a substitute for other types of monitoring instrument.[37] However, none of these empirical studies elaborates extensively on the links between the characteristics of the deal and its capital structure. The exception to this is the level of free cash flow giving rise to the use of debt as a disciplinatory instrument in the sense of JENSEN (1986).[38] Characteristics other than free cash flow may be included for control purposes but are not discussed in a theoretical context. In contrast to buyout financing research, most prior corporate finance research does not investigate the influence of the capital structure on firm performance.[39] Consequently, a link between buyout financing and corporate financing research can hardly be established.

2.) A second group of research studies puts less emphasis on exploring the consequences of capital structures on firm performance. Instead, they discuss how the different aspects of the transaction settings affect the agency cost of equity mitigated by debt capital.[40] Accordingly, these articles can be considered derivatives of the first group. They most closely follow the same motivation as this thesis because they provide answers to the ex-ante decision on the

[35] Well known articles are Opler, T./ Titman, S. (1993); Lichtenberg, F./ Siegel, D. (1990); Palepu, K. (1990); Marais, L. et al. (1989); Kaplan, S. (1989); Amihud, Y. (1989); Bull, I. (1989); Hite, G.L./ Vetsuypens, M.R. (1989); Lowenstein, L. (1985).

[36] E.g. Phan, P.H./ Hill, C.W.L. (1995); Long, W.F./ Ravenscraft, D.J. (1993a); Smith, A. (1990); Muscarella, C.J./ Vetsuypens, M.R. (1990); Lehn, K./Poulsen, A. (1989).

[37] E.g. Thompson, R.S./ Wright, M./ Robbie, K. (1991); Palepu, K. (1990).

[38] See chapter 3.3.2.2.

[39] Chapter 5.2. provides an extensive review of prior corporate finance research.

[40] An example would be the impact of ownership structure on the role of debt, see Green, S. (1992). Another example of this category is Cotter, J.F./ Peck, S.W. (2001), who examine the influence of the financial investor's activity level on the capital structure.

[41] For example, the interpretation of the likelihood ratio index ('LR test') is alleged to be wrong in the way that it cannot be interpreted as the logit counterpart to the R^2 metric in OLS regressions. For an exact definition of the LR test, see chapter 6.3.4.2.

optimal capital structure. However, in these studies transaction characteristics predominantly explain the use of debt with regard to the influence on the agency cost of equity and less on other cost and benefits of debt. In addition, no studies specifically control for a larger set of characteristics. This appears quite surprising since many empirical studies on usual corporates have been published to understand the impact of different characteristics. Practically no two studies on buyouts pursue the same method so that direct comparability and a thorough discussion of potential differences are ruled out. The only exception is a framework offered by RODEN / LEWELLEN (1995) that is very similar in spirit to the one underlying this thesis. However, their analysis must be considered rather rudimentary given the thin theoretical discussions and the technically insufficient use of a multinomial logit model.[41] Another shortcoming of the model is the failure to specifically address one type of leveraged buyout. Instead, different types appear to be mixed up with no consideration that the management's perspective and investor's perspective may differ as regards the reasons for their financial policies.[42] This could also be a reason for the rather poor quality of the model.

3.) Other purely theoretical articles develop models on financial policies from the perspective of the management. They develop or extend existing models regarding the marginal use of debt or external equity financing.[43] For example, SCHMID (1994)[44] builds on a formal model developed by GRAMMATIKOS / MAKHIJA / THOMPSON (1988).[45] A model is outlined which combines a portfolio theoretical approach and signalling aspects, where the management's equity stakes signalize the target's quality to external equity investors. Moreover, the personal setting of management is related to various transaction characteristics and evaluated using a portfolio optimisation approach.[46] These articles fail to consider the perspective of the investor as the key decision maker in the process and are therefore unable to explain financial policies in IBOs.[47]

[42] The insufficient consideration of one type will be discussed again at the end of the chapter.

[43] For example Krebs, A. (1990) and Arzac, E.R. (1992). The latter does not explicitly distinguish between management and external investors, but the model outline reflects the approach developed by Ross, S.A. (1977), which accounts for the management as producer of the signal.

[44] Schmid, H. (1994). For a similar article, see Then Bergh, F. (1997).

[45] Grammatikos, T. / Makhija, A./ Thompson, H. (1988).

[46] Schmid, H. (1994), pp. 200-212.

[47] See chapter 2.1.3.2 for the role of the financial investor in the transaction.

4.) Buyout financing has been frequently discussed in practitioners' guides, often in the context of M&A acquisition financing.[48] However, many of the articles to date have simply described the financial structure and made little attempt to transfer broader knowledge from traditional corporate finance into the world of buyouts.[49] Obviously, these sources do not contribute to identifying the relevant determinants of IBO financing.

Apart from the shortcomings already mentioned, the different research categories have further deficits in common that need to be filled.

- As indicated, none of the articles specifically addresses the importance and nature of IBOs.[50] The bulk of the research presents a limited view of the decision-making mechanism by largely entitling the management to structure and develop the transaction.[51] In fact, IBOs are structured by the financial investor and not by the management. Research papers virtually ignore this aspect with the consequence that their findings are partly imbalanced.[52] This negligence is surprising for two reasons: first, buyouts in which financial investors play the key role not only account for the largest share of all buyouts. They also represent the most popular ones discussed by numerous articles in the business press.[53] Second, decisions taken by management are based on far more complex considerations than those taken by the financial investor whose sole aim is to maximise his return on investment. Management decisions comprise more aspects than just the maximisation of their financial investment.

[48] A frequently cited book on M&A financing is Lajoux, A.R./Weston, J.F. (1999). Fromman, H. (1992) is one of the best known articles in Germany specifically on buyout financing. Other examples are Hug, J./Ernst, D. (2003); Krebs, A./Eckhardt, U. (1998) and Krebs, A. (1990). A frequently cited early German article is Milde, H. (1990). A recent article discussing the buyout of Messer Griesheim as a case study is Schierek, D./ Klab, A./Kitzmann, J. (2004).

[49] International contributions on the subject are Kaplan, S.N./ Stein, J.(1993) and Allan, J. (1999).

[50] To the author's knowledge the only article which specifically highlights the nature of IBOs is Wright, M./ Robbie, K. (1996). However, the article does not discuss financing issues but the process and success factors of corporate divestments. The only finance-related buyout article to mention IBOs is Mittendorfer, R. (2001). It has to be emphasised that some articles – both of a theoretical and empirical nature – implicitly refer to IBOs as their object of research without specifically naming them. Particularly the articles that place their line of argument around the above-mentioned disciplination hypothesis from Jensen (1986) discuss transactions in which the management is controlled by the disciplinary effect of debt. Clearly, this cannot be a discussion of deals where the management decides on the financial structure as they lack the incentive to limit their own discretionary power. Examples of such articles are Jensen, M.C. (1989a); Jensen, M.C. (1989b); Muscarella, C.J./ Vetsuypens, M.R. (1990); Liebeskind, J. et al. (1992). However, none of these articles has a similar objective to this thesis.

[51] Examples are Then Bergh, F. (1997); Schmid, H. (1994); Frankfurter, G.M./ Gunay, E. (1992); Fox, I./ Marcus, A. (1992); Luippold, T. (1991); Singh, H. (1990). Occasionally, the external investor and the management are grouped together as a "promoters group", see e.g. Arzac, E.R. (1992), p. 17.

[52] While for most aspects of a buyout (e.g. value levers in general) a distinction between the perspective of the PE investor and the management might not be necessary, this results in serious consequences regarding the relevant theories and should not be neglected. See chapter 3.1.6.

[53] Examples are the buyouts of Celanese by The Blackstone Group, Dynamit Nobel and MTU by KKR, Debitel by Permira, Flender by CVC, Symrise by EQT, and Tele Columbus by BC Partners or Minimax by Investcorp.

Notably the investment in human resources and the implications for their employment are parameters in their utility functions.[54]

- Finally, no theoretically driven empirical study on buyout financing has been published to date in Europe despite the size of the European market. Given the enormous relevance of private companies compared to public companies here, a study of European deals would produce valuable results for the private sector. Most probably, the main reason for the lack of European studies can be attributed to the difficulty of retrieving appropriate data. While in the US data on buyouts can be obtained from various sources,[55] corresponding data in Germany is only available as long as public-to-private buyouts[56] or reverse leveraged buyouts are under review, hence when they are listed either before or after the buyout. Results, however, exclusively based on these transactions would be deluted by the sample selection.

Overall, buyout capital structures have been the subject of a large body of literature, practical, theoretical and empirical articles. However, the question of why buyouts and particularly IBOs are financed the way they are is still not answered in its entirety. Apart from some anecdotal evidence, few empirical tests have attempted to draw a complete picture of IBO capital structure decisions. This leaves room for an empirical study which derives a set of hypotheses, consistently based on established capital structure theories, for a homogenous group of buyouts.

1.3. Objective of the thesis

Following the previous discussions, the present thesis attempts to fill the gap that is left by existing research:

The objective of the thesis is to examine to what extent established corporate finance theories are able to explain capital structures of institutional buyouts.

In line with other empirical studies, the major aim is therefore to *confirm* or *reject* hypotheses derived from theoretical approaches and supplemented by interviews.[57] The intention is not, however, to *explore* relationships, i.e. identify hitherto undetermined and unexplained

[54] Schmid, H. (1994), pp. 214-217.
[55] E.g. proxy statements, prospectus and 10k filings, Compustat, etc.
[56] For a definition of public-to-privates see chapter 2.1.2.1, reverse leveraged buyout denotes the action of offering new shares to the public by companies that initially went private through past LBOs.

relationships.[58] Exploratory, hence theory-building, approaches require different, more qualitative research methodologies.[59]

The specific nature of IBOs, their private character, and the simultaneous decision on the financial structure should provide a robust basis for partly closing the gap between abstract theoretical approaches and actual financing practices. In particular, it should constitute an incremental step towards better understanding cash flow lending, an increasingly relevant yet under-researched field of corporate finance, as these transactions are particularly threatened by agency cost.[60] Therefore, if the empirical results generally support one or more of the theories, this study should help to mitigate the ongoing controversy about the relevance of established theories.

If the results are not confirmatory, there remains at least some hope that the study identifies specific gaps in the existing literature on capital structure. M. MILLER once put the merit of this type of research in a nutshell by stating that "showing what doesn't matter can also show, by implication, what does".[61] Accordingly, even non-confirmatory empirical results will help narrow down future research questions and trigger discussions on theory amendments.

Beyond understanding the debt-/equity choice, the study will be enriched by examining the use of other available financial instruments. Apart from senior debt, decision makers may choose other instruments, in particular sub-ordinated debt. This not only extends the coverage of the practitioner's view, but also adds to theoretical studies that have addressed the choice of other instruments. In addition to sub-ordinated debt, other instruments are available within the classes of equity, senior debt and sub-ordinated debt giving rise to a multi-layered financing decision, which shall be addressed, however, without developing hypotheses in advance.

Therefore, given the above objective, an approach geared towards the following three research questions will be adopted:

---

[57] Notably Frank, M./ Goyal, V. (2003); Fama, E./ French, K. (2002); Rajan, G./ Zingales, L. (1995); Titman, S./ Wessels, R. (1988) and Bradley, M./ Jarrell, G.A./ Kim, E.H. (1984).

[58] See Bortz, J./ Döring, N. (2002), pp. 53-54 for a characterisation of confirmatory and exploratory studies.

[59] Qualitative and quantitative research must be delineated in a context of contrary understandings of empirical work. To compare these opposing poles, see, e.g. Bortz, J./ Döring, N. (2002), pp. 298-307. For an overview of different qualitative data collection and assessment techniques, see Bortz, J./ Döring, N. (2002), pp. 307-352.

[60] Wolf, B./ Hill, M./ Pfaue, M. (2003), p. 41. See also Backhaus, K./ Werthschulte, H. (2003) and Nevitt, P./ Fabozzi, F. (2000) for project financing deals in general.

[61] Miller, M. (1988), p. 100.

1.) Which established corporate finance theories best predict the financing of IBOs?

2.) What particular influence do the various transaction-specific characteristics have on capital structure decisions?

3.) Which factors determine the use of financial instruments beyond the debt-/equity choice?

1.4. Research design

Empirical corporate finance research may pursue two objectives: While the exploration of actual finance decisions aims to develop theories, confirmatory empirical work is designed to assess actual policies in light of existing theoretical approaches and potentially suggest changes to them.[62] This thesis clearly belongs to the latter category.

In general, confirmatory empirical studies include three generic steps, a description of the research object, the development of hypotheses based on a theoretical framework, and the testing of these hypotheses in practice. This represents the backbone of the present thesis, which is organised in seven chapters following the introductory section:

Chapter 2 characterises the distinct nature of IBOs. The specific features of IBOs need to be understood in order to put financing in the context of the transaction itself and to ascertain what position the financial structure assumes as a value driver vis-à-vis other strategic and operational levers. In addition, and most significantly, an understanding of the characteristics provides the basis for selecting the appropriate theory and for correctly interpreting the empirical results.[63]

The subsequent chapter 3 outlines the theoretical framework. On the basis of the discussions in chapter 1, two appropriate theories will be selected from the total body of corporate finance theories and presented in more detail.

Chapter 4 presents the different financial instruments available for IBO financing. This not only completes the picture on buyout financing but rather helps us to understand the economic characteristics of the instruments. Together with the existence of market frictions, the nature of the attached claims constitutes the economic basis for the different theories.

[62] Breuer, W. (1998), p.1.
[63] Zingales, L. (2000), p. 1630.

Incorporating the discussions of previous sections, chapter 5 is primarily dedicated to developing hypotheses on the influence of seven relevant transaction characteristics. Chapter 6 then outlines the methodology of the empirical study to test the validity of these hypotheses. It is split into two paragraphs, the design of the survey (data collection) and the methods to investigate the relationships (data analysis).

The main chapter 7 discusses the empirical results of the study. After a paragraph that describes the sample itself, several statistical tests will be conducted to answer the three research questions at the centre of this thesis. The final chapter 8 provides a conclusion of the results and discusses implications for future work.

Figure 2: Research design

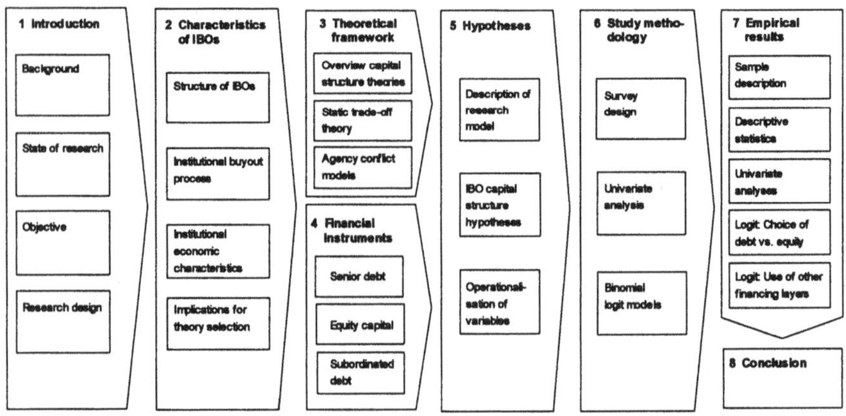

Source: Author.

2. Characteristics of institutional buyouts

IBOs exhibit specific characteristics which deviate from usual corporate entities in various respects. In light of the objective of this thesis, an understanding of these characteristics serves to

- select a suitable theoretical framework since not all corporate finance theories fit the nature and structure of IBOs
- interpret the financing patterns of IBOs, particularly in comparison to empirical results on the financial policies of usual corporations

The presentation of IBO characteristics follows a four-step procedure. First, an introduction to the structure of IBOs will be provided, followed by a description of the distinctive private nature. The main levers for value creation will then be briefly discussed in order to gain a more comprehensive understanding of this phenomenon. Finally, the findings will be reviewed in light of their implications for the selection of suitable capital structure theories.

2.1. Structure of institutional buyouts

Before considering the private nature of buyouts and the ways in which value can be created, this paragraph describes what characteristics constitute a buyout and which parties are typically involved in a transaction.

2.1.1. Definition of institutional buyouts

The general term "buyout" first appeared in 1974 in a wider context than is used today.[64] However, a review of existing buyout research reveals that to date neither practitioners nor academics have agreed on a common definition of the term.[65] This thesis follows the straightforward definition coined at the renowned Center for Private Equity and Entrepreneurship at Amos Tuck University, which denotes a buyout as "*the purchase of a controlling interest of a company by an outside investor and/or a management team*".[66]

[64] Vignola, L. (1974), p. 12.

[65] Downes, J./ Goodman, J.E. (2003), p. 86; Neukirchen, D. (1996), pp. 4/6; Honert, J. (1995), pp. 7-8; Schmid, H. (1994), p. 5; Huydts, H.J. (1992), p. 19; Hoffmann, P./ Ramke, R. (1992), p. 22; Forst, M. (1992), pp. 5-6; Luitpold, T.L. (1991), p. 9.

[66] Center for Private Equity and Entrepreneurship at Amos Tuck University (2002), no page.

In general, the term buyout needs to be specified in order to narrow down the wide range of possible occurrences. This specification can be done along three dimensions: the type of buyer, the motive for the deal, and the source of financing.[67]

In this sense, IBOs are clearly distinguished from other buyouts through a specific type of buyer: an institutional investor, typically a "professional entity that invests capital on behalf of companies or individuals"[68] Institutional investors that are active in the buyout industry are usually called "private equity firms"[69]. Therefore this type of buyout is referred to as an institutional buyout[70]. While existing research lacks a consensus definition, IBOs share certain characteristics:

- PE firms take the lead in structuring and developing the buyout[71]
- The stake held by the institutional investor is a priori planned to be exited after 5-8 years[72]
- The institutional investor either retains the incumbent management or brings in new external managers who receive a small equity share[73]
- The buyout deal is executed in a very professional way with a complex financial and legal structure orchestrated in co-operation of the key parties and their advisors[74]

For the purpose of this research work a proprietary definition of an IBO should be established. Based on the characteristics mentioned above, an IBO is defined as follows:

An IBO denotes a transaction that is driven by a private equity firm taking the lead in structuring, developing and exiting the buyout in co-operation with an internal or external management team, which is entitled to hold a minority interest in the target company.

---

[67] Jakoby, S. (2000), p. 11. Chapter 2.1.2 will elaborate on these dimensions.

[68] Center for Private Equity and Entrepreneurship at Amos Tuck University (2002), no page. Originally, the term "institutional investor" describes "an organisation that trades large volumes of securities", e.g. mutual funds, pension funds or insurances, see Downes, J./ Goodman, J.E. (2003), p. 335.

[69] As will be discussed in chapter 4.2, private equity firms do not necessarily provide solely equity capital in the form of common/preferred equity. Rather, much of the capital is induced as shareholder's loans, which does not necessarily have clear equity characteristics. However, the term "private equity firm" is widely acccepted in the industry and will therefore be used throughout this thesis.

[70] The terms "investor-led buyout" and "investor-driven buyout" are used synonymously.

[71] Weitnauer, W. (2003), p. 65; Wright, M. et al. (2000), p. 11; Haynes, M./ Thompson, S./ Wright, M. (1999), p. 220. The lead becomes manifest, though not mandatory, in a majority shareholding of the private equity firm.

[72] Bader, H.P. (1996), p. 14.

[73] Weitnauer, W. (2003), p. 3; Wright, M./ Robbie, K. (1996), pp. 691-692. In some rare cases the private equity firm may even manage the company by itself (source: interviews). Controversial discussions exist regarding the optimal management equity share. Practitioners consider an investment of 1-3 times an annual gross salary to be the minimum amount without specifying a percentage of total equity.

[74] Weitnauer, W. (2003), p. 3; Eichner, C.A. (2002), pp. 15-16.

In essence, the "key difference between an IBO and an MBO is that in the former venture capitalists are working with the management rather than backing them"[75]. The sovereignty of the PE firm results in a view on the financial structuring which is different from other types of buyouts. Here, the investor, usually endowed with substantial financing experience, decides on each financing layer simultaneously by trading off benefits against the cost of each source of capital. In contrast, buyouts where the management is in control of the financing process[76] are driven much more by the personal situation of the managers.[77] For that reason, the present thesis focuses on IBOs exclusively.

2.1.2. Delineation of related terms

Having accepted this definition, an IBO may now be delineated from related terms which are often used in similar contexts but which encompass different characteristics and hence are likely to result in different hypotheses with regard to financing structures. These are different types of buyouts on the one hand and spin-offs on the other.

2.1.2.1. Delineation of different types of buyout

Based on a review of the literature, the following three dimensions can be identified to specify buyouts: the type of buyer, the motive, and the source of financing. In addition, combinations of these criteria can classify a type of buyout.[78]

Type of buyer

Buyers fall into five categories: incumbent managers, external managers, employees, institutional investor, and the current owner.

A buyout is called a **management buyout** (MBO) if the incumbent (senior) managers invest their own money and become partial or 100 per cent owners of a company or a division of it.[79] Moreover, the initiative to buy out the firm is usually triggered by the incumbent management and not by the

[75] Wright, M./ Robbie, K. (1996), p. 700.
[76] See chapter 2.1.2.1.
[77] Schmid, H. (1994), p. 193.
[78] Schwenkedel, S. (1991), pp. 9-18.
[79] Beaver, G. (2001), pp. 307-308; Huydts, H.J. (1992), p. 20.

owner or other parties.[80] The management team should typically hold the majority of the equity capital and voting rights.[81]

The buyout should be denoted as an **institutional buyout**[82], when a private equity firm and not the management holds the controlling interest.[83]

When an *external* management assumes a controlling majority, a buyout is called a **management buyin** (MBI).[84] When internal and external managers take over the company jointly, the deal becomes a **buyin management buyout** (BIMBO).[85]

In an **employee buyout** (EBO) all or at least a large number of employees across all hierarchies[86] acquire a substantial share of the company's equity.[87] As regards the operationalisation of a substantial share, BERGER claims that more than 5 per cent of the voting rights must be controlled by employees not belonging to the top management.[88]

When the seller plays a dual role by selling parts of the company and acquiring the interest at the same time, the buyout is called an **owner buyout** (OBO). Here, the company (or parts of it) has to be transferred to a new entity, which the seller owns.

Motive

A buyout can be triggered by various motives. Existing literature largely distinguishes five different types: succession, divestment, turnaround, privatisation and going private. They describe reasons for the seller to divest assets and motives to choose a buyout as the preferred exit route.[89]

Frequently, family-owned companies face a **succession** issue.[90] Where no family member appears willing or able to take over the helm, the incumbent management is forced to look for alternatives to

---

[80] Luippold, T.L. (1991), p. 15; Schmid, H. (1994), p. 35.
[81] Neukirchen, D. (1996); Honert, J. (1995), p. 8. See Schmid, H. (1995), pp. 32-33 for a different opinion.
[82] See chapter 2.1.1.
[83] Berger, M. (1993), p. 7; Huydts, H.J. (1992), p. 21.
[84] Wright, M. et al. (2000), p. 140.
[85] Luippold, T.L. (1991), p. 16.
[86] Honert, J. (1995), p. 12.
[87] Forst, M. (1993), p. 10; Nadig, L. (1992), p. 23; Hoffmann, P./ Ramke, R. (1992), p. 24.
[88] Berger, M. (1993), p. 14.
[89] See Jakoby, S. (2000), p. 163 for an overview of studies examining the relative importance of the various motives.
[90] Hoffmann, P./ Ramke, R. (1992), p. 39; Schwenkedel, S. (1991), p. 14.

ensure the continuation of the business. Succession in the form of a buyout represents an attractive option.[91]

The disposition of an asset (usually parts or subsidiaries of a company) is called **divestment** (or divestiture).[92] Several rationales may drive the decision to divest. Among them are the lack of strategic fit, weak performance, or the need to generate liquidity to fund other investments or pay back company debt.[93] Another occasion arises when incumbent investors in a company attempt to divest their current stakes (e.g. venture capitalists).

A **turnaround**[94] buyout constitutes a countermeasure to overcome a company crisis or to prevent an anticipated bankruptcy. It can be defined as the acquisition of a whole company or part of a company going through a crisis. It has to be differentiated from the sale of profitable parts or subsidiaries designed to enhance the financial position of the vendor company. This case should be regarded as a spin-off. Accordingly, the constitutive criterion is the objective of turning around the bought-out company and not the vendor company.[95]

Transferring former state-owned companies into private ownership is commonly known as **privatisation**. In Germany, a wave of privatisation occurred in Eastern Germany after reunification in order to refocus the economic structure towards a market-oriented economy. Previously large and inefficient state-owned companies dominated the economic landscape. Due to tax and regulatory restrictions, medium-sized businesses were very poorly developed. Buyouts represented a feasible option to amend the economic structure by creating smaller, profit-oriented entities.[96]

Finally, the **going private**[97] ("delisting" or "public-to-private") of a company on the stock exchange also represents a buyout motive when one or more financial investors take the company private if the stock market valuation falls below the intrinsic value of that company.[98] In Europe, going privates are the least common type of buyout, with a mere 2.7 per cent share in terms of number of transactions in 2002.[99]

[91] Jakoby, S. (2000). For a detailed discussion of buyouts as an option for succession, see Bieler, S. (1996), pp. 124-134 and also Huydts, H.J. (1992); Wagner, K.R. (1993).
[92] Downes, J./ Goodman, J.E. (2003), p. 184; Luippold, T.L. (1991), p.18.
[93] Berger, M. (1993), p. 25; Forst, M. (1992), pp. 63-66; Luippold, T.L. (1991), p. 19.
[94] For a detailed description of the terms turnaround and restructuring see Kraft, V. (2001), pp. 64-65.
[95] Jakoby, S. (2000), p. 43. Some authors do not agree with this opinion, see, e.g. Kropp, M. (1992), p. 20.
[96] Laub, J. (1995), pp. 38-39 and 47; Schwien, B. (1995), pp. 30-33.
[97] For an exhaustive definition, see Siemes, M. (2003), p. 15.
[98] Jakoby, S. (2001), pp. 47-48. For further reasons for "going private" see DeAngelo, H./ DeAngelo, L. (1987), pp. 44 - 45; DeAngelo, H./ DeAngelo, L./ Rice, E.M. (1984), pp. 371-373.
[99] In value terms, going privates accounted for 15.2% in 2002, see CMBOR (2003), p. 22.

Source of financing[100]

A buyout can be basically financed with equity and debt capital as well as with hybrid forms of capital.[101] If the buyout is financed with a substantial share of (senior) debt, it is termed a **leveraged buyout** (LBO).[102] However, the adjective "substantial" is not clearly defined.[103] SCHMID suggests applying the definition "highly leveraged transaction" (HLTs) coined by the US supervisory authorities[104] in 1989 to refer to LBOs. The definition of HLTs envisages two criteria of which one must apply to constitute an LBO. Either the debt must increase by at least 50 per cent resulting in a total share of debt of more than 50 per cent, or the total share must exceed 75 per cent irrespective of the percentage increase in debt.[105] In turn, all other buyouts, which do not satisfy the criterion of a substantial share of debt, shall not be considered a leveraged transaction.

In summary, buyouts can be categorised along the three dimensions outlined above. For the purpose of this study, the term "buyout" is narrowed down by the single criterion "type of buyer" towards an IBO as the focus of investigation due to the distinctive characteristics described in chapter 2.1.1. The criteria "motive" and "source of financing" are left unspecified as the former represents an exogenous factor within our empirical study while the latter constitutes the endogenous variable.

2.1.2.2. Delineation of spin-offs

Apart from distinguishing an IBO from other types of buyouts, a differentiation vis-à-vis the frequently encountered term "spin-off" should also be made although it is often difficult to draw the line unambiguously.[106]

Spinning-off parts of a company or the subsidiary of a parent company results in an independent new entity, of which the shares "are distributed to the parent corporation's shareholders of record on a pro rata basis".[107] In this sense, a spin-off deviates from a buyout in which outside investors are usually involved. An overlap exists when the incumbent management rather than outside investors acquire shares. This case is called an MBO spin-off, which shows that buyout and spin-off are not

100 As the examination of the financial structure represents the central goal of the thesis, this paragraph does only marginally cover the topic of financing simply differentiating leveraged buyouts and non-leveraged buyouts.

101 Chapter 4 will elaborate in detail on the different sources of financing for buyouts.

102 Then Bergh, F. (1998), p. 8; Honert, J. (1995), p. 32; Baker, G.P./ Montgomery, C.A. (1994), p. 1; Huydts, H.J. (1992), p. 22; Arbeitskreis Finanzierung der Schmalenbachgesellschaft (1990), p. 832.

103 Then Bergh, F. (1998), p. 9; Schmid, H. (1994), p. 41; Forst, M. (1993), pp. 6-7; Luippold, T.L. (1991), p. 9.

104 Federal Reserve Board, Federal Deposit Insurance Corporation (FDIC) and Controller of the Currency (COC).

105 Schmid,H. (1994), p. 42. Schmid subsumes both senior and sub-ordinated debt under the term "debt".

106 Hoffmann, P./ Ramke, R. (1992), p. 22.

necessarily mutually exclusive terms.[108] The definition by DOWNES / GOODMAN appears to limit the term "spin-off" to a narrow meaning, which SCHMID considers to be only one specific type of spin-off.[109] Moreover, he regards a spin-off as comprising a far broader set of meanings, which includes a buyout as a spin-off where parts of the parent company become independent with no further specification of the new ownership structure.[110]

However, he acknowledges that although the understanding of a spin-off as a corporate transaction has been diluted, given the vast number of possible meanings, the terms spin-off and buyout need to be clearly separated.[111] Moreover, as the term "buyout" has matured and assumed a proprietary meaning, the original meanings of the two terms have drifted apart. The key argument here consists in the ongoing relationship[112] of the spun-off entity and the parent company, which does not constitute a main characteristic of a buyout.[113] For the remainder of the thesis, SCHMID'S opinion will be adopted, as the focus lies on IBOs where an ongoing business relationship with the selling company may exist initially but does not usually last.[114]

2.1.3. Key parties involved

The following paragraphs discuss the main parties that participate in a buyout transaction. These key parties are the vendor, the private-equity firm, debt / mezzanine providers, the management, and the target company. In addition, various types of advisors support the main parties during the buyout process.[115] Figure 3 presents an overview of the main parties.

[107] Downes, J./ Goodman, J.E. (2003), p. 658. A similar definition is provided by Ross, S.A./ Westerfield, R.W./ Jaffe, J.F. (2005), pp. 815-816.
[108] Eichner, C.A. (2002), p. 18.
[109] Schmid, H. (1994), p. 11.
[110] Schmid, H. (1994), p. 13.
[111] Although following a different reasoning, Luippold, T.L. (1991), p. 17 arrives at the same conclusion.
[112] Weitnauer states that this relationship usually manifests itself in a minority shareholding of the parent company, see Weitnauer, W. (2003), p. 30. Compare also Wright, M./ Coyne, J. (1985), p. 2.
[113] Schmid, H. (1994), p. 60. Some authors, e.g. Jakoby, S. (2000), p. 41, explicitly contradict this view, while others avoid making a tangible comparison, e.g. Weitnauer, W. (2003), p. 30.
[114] Interestingly, in the US where the term "spin-off" originated, buyouts from larger corporations are not referred to as spin-offs but rather as "divisional" or "unit" management buyouts, see, e.g. Jensen, M. (1989), S. 62.
[115] For a comprehensive overview and description of the various advisors see Fenn, G./ Liang, N./ Prowse, S. (1997), pp. 78-87.

Figure 3: Parties involved in an IBO transaction

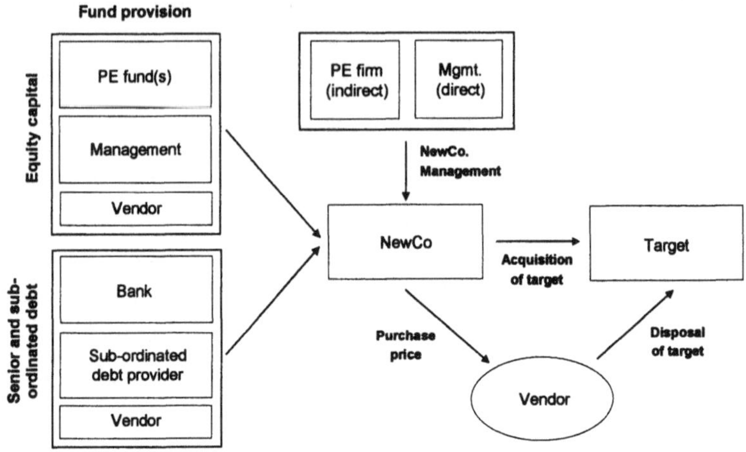

Source: Author.

2.1.3.1. Vendor

As indicated, companies or private persons may have various motives to sell parts or 100 per cent of a company they own.[116] The vendor usually initiates the buyout and subsequently engages advisors (e.g. investment banks) to identify and contact potential investors in co-operation with the incumbent management.[117]

Quite frequently, the vendor's involvement does not stop with the financial close of the deal. Rather, he continues to be involved in the financing by granting a seller's note[118] or keeping a minority share in the target company.[119]

The continued participation in the deal can be explained by

- an ongoing interest from the vendor companies' perspective in the case, e.g. of a spin-off IBO
- a continuation of business relations

[116] See chapter 2.1.2.1.
[117] Sometimes these buyouts are also referred to as vendor-initiated management buyouts (VIMBO), see Golland, F. (2003a), p. 175.
[118] See chapter 2.3.2.2.3.
[119] Tobler, S. (1998), p. 50.

- further participation in value appreciation
- a stepwise sales process due to tax or accounting considerations[120]

2.1.3.2. Private equity firm

In IBOs the private equity firm acts as the lead acquirer in the transaction. In fact, however, it represents an intermediary between investors and target companies and invests on behalf of the institutions which endow the PE fund with capital. BADER (1996) defines five different functions of a private equity firm:[121]

- *Investment* of raised funds
- *Assessment* and *evaluation* of investment opportunities
- *Financing* of target companies
- *Monitoring* and *mentoring* of target companies
- *Exit* of investments for realisation of capital gains

Three different types of private equity firms can be distinguished: independent funds (private and public), captives and government funds. While independent funds are privately held, public firms are listed on the stock exchange. Captives are not legally independent. They are typically subsidiaries or divisions of financial institutions[122] (e.g. insurance company, bank, pension fund), which account for 100 per cent of total funds. Government funds manage PE capital sponsored by the government.[123] 95-99 per cent of the capital of a PE fund comes from external investors,[124] who take the position of limited partner in the PE firm. The remainder is provided by the general partners, the management of the private equity firm which advises the PE fund.[125]

In IBOs, the PE firm founds an investment vehicle (NewCo), which in turn acquires the shares or assets of the target company.[126] Subsequently, the private equity firm endows the NewCo with the majority of the equity in the form of common/preferred equity or as shareholder loans.[127]

---

[120] Berger, M. (1993), p. 192 or Schwenkedel, S. (1991), p. 100.
[121] Bader, H.P. (1996), p. 17.
[122] Likewise, some non-financial institutions have founded subsidiaries which invest in related businesses (e.g. T-Venture of Deutsche Telekom or E.ON Ventures of E.ON). However, as the names indicate, these firms are mostly engaged in early-stage investments.
[123] Bader, H.P. (1996), p. 114.
[124] For an overview and comparison of the European and US sources of funds see EVCA (2003) and NVCA (2003).
[125] Bader, H.P. (1996), pp. 156-157 presents an overview of a private equity firm structure.
[126] Weitnauer, W. (2003), p. 9. See also chapter 2.3.2.1.
[127] See chapter 2.3.2.2.1.

Large buyouts are often realised through more than one private equity firm. In order to share the risk, the lead private equity firm subsequently syndicates the initial stake.[128]

2.1.3.3. Senior / Sub-ordinated debt provider

Alongside equity from the PE fund and management, commercial banks are engaged to capitalise the buyout with senior debt.[129] Specialised structured finance departments[130] provide senior debt which ranks highest in the priority order in the event of the company's insolvency.[131]

Banks' incentives to engage in buyouts are threefold. First, they get a variable interest on their senior debt engagement.[132]

In addition, up-front fees amounting to 1-2 per cent of the amount of debt are granted to cover initial cost (e.g. evaluation cost) as well as so-called agency fees of at least EUR 25.000 p.a. as arranger of the syndicate.[133] As banks do not set out to have a stake in a potential company value increase and focus solely on debt amortization, they are primarily concerned with the probability of a company default.[134]

To fill a potential gap between equity and senior debt, additional providers of sub-ordinated debt are invited to inject funds that are of lower priority than senior debt but rank ahead of equity capital.[135] In practice, providers of sub-ordinated debt come into the financing process late,[136] which reinforces the common understanding of this financing layer as a "gap filler".[137] The return structure for providers of sub-ordinated debt differs from that of senior lenders.[138] Depending on the actual type of instrument, the return may range from significantly higher interest rates of on average

[128] Fromman, H. (1992), p. 123. In rare cases the limited partners invest in the transaction both indirectly through the PE fund and directly (Source: interviews).

[129] Fromman, H. (1992), pp. 121-123. In IBOs, the incumbent house bank usually does not continue to be involved through substantial lending (only for day-to-day payment transactions or financing of parts of the operating assets).

[130] The main players in the German market are JP Morgan, Royal Bank of Scotland, IKB, HSH Nordbank, Hypovereinsbank, Barclays Capital, and BNP Paribas.

[131] See chapter 4.1.2. for a discussion of different types of senior debt.

[132] According to the 2003 Leveraged Finance study, the return ranges between 200 and 300 base points above EURIBOR, depending on the specific deal and debt tranche, see Golland, F. (2003b), p. 84.

[133] Source: Interviews.

[134] Nevitt, P./ Fabozzi, F. (2000), pp. 10-12.

[135] Tobler, S. (1998), p. 51.

[136] Brealey, R.A./ Myers, S.C. (2000), p. 408.

[137] Willis, J./ Clark, D. (1993), p. 245. However, concerning the function of mezzanine, academics increasingly regard it as a means to optimise the capital structure by solving specific problems, see, e.g. Müller, O. (2003), p. 12.

[138] However, in some cases banks themselves provide sub-ordinated in addition to senior debt. Here, banks just aim to benefit from the higher interest rates.

12-18 per cent to match higher risk to a reduced interest level but with an adjunct right to participate in the creation of equity value. The latter structure is commonly referred to as an equity kicker.[139]

2.1.3.4. Management

Depending on the size of the transaction, it will involve the members of the first and second management levels.[140] This involvement takes the form of a dual role that of the co-owner of the company with an equity share of less than 100 per cent and that of the agent to other financiers.[141] This dual role creates conflicts that undermine the value of a firm and are further discussed in chapter 2.2.3. However, the management continues to be crucial for the success of a transaction. Quite early empirical studies have revealed the importance of a highly qualified management in buyout transactions.[142]

2.1.3.5. Target company

Target companies are typically established companies with limited liabilities and business activities in mature, non-cyclical markets with highly predictable and stable cash flows, low investment demand, and minor organic growth rates.[143] These characteristics are commonly seen as increasing the debt capacity and allowing a greater amount of senior debt to finance the buyout.[144]

---

[139] See chapter 4.3.

[140] Schmid, H. (1994), p. 20. The monetary involvement usually amounts to 2-3 times the per annum gross salary, source: interviews.

[141] For the remainder of the thesis the term "manager" denotes a manager with equity ownership, or synonymously "owner-manager".

[142] See, e.g. Lang, L.H./ Stulz, R.M./ Walking, R.A. (1989), pp. 138-139 or Morck, R./ Shleifer, A./ Vishny, R.W. (1990), p. 47. Although the results were related to corporate acquisitions, there is no reason why they should not also apply to buyouts.

[143] However, buyouts may occasionally be initiated to enable further growth when a firm cannot achieve the next level of firm development with its existing capitalisation.

[144] Honert, J. (1995), pp. 54-59; Hoffmann, P./ Ramke, R. (1992), pp. 51-52 and 58-59.

Figure 4: Positioning of buyout within a company's lifecycle

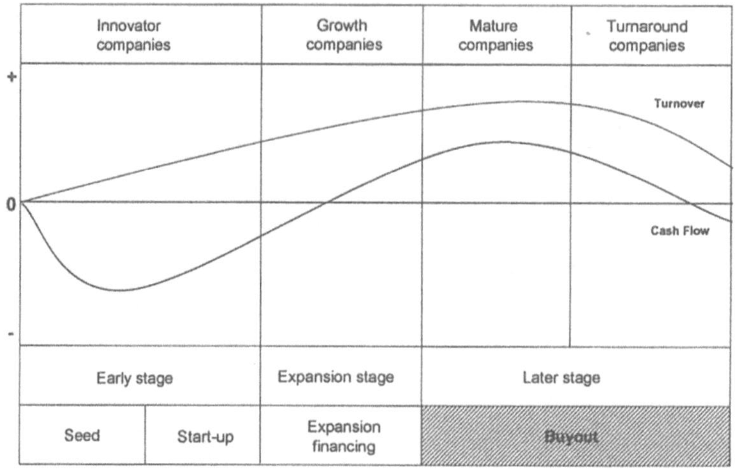

Source: Author, following Hoffmann, P./ Ramke, R., p. 63.

Private equity firms usually target firms that are in the second half of their lifecycle.[145] Early-stage financing tends to be provided by dedicated venture capital firms aiming to invest in companies which have not yet achieved a positive cash flow and whose characteristics aggravate access to traditional financing sources.[146]

The previous section has outlined the structure of IBOs, including the definition and main parties involved. The main result for the remainder of the thesis is that in IBOs the private equity investor takes control of the whole process. As opposed to a classic MBO, the structure of an IBO is entirely designed by the PE investor. All other parties are invited to participate in the deal.

2.2. Institutional economic characteristics

As discussed above, buyouts are transactions that are not carried out via public organised markets. Rather, all relations among the main parties involved in the deal are embodied in a private setting, and hence the claims resulting from these relations are also traded in a private market. This implies

[145] Turnaround companies are increasingly targeted by specialised vulture funds (e.g. Cerberus, Orlando).
[146] Gompers, P.A./ Lerner, J. (2000), p. 127. For a detailed overview of the financing stages, see Kraft, V. (2001), pp. 42-47.

certain inefficiencies which hamper the functioning of the market and which may therefore affect the financing patterns of IBOs. The next section gives an account of the most important implications.

At first glance, it is not obvious why claims resulting from buyout transactions are traded entirely separated from other capital market segments. Like other capital markets, these transactions are determined by a number of contracts among the participants, in which financial intermediaries assume central roles.[147] In the case of IBOs the private equity firm acts as the key intermediary between investors and target companies.

However, there is no room for intermediaries as long as a world with perfect capital markets is assumed. But the world is not perfect, transactions cannot be carried out free of cost, and market participants do not share the same set of information.[148] A market "in which prices always fully reflect available information"[149] are considered efficient markets. Here, all market participants have access to the same information and agree on their implications.[150] Obviously, this does not describe real capital markets. Even for stock markets empirical tests only accept the weak form and to some extent the semi-strong form of market efficiency.[151] Clearly, buyouts as private transactions are likely to be even less efficient.[152] Market frictions in the buyout segment are no different from those arising in other capital markets but the degree to which they occur is different. The market for private equity is characterised by particularly high inefficiencies. While the private nature of the deals already implies these substantial inefficiencies, the fact that most transactions concern small to medium-sized companies reinforces the degree of inefficiencies faced by transactors.[153]

These inefficiencies are at the core of the development of neo-institutional corporate finance theories. The subsequent chapter briefly reviews the two key market inefficiencies: the existence of information asymmetries and transaction cost as well as the central theory based on the existence of these frictions: the principal-agent theory.

---

[147] Bader, H.P. (1996), p. 17.
[148] Franke, G./ Hax, H. (2003), p. 458.
[149] Fama, E.F. (1970), p. 383.
[150] Fama, E.F. (1970), p. 387.
[151] Ballwieser, W. (1987), p. 178. For the definition of weak, semi-strong and strong forms of market efficiency, see Fama, E.F. (1970), pp. 389-409.
[152] Here, a distinction between "public-to-private" and "private-to-private" transactions needs to be made as the former are – prior to the buyout – listed and exposed to the same disclosure requirements as other quoted companies. However, as public-to-private deals are exceptions in the buyout landscape, this distinction will not be further elaborated.
[153] Bader, H.P. (1996), pp. 20-21.

2.2.1. Information asymmetries

The central problem in the co-ordination of economic activity is the fact that nobody possesses all the information as a whole and the level of knowledge differs among market participants.[154] Two types of information asymmetries can be distinguished which aggravate the initiation and accomplishment of transactions: *hidden information* and *hidden action.*[155] A third type of asymmetry, the *hold-up problem ("hidden intention")* will not be treated as an independent class.[156]

Hidden information

Hidden information[157] describes a form of asymmetrical distribution of information about the quality of an object or a person which or who might be subject to a contractual agreement. Therefore, the hidden information problem gets relevant before or at the time the contract is concluded.[158]

AKERLOF (1970) was among the first to substantiate the hidden-information problem by means of his famous lemons market. He showed for the car market how hidden information could lead to *adverse selection* and ultimately a potential market failure.[159] ROSS (1977) and LELAND / PYLE (1977) were among the first to discuss the implications of hidden information for the financing behaviour of companies and the ways in which capital structure can send out signals about the quality of the company. JAFFEE / RUSSEL (1976) and STIGLITZ / WEISS (1981) published papers on possible adverse selection by banks, which initiated the research on credit rationing.

An initial source of information consists in the official accounts published by the target company. Accounting standards are basically designed to prevent a market failure due to information deficits.[160] An important function of official disclosure is the support of potential investors.[161] However, German GAAP especially does not provide an adequate basis on which investors can take

[154] Hayek, F.A. (1945), p. 519.
[155] Franke, G./ Hax, H. (2003), p. 420.
[156] As opposed to hidden action the actual behaviour of the agent can be perceived ex-post by the principal. This feature does not play an important role for the classes of capital structure theories presented and tested subsequently; see Wohlschieß, V. (1996), p. 12. However, it is frequently discussed in the context of financial contracting theory, because the inability to formulate complete contracts anticipating any contingencies is a major cause of hold-up problems, see Milgrom, P./Roberts, J. (1992), p.136. The issue will be touched upon again in chapter 2.3.2.2.2 where contractual covenants are discussed.
[157] The nomenclature dates back to Arrow, K.J. (1985), pp. 37-39 and was also adopted by other scholars, e.g. Franke, G./ Hax, H. (2003), p. 420.
[158] Franke, G./ Hax, H. (2003), p. 420.
[159] Akerlof, G.A. (1970), pp. 488-500.
[160] Ballwieser, W. (1985), pp. 47-48.
[161] Busse v. Colbe, W. (1993), p. 13.

their decisions,[162] although even international accounting standards are not considered to be sufficient in terms of investor-related content. The main deficit is the lack of future-oriented information.[163] Given that official disclosures focus on past-oriented financial data, the asymmetry of information is particularly relevant for different kinds of non-financial information (strategic positioning, intangible assets, customer / supplier-relationships, etc.).[164]

For publicly quoted companies the level of information provided to investors has been improved mainly due to pressure from institutional investors and business failures.[165] The requirements for privately held companies are, however, still limited.

In a buyout, hidden information is a serious problem particulary for the PE firm and financing banks. While they share the same information when they first make contact with the potential target, they differ with regard to their information requirements.[166] Managers, however, may also face the same hidden information problem when they are brought in from the outside (MBI).[167] Nonetheless, as they are usually from the same industry, they should be familiar with some characteristics of the target company and are likely to be better informed than both PE firm and banks.

Hidden action

Hidden action is how economists describe an ex-post information asymmetry in a setting where the level of profits of one contractor A depends on the level of activity of another contractor B. Once the transaction is concluded, contractor A faces the *moral hazard* that contractor B may behave opportunistically and change the endogenous characteristics of the good, which was subject to the agreement. Unlike the hold-up problem, the hidden action cannot be perceived by contractor A.[168] Basically, it denotes a problem of external effects, as the behaviour of A also affects the welfare of B.[169] The term "moral hazard" refers specifically to the exogenous uncertainty[170] of the results of

162 See Günther, T. (1997), pp. 54-58 for the main shortcomings of the German GAAP.
163 Küting, K.H. (2000), pp. 154-156.
164 Amir, E./ Lev; B. (1996), pp. 3-30 have demonstrated for the wireless communication industry that financial information is largely irrelevant for security valuation as opposed to non-financial measures.
165 In Germany, quoted companies must disclose according to the requirements of a large corporation, see §267 Abs. 3 S. 2 HGB; in addition, disclosure requirements stipulated by the stock exchange act (BörsG) and securities code (WpHG) need to be fullfilled.
166 While for owners the likelihood of a company default is a necessary item of information, only the assessment of the upside potential to match their expected return sufficiently satisfies their requirements. In contrast, lenders of (senior) debt look exclusively at the probability of default.
167 Coenenberg, A.G./ Jakoby, S./ Maas, G. (1996), p. 529.
168 Franke, G./ Hax, H. (2003), p. 420.
169 Feess, E. (1997), p. 639.

B's activity level, which hampers A to ex-post back out the actual activity level of B and possibly to call B to account afterwards. In this case, A faces an endogenous uncertainty in the form of a moral hazard.[171]

PE investors and banks are particularly exposed to hidden actions of their contractors as they provide their capital upfront, while, for example, the management delivers their service later. This means that investors are locked in the relationship and face uncertainty as regards management performance.[172]

2.2.2. Transaction cost

Both types of information asymmetry hamper the functioning of markets.[173] However, in addition to these market frictions, mainly the cost of the transaction lead to efficiency losses in the market. The term transaction cost can be traced back to the work of COASE in 1937 when he tried to explain why people are organised in firms instead of being self-employed and having contracts with one another.[174]

Different types of transaction cost have come to be known by particular names. *Search and information cost* arise as a result of determining that the required good is available on the market, which product has the lowest price, etc. *Bargaining cost ('haggling')* are the cost of negotiating an acceptable agreement with the other party to the transaction, drawing up an appropriate contract, etc. *Policing and enforcement cost* are the cost of ensuring that the other party adheres to the terms of the contract and taking appropriate action (often through the legal system) if this turns out not to be the case.[175]

The level of transaction cost depends largely on the characteristics of the firm and the market setting. For small and medium-sized firms, and even more so in the case of privately held firms, transaction cost are particularly significant. The following factors push transaction cost up:[176]

- Intransparency of the market
- Strong information asymmetries

---

[170] Knight, F.H. (1921), p. 256 was among the first to analyse uncertainty and its impact on profits.
[171] Feess, E. (1997), p. 639; Then Bergh, F. (1998), p. 100.
[172] Richter, R./ Furubotn, E.G. (1999), p. 279; Grossman, S./ Hart, O. (1986), pp. 691-719.
[173] Franke, G./ Hax, H. (2003), p. 420.
[174] Coase, R. (1937).
[175] Williamson, O.E. (1985), p. 21.
[176] Bernet, B./Denk, C.L. (2000), pp. 47-53.

- Highly fragmented markets
- Underdeveloped disclosure policy

The modern interpretation of the transaction cost theory is known as *"incomplete contracts theory"*.[177] Central to these contracts is the allocation of control (decision) rights that determine who decides what if unforeseen events arise.

2.2.3. Principal-agent relations

The relations among the parties involved in an IBO are established through certain claims. Whether these claims are fully redeemed depends largely on the efforts of the contract partners. In IBOs two main types of claimholders are involved namely shareholders and debtholders, with the shareholders sub-dividing into the PE firm and the management. Within this context, the management assumes the role of ensuring that the claims of both PE firm and banks are satisfied. Presuming the existence of information asymmetries as presented in chapter 2.2.1, this allocation of roles gives rise to conflicts which the academic literature discusses under the heading "principal-agent relations".[178]

Understanding principal-agent relations has been among the most substantial theoretical advancements in economic studies over the last three decades.[179] Academic literature does not provide a consensus definition for a principal-agent relation. However, three characteristics are pointed out:[180]

- The setting comprises two acting parties (agent and principal), both of which may consist of more than one person
- An action undertaken by the agent affects the welfare of both parties
- Both parties act rationally and aim to maximise their own utility

The relation between the agent and the principal is determined by the two phenomena described in the previous paragraphs, information asymmetries and transaction cost.

However, not only hidden action but both types of information asymmetries have an impact on the relation, either jointly or separately. On the one hand, the principal does not have the same

[177] For a very good introduction, see Hart, O. (1995).

[178] Representative of a large body of literature on principal-agent models, see Varian, H.R. (1994), pp. 443-445.

[179] Particularly Jensen, M.C./ Meckling, W.H. (1976) building on the work of Fama, E./ Miller, M. (1972). Another important finance-related article is Easterbrook, F.H. (1984). A major early contribution on principal-agent conflicts in general can be found in Berle, A./ Means, G. (1932).

information about the quality (education, experience, personal relations, etc.) of the agent as the agent himself (hidden information). On the other hand, the principal is uncertain about and cannot observe the activity of the risk-averse[181] agent (hidden action).[182]

The level of information should not be treated as a given. Rather, it can be endogenous through an incentivation of the agent, but this is costly and must be traded against the benefits of improved information.[183] For the incentivation of the agent the literature distinguishes *monitoring* and *bonding* measures.[184] However, these incentives will not ensure a complete alignment of interests between principal and agent. Costs associated with the harmful behaviour that remains for the principal are referred to *residual loss*. Therefore, three types of agency cost arise in a principal-agent relation:[185]

- Monitoring cost
- Bonding cost
- Residual loss

For an IBO two conflicts are crucial, namely the relation between the PE firm (outside shareholder) and the manager (inside shareholder) as well as the relation between debtholders (banks) and shareholders (PE firm and manager).[186] The agency cost associated with the former conflict are called **agency cost of equity** (1) as they are borne by outside shareholders. Conversely, the cost associated with the latter conflict are borne by debtholders and hence termed **agency cost of debt** (2).

1.) The role of managers in IBOs creates risks for the deal that are related to both human and financial capital. First of all, as opposed to financial capital, the inherent risks that are associated with human capital (e.g. job loss) are not widely diversifiable.[187] While outside

[180] Neus, W. (1989), p. 472.
[181] Feess, E. (1997), p. 642.
[182] Feess, E. (1997), p. 585.
[183] Feess, E. (1997), p. 587.
[184] The prinicipal difference between monitoring and bonding is that the costs associated with the former are borne by the principal, while the costs of the latter are borne by the agent.
[185] Betsch, O./ Groh, A./ Lohmann, L. (2000), p. 248.
[186] However, as chapter 3.3 elaborates in detail on the conflicts arising from principal-agent relations, they are discussed only very briefly here. Also, the discussion shall be limited to these two relations as they have been debated intensely in the financial literature and have been subject to empirical tests. At times, a potential conflict between a non-shareholding management and debtholders is emphasized separately. However, because these managers are paid fixed – not performance-based – salaries, their claim structure is comparable with debtholders, which should prevent potential conflicts. Jensen, M.C./ Meckling, W. (1976) have already stressed that "... in some respect the claim managers' hold on a firm in the form of his wage contract has some characteristics of debt" (p. 353).
[187] Amihud, Y./ Lev, B. (1981), p. 606. See also Hart, O./ Moore, J. (1994).

investors can reduce firm-specific risk and only bear systematic risk, managers have to bear both risk types in full.[188] Similarly, the cost of acting as a manager in the firm, particularly the work effort, cannot be shared among the owners. Though the cost are fully borne by the management, they only benefit in accordance with their management equity share of $\alpha < 1$ from the profits they generate. The lower the management equity share, the more obvious are the disincentives to maximise shareholder value.[189]

2.) Besides the agency cost attributable to the (partial) separation of ownership, another conflict consists in the relation between providers of debt and equity capital, which is a result of the spread of financial claims[190] over different claimholders.[191] Whether the fixed claims of debtholders can be satisfied depends again largely on the actions of the owner-managers. Owner-managers have an incentive not to act in the interest of debtholders once the contract with them has been signed. Rather, they can increase the shareholder value by expropriating wealth from debtholders through actions that jeopardise the value of the creditor claims. The larger the debt position is the stronger will be the incentive for the wealth transfer.[192]

2.2.4. Typical information structure in IBOs

Having described the different types of information asymmetries and how the various claimholders relate to each other in light of these asymmetries, a typical picture of "who knows what" in IBOs will now be drawn.

The structure determines to a high degree which theories are applicable to IBOs. As already discussed, three main parties are involved in IBOs: the PE investor, banks and the (external or incumbent) management. All three share certain levels of information at the time of the acquisition.[193] If incumbent managers are involved, they have the best knowledge about the quality of the firm.

---

188 Bader, H.P. (1996), p. pp. 59-50.
189 Breuer, W. (1998), p. 154. For a further discussion, see chapter 3.3.2.
190 As opposed to real claims (supply of goods). Real claims can also be subject to principal-agent relations. However, as this work is concerned exclusively with financial claims, other relations will be disregarded.
191 Milde, H. (1990), p. 656.
192 See e.g. Gavish, B./ Kalay, A. (1983) or Green, R.C./ Talmor, E. (1986). See also chapter 3.3.1.
193 Again, this thesis only covers the financing mechanism at the time of the acquisition and thus does not account for the changing levels of information during the holding period. An ongoing relationship between the investment and the bank and PE investor obviously has an impact on the optimal financial structure after the closing, but will not be considered here. For related readings, see e.g. Diamond, D. (1991) or Sharpe, S. (1990).

Conversely, external managers who join the transaction are less informed about the deal although in most cases they stem from the same industry and hence have certain knowledge of the company and are well-informed about the future potential of the industry as a whole.

Initially then, banks and PE investors have the same level of information, which means they go through the process of evaluating the firm on equal terms.[194] Given the closer contact between PE investor and management, the PE firm is usually in a slightly better position. However, in the acquisition phase, the difference in the level of information is probably neglegible. While the asymmetry between PE firm and bank as regards the management itself might be substantial, it is certainly not the case as regards the quality of the target. Both parties share the same information sources to ameliorate their position vis-à-vis the management. The fact that the comparatively ill-informed PE investor determines the financial package of the acquisition must be considered in the appraisal of the financing behaviour.

2.3. Institutional buyout process

An institutional buyout process can be basically subdivided into four different phases: evaluation, structuring, post-investment value generation and exit.[195] Figure 5 illustrates these phases.

Figure 5: Overview of an IBO process

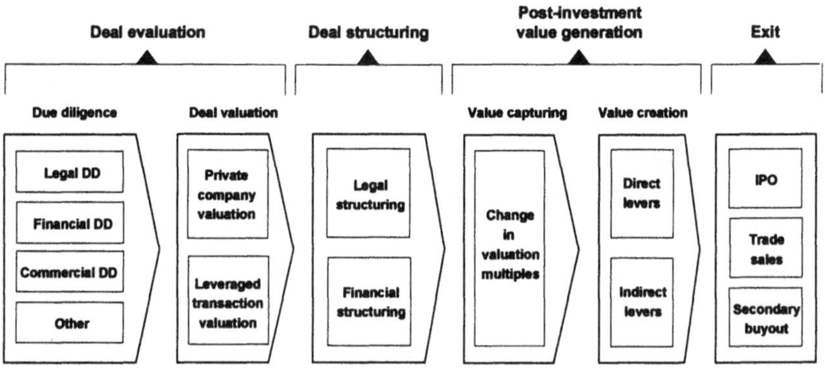

Source: Author.

[194] See chapter 2.3.1.

[195] Clearly, prior to these phases the target needs to be identified (deal generation). However, this will not be treated as a separate phase as the way targets are identified differs randomly and is not linked to the subsequent phases of the transaction.

Each phase has a distinctive impact on the return that the PE firm ultimately realises on the investment. The subsequent paragraphs will outline each phase briefly.

Understanding the value-creation process not only puts the financial structuring into context but also highlights potential interlinks between the financial structure and other aspects of a buyout transaction. Given the focus on the financial aspects of an IBO, the main body will be dedicated to the structuring of buyouts.

2.3.1. Deal evaluation

Once a potential target company has been identified, the process enters the evaluation stage when the attractiveness and inherent risks and ultimately the fair value of a company need to be assessed. In terms of impact on the return, the due diligence and valuation of the target company are the most significant steps to take in the evaluation phase.

2.3.1.1. Due Diligence

After initial discussions between the seller and a potential acquirer over the general terms of a buyout, several advisers are mandated to carry out a due diligence.[196] It aims to critically assess various risks which might arise in the future and jeopardize the return on investment.[197] Therefore, it represents the most critical step towards reducing the information asymmetry about the quality of both the target company and the incumbent management. The due diligence serves four distinct functions:

- **Identification of risks and opportunities:** A systematic review of the company within its environment identifies hidden risks and confirms or clears out assumed risks.[198] However, while the focus lies on risks, the due diligence also looks at potential upsides which are not obvious to external parties either.
- **Validation of strategic plan:** Review of main strategic steps envisaged by management and overall validation of sales and cash flow forecasts.[199]

---

[196] Bing, G. (1996), p. 1. Depending on the size of the transaction and general process, the due diligence may be split into several parts. The level of detail increases according to the progress in the acquisition process. A full-fledged due diligence requires exclusivity. For a description of each phase see Binder, P./ Kanz, R. (1993), p. 19.

[197] Ganzert, S. / Kramer, L. (1995), p. 577.

[198] Blex, W./ Marchal, G. (1990) and Krallinger, J. (1997), p. 94.

[199] Binder, P. / Lanz, R. (1993), p. 17.

- **Management quality:** The due diligence in itself reveals information about the quality of the management. Conversations provide additional information about the capability and the willingness to co-operate with external investors.[200]
- **Contractual assignment of risks:** The documentation of identified risks helps to assign risks and liabilities and hence to reduce uncertainty. In case of disputes a documented due diligence helps to determine the extent to which the acquirer has been informed by the seller prior to the acquisition.[201]

A due diligence consists of various parts of which the legal, financial and commercial due diligence are carried out in every buyout. Depending on the transaction, these might be complemented by further due diligences (e.g. tax, environmental, IT, human resources).[202]

The **legal due diligence** covers all risks that may be inherent in existing or lacking contracts and legal relationships.[203] Relevant contracts relate to both internal and external parties. Internally, any type of formal agreement between groups or persons of major relevance, e.g. owners, workers' council, etc., needs to be examined. But also relations with external parties are subject to the legal due diligence. These parties include predominantly authorities, major suppliers, lessors, and joint venture partners.[204]

The objective of the **financial due diligence** is to examine all risks and opportunities associated with the financial position of the target company. Accordingly, the company's assets, liquidity and profitability positions are reviewed. The underlying question is whether the acquirer can trust the numbers provided by the vendor and management.[205] For example, in first place they discuss the results of the current trading. Inreasingly however, financial due diligences begin to comment on assumptions of the management plan as regards operating costs, working capital and capex projections.

While the legal and financial due diligences primarily focus on past and present conditions, the **commercial due diligence**[206] exclusively concerns future conditions.[207] The objectives are twofold: first, the validation of the management sales plan and second, the identification of risks arising from

[200] Bing, G. (1996), pp. 130-131.
[201] Berens, W./ Schmitting, W./ Strauch, J. (1998), p. 69.
[202] Natusch, I. (2002), pp. 543-549.
[203] Ganzert, S./ Kramer, L. (1995), pp. 576-578.
[204] Fritzsche, M. (2002), pp. 376-384.
[205] Harvey, M./ Lusch, R. (1995), pp. 16-19.
[206] The terms *market* and *strategic due diligence* can be used synonymously.
[207] Sebastian, K.H./ Niederdrenk, R./ Tesch, A. (1998), p. 207.

the market and competitive environment. While the former objective primarily serves the interest of the PE firm, the latter objective is also of great relevance for the banks in order to assess the downside risk. Unlike the other due diligences, internal data does not suffice to examine these issues.[208] Instead, additional information must be gathered externally in order to estimate market development, identify key trends, assess the competitive landscape and derive the current and likely future positioning of the target company.[209]

2.3.1.2. Valuation of Buyouts

At the same time the price of the target needs to be negotiated ultimately on the basis of the results of the due diligence. Determining the intrinsic value of a company as a basis for purchase price negotiation represents perhaps the most critical moment in a buyout transaction.[210] The valuation of buyouts in general and IBOs in particular is not subject to a separate methodology.[211] However, well-known methodologies must be amended to reflect the specific nature of IBOs; particularly the private ownership and a usually high portion of debt require slight adjustments. Both considerations will be briefly described below.[212] The subsequent paragraphs discuss the use of the discounted cash-flow method for IBOs. Since the use of market multiple valuation techniques does not differ between IBOs and other settings, the presentation shall be forgone here.[213]

2.3.1.2.1. Valuation of private companies

The valuation of a privately held company is a difficult process. As opposed to publicly traded companies, private companies do not have their shares listed with daily prices which reflect the market value.[214]

The popular DCF method has been developed for quoted companies. Accordingly, two main assumptions are made, neither of which complies with the nature of private companies:[215]

---

208 Sebastian, K.H./ Niederdrenk, R./ Tesch, A. (1998), p. 208.
209 Reed, S./ Lajoux, A. (1995), pp. 378-380.
210 Hölters, W. (2002), p. 31.
211 See Weitnauer, W. (2003), pp. 41-65 for an overview of the different valuation techniques applied in buyouts.
212 Familiar methods are not presented here, as a huge body of literature exists on company valuation techniques. For a general overview see e.g. Betsch, O./ Groh, A./ Lohmann, L. (2000), pp. 179-232; Drukarczyk, J. (2003), pp. 119-448. Concerning the relevance of the different techniques for buyout valuation, see e.g. Jakoby, S. (2000), pp. 236-239.
213 For a discussion, see e.g. Kraft, V. (2001), pp. 191-192. However, chapter 2.3.3 will briefly return to the technique as it provides a basis for the value generation framework outlined in that chapter.
214 Koeplin, J./ Sarin, A./ Shaprio, A.C. (2000), p. 94.
215 Weitnauer, W. (2003), p. 54.

- Fungibility of shares
- Elimination of firm-specific risk through diversification

These assumptions do not hold for private companies because the market is highly illiquid and shareholders, even PE firms with large portfolios, are not able to fully diversify firm-specific risk. Therefore, a discount rate different from those for quoted companies, needs to be applied.[216] Several empirical studies estimate that accounting for the market illiquidity and the firm-specific risk results in a discount of roughly 30-40 per cent on average on a firm value of a publicly quoted company.[217]

At the same time, the valuation of IBOs should also reflect a premium for the control over the target company. Control has a positive impact on a firm's value from the viewpoint of the controlling party. Empirical studies have identified an average premium of about 30 per cent.[218]

2.3.1.2.2. Valuation of highly leveraged companies

Almost all IBOs are financed with a substantial debt burden.[219] The valuation of such firms is a particularly difficult task as future leverage ratios are uncertain. Two commonly used methods of valuing firms on the basis of the way they are financed are the adjusted present-value approach (APV) and the weighted average cost of capital approach (WACC), both of which demand predetermined debt levels.[220] However, neither method is appropriate owing to the uncertain amount of debt the firm will carry in the future. That is since banks which finance highly leveraged transactions demand the use of free cash flow to pay down outstanding debt.[221] Debt reduction is hence a function of future cash flow.[222] Consequently, the tax shield is uncertain and needs to be discounted at a rate different from the cost of debt. MILES / EZZELL (1980) have shown that the cost of equity is the correct discount rate only if a constant leverage ratio is assumed and hence the absolute level of debt fluctuates with the value of the unlevered firm.[223]

LÖFFLER (1998) has even showed that the cost of equity for the unlevered firm can still be applied if the absolute level of debt is deterministic.[224] This can, e.g. be the case if the post-acquisition plan

---

[216] Weitnauer, W. (2003), p. 55.
[217] Koeplin, J./ Sarin, A./ Shaprio, A.C. (2000), p. 95. Bader, H.P. (1996), p. 93 also cites further studies.
[218] Bader, H.P. (1996), p. 90.
[219] See chapter 2.3.2.3.2.
[220] E.g. Drukarczyk, J. (2003), p. 209-258.
[221] This is a common covenant in financial contracts. See chapter 2.3.2.2.2.
[222] Arzac, E.R. (1996), p. 42.
[223] Miles, J.A./ Ezzell, J.R. (1980), pp. 719-730.
[224] Löffler, A. (1998), pp. 4-7.

for the target company foresees certain divestments which are fixed in terms of volume and timing, so that the debt reduction follows a non-stochastic plan.

However, this appears very unlikely and it stands to reason that the cost of equity is not an appropriate rate if debt reduction primarily follows the available operating cash flow.

A problem here is that the tax shield is negatively correlated with the unlevered cash flow, as profitable firms pay back their debt more quickly and therefore have lower tax shields during the investment period. As a result, the discount rate for the tax shield must be lower than the cost of equity.[225] The literature even proposes that the discount rate of the tax shield must be lower than the riskless rate since firm performance is closely linked to the overall health of the economy and hence the tax shield possesses a negative beta.[226]

The valuation of the tax shield therefore depends on the assumptions made about the future development of the firm's debt. In short, the investor may apply three different approaches to determine the value of a highly leveraged company given by

$$V_0^l = V_0^u + T_0$$

where V_0^l denotes the value of the levered firm, V_0^u the value of the unlevered firm and T_0 the value of the tax shield.[227]

First, the investor can assume a constant absolute level of debt and therefore apply the APV equation[228]

$$V_0^l = \sum_{t=0}^{T} \frac{E[\tilde{X}] - \tau E[\tilde{O}]}{(1+k_E)^t} + \sum_{t=0}^{T} \frac{\tau r_f D_t}{(1+r_f)^{t+1}}$$

where T denotes the number of periods considered, $E[X]$ the expected free cash flow, $E[\tilde{O}]$ the expected operating income, τ the tax rate, k_E the cost of equity, r_f the riskfree rate, and D_t the amount of (riskless) debt in period t.

225 Arzac, E.R. (1996), p. 44.
226 Grinblatt, M./ Titman, S. (1998), p. 459.
227 Betsch, O./ Groh, A./ Lohmann, L. (2000), p. 221.
228 Myers, S.C. (1974), p. 22.

Second, where the investor assumes a deterministic leverage ratio or absolute debt level, the formula developed by LÖFFLER may be applied.[229]

Finally, if the absolute debt level is random and the leverage ratio is equally stochastic, the tax shield shall be considered a derivative of the unlevered firm value and a method of derivative pricing may be applied.[230] Alternatively, methods that avoid explicitly valuing the tax shield may be also applicable.[231]

In any case, the use of standard valuation approaches and the degree of adjustment requires a high degree of clarity about the future development of the capital structure. Otherwise, the valuations will certainly generate biased results.

2.3.2. Deal structuring

Once a PE firm has decided to acquire a target company, the next major step represents the structuring of the deal in collaboration with the seller, management, banks and advisor parties. The main elements are the legal and financial structuring.[232] In this, the *PE investor* pursues five different objectives:[233]

- Tax minimisation
- Reduction of default risk
- Satisfying seller interests
- Influence / Control of management
- Ensuring exit route

The subsequent paragraphs are designed to provide an overview of the two steps. The legal structuring is described only briefly since a large body of dedicated (country-specific) literature exists and the legal environment is in a state of constant flux. In contrast, the mechanism of financial structuring has remained much the same over the last years and must be discussed in depth to provide a basis for grasping the different aspects of the overall topic.

---

229 Löffler, A. (1998), p. 7.

230 Löffler, A. (2000) applies a martingale approach, which shall not be discussed in detail. For further readings on martingales and company valuation see, e.g. Musiela, M./ Rutkowski, M. (1998).

231 Arzac, E.R. (1996), pp. 44-49.

232 Some publications consider tax structuring to be a separate element, e.g. Weitnauer, W. (2003). However, taxes are assumed to be primarily a result of the legal and financial structuring. For further discussions on the links between tax and legal structuring, see e.g. Diem, A. (2005), pp. 15-18.

233 Cole, J.E./ Sokol, A.L. (1998), pp. 36-39.

2.3.2.1. Legal structuring

In many aspects, a buyout does not differ from a "usual" corporate acquisition as regards the legal conditions.[234] However, as opposed to a corporate acquisition, the IBO is executed using a transaction vehicle, a so-called "NewCo".[235] Two key decisions have to be made regarding the structure of the NewCo, namely on the legal form of the NewCo and on the actual process of the transaction in legal terms.

Choosing the **legal form** follows two considerations:[236]

- Limitation of the investor's and management's liabilities associated with the buyout transaction
- Balancing the interdependent interests of all parties and facilitating the timing of the structuring

While the regulatory environment differs substantially among European countries, the directives in most countries favour the limited liability company.[237] In some cases the public corporation constitutes the appropriate vehicle when an exit is planned via floatation and a change in the legal form is considered too expensive. However, the benefits must be balanced against the specific cost of a public corporation (e.g. disclosure).[238]

When the NewCo is structured as a company with limited liability, the target company may either be taken over in the form of a **share deal** or an **asset deal**. While in a share deal the target company is acquired in the way the company exists, in the asset deal the individual assets are taken over together with the attached claims and liabilities. Accordingly, on the one hand the shares may serve as collaterals granted by the NewCo, on the other hand the company's assets ideally provide the backing of the bank debt ("Upstream Guarantees").[239] Quite frequently, however, the assets serve as collaterals for loans to the operating units, so that they cannot back the acquisition loan. In this case, the acquisition bank and housebank have to commit themselves to an intercreditor agreement

---

234 Beisel, W./ Klumpp, H.H. (1996), p. 211; Müller, H.P. (1996), p. 317. Diem, A. (2005) is a comprehensive recent publication on the legal aspects of financing leveraged transactions.

235 Weitnauer, W. (2003), p. 101. Alternative denominations for the NewCo. are Special Purpose Vehicle (SPV) or HoldCo.

236 Weitnauer, W. (2003), p. 170.

237 E.g. GmbH (Germany), SARL (France), Ltd. (UK).

238 Weitnauer, W. (2003), p. 173; Jakoby, S. (2000), pp. 244-246.

239 Eichner, C.A. (2002), pp. 123-124.

settling different aspects of their financing relations such as the rank of the claims.[240] Figure 6 depicts the relationships in an IBO.

Figure 6: Typical IBO deal structure

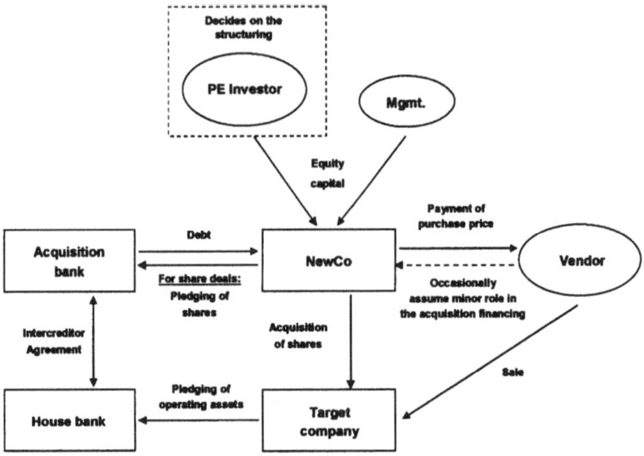

Source: Author, following Nussbaum, P. (1995), p. 255.

In practice, many buyouts are structured in the form of a share deal, as total cost are typically lower than for an asset deal (e.g. due to the complexity of contracts).[241] However, whether an asset deal or share deal is the appropriate way depends on several factors and relates primarily to the effect on the actual tax burden for both vendor and acquirer.[242] Though tax regulations differ among European countries, they share the fact that the legal form of both the selling and acquiring parties largely determines the tax status. The taxation aspects of a buyout are highly relevant in general but will not be discussed in any further depth. First of all, regulations are constantly being changed[243] and differ across countries. This makes it impossible for an empirical study to grasp all details of taxation. In addition, PE firms are likely to structure their deals in such a way that regulatory barriers are overcome.[244] From this perspective, the generic treatment of taxes in finance theories

[240] Ticknor, G./ Ruediger, D./ Kacoyannakis, J. (2004), p. 2.
[241] Boxberg, F. v. (1991), p. 267; Kraft, V. (2001), p. 212.
[242] Weitnauer, W. (2003), 128-156.
[243] In the years 2000-2002, for example, the German government enacted several laws (StSenkG, StÄndG, StVBG, StSenkErgG, StVerAbG) which have had a material impact on the structuring of buyouts, see Weitnauer, W. (2003), pp. 119.
[244] An example in Germany would be a specific legal structure to allow the so-called step-up that was abolished in the course of the 2001 tax reform.

can be justified. Accordingly, no empirical study hitherto has particularly discriminated between different tax regulations.

2.3.2.2. Financial structuring

From the viewpoint of this study, the financial structuring constitutes the main step in the buyout process. Although it is tightly linked to the legal structuring as regards collateralisation, the financial package itself is designed primarily on the basis of the target company's characteristics.[245] The subsequent paragraphs look at some basic considerations on the financing of buyouts. Besides determining the financings needs and subsequently structuring the package, two further aspects are raised. Both are frequently the subject to academic publications and have to be discussed in the context of buyout financing as they represent both complementary and substitutive elements to financial instruments.

2.3.2.2.1. Determining total financing needs, the appropriate equity stake, and the optimal financing mix

In a first step, the envisaged equity stake and the purchase price have to be determined. The equity stake reflects the control level which the financial investors aim to achieve.[246] As characterised in the definition of IBOs, the PE firm strives for a controlling interest, which does not necessarily imply a majority ownership. However, in most cases, one lead PE firm takes over the majority of the shares, assigns a minority stake to the management and invites further equity investors (or the vendor) to participate in the transaction ("syndication").

Closely related to the allocation of shares is the calculation of the purchase price, which in turn may have implications for the optimal equity share of the lead PE investor. Two elements mainly determine the price with which the PE firm enters negotiations with the vendor: the potential exit value and the return requirements of the PE investor.[247] In a first step, based on a verified business plan, the potential exit value of the target company needs to be determined.[248]

The value is then discounted at the required return over the investment horizon to yield the maximum price which the PE investor is willing to pay (marginal purchase price) or which is at

[245] Weitnauer, W. (2003), p. 70.
[246] Kraft, V. (2001), p. 212.
[247] Mittendorfer, R. (2001), p. 154.
[248] See chapter 2.3.1.2 for the valuation of buyouts.

least the starting point for actual price negotiations.[249] Upon agreement on a price the company is bought out on a cash and debt-free basis. In some cases, existing debt may be assumed as long as the conditions are favourable (e.g. working capital facility).[250] Considering transaction cost (e.g. consultants, banks, etc.) in addition to the purchase price that usually account for 3-5% of the enterprise value the total sum yields the transaction value.[251]

The next step refers to the optimisation of the acquisition financing structure, which constitutes one of the most momentous decisions in a buyout transaction.[252] It has long been acknowledged as a primary source of value creation. Three aspects will be mentioned briefly in this context: First and foremost, the reduction of corporate tax was identified early on as an important source of value creation due to the tax deductibility of interest payments, providing a tax shield with a positive impact on cash flows.[253] Second, as a rather indirect lever, an appropriate financial structure enables the PE investor to reduce agency cost, mainly due to the limitation of managerial discretion. JENSEN has emphasized the effect of debt to reduce the waste of free cash flow.[254] Third, as a professional and experienced borrower at stake, PE firms are in a position to negotiate better conditions than would the target firm on a stand-alone basis.[255]

In developing the financial structure, four factors can be distinguished that determine the optimal mix of instruments:

- PE fund constraints and policy
- Debt market conditions
- Characteristics of the transaction
- Value impact of the different financing layers in light of existing market frictions

First of all, there may be certain constraints regarding the fund, e.g. pressure to invest a certain share of the total fund or to pursue a specific policy in terms of leverage ratio.[256] For the remainder of this thesis, however, it is assumed that PE fund constraints/policies do not differ among PE firms

---

[249] Hafner, R. (1993), p. 80.
[250] Krebs, A./ Eckhardt, U. (1998), p. 18; Mittendorfer, R. (2001), p. 157.
[251] Tobler, S. (1998), p. 49.
[252] Williamson, O.E. (1988), pp. 586-587; Opler, T./ Titman, S. (1996), pp.19996-1998.
[253] Lowenstein, L. (1985), pp. 759-764; Bull, I. (1989), p. 276; Kaplan, S.N. (1989), p. 630; Leland, H.E. (1989), p. 26; Smith, A. (1990), p. 21; Long, W.F./ Ravenscraft, D.J. (1993), p. 12.
[254] Jensen, M.C. (1986, 1989a, 1989b). See also chapter 3.3.2.2.
[255] Kaufman, A./ Englander, E. (1993), pp. 94-96.
[256] Interviews have confirmed that occasionally PE firms aim not to exceed a certain leverage ratio irrespective of the actual transaction.

and hence are of negligible relevance compared to the other factors.[257] This implies that their policy will not affect the the development of hypotheses, although these aspects may be considered when interpreting results.

In addition, the availability of debt capital affects the financial structure.[258] Various factors determine the health of the debt capital market. However, while the debt market conditions might certainly be of relevance,[259] it appears reasonable to assume that the debt market conditions in general apply to all deals alike and are thus not able to explain capital structure variations based on differences in the characteristics.[260]

The remaining two factors, however, constitute the foundation of this thesis. As will be elaborated in detail in chapter 3, market frictions have a certain impact on the value of a firm. In turn, the characteristics of the transaction determine the actual relevance of market frictions and consequently the potential value impact of the financial instrument (e.g. the profitability of a firm influences the value impact of tax deductibility). Hence, the optimal capital structure depends both on transaction characteristics and market frictions.

Of course, the elements purchase price, equity share and financial structure are not strictly consecutive steps but rather simultaneous considerations which are interdependent. For example, a substantially constrained debt market may force the PE investor to reduce the marginal purchase price if he wants to maintain a certain leverage ratio. Whether the bank displays generosity in terms of volume and conditions depends mainly on the characteristics of the transaction such as the level and volatility of the free cash flows.[261] The same characteristics also determine the actual impact of the financing layers on firm value. These functions of the financing elements are the subject of chapter 3 and represent the largest share of contributions in corporate finance theory.

---

[257] In fact, none of the interviewees has ever been involved in a deal where fund considerations have substantially altered the financial structure.

[258] Fromman, H. (1992), p. 121.

[259] In particular, the syndication has an impact on the structure of the debt package, especially the interest conditions. See Hug, J./ Ernst, D. (2003), p. 444.

[260] Clearly, market conditions change over time, providing different market settings for buyouts of different years. Unfortunately, for confidentiality reasons, the year of the buyout could not be recorded, leading to some time-dependent blurring of the study. However, the most important macroeconomic determinant, the long-term interest rate, has not changed significantly over the last 7 years, which leaves the study results controlled for the level of market interests. See appendix 7 for the development of the interest level.

[261] Of course, other aspects may be of relevance here, too (e.g. personal relations). They are not, however, verifiable and hardly follow certain patterns.

2.3.2.2.2. Financial contracting and covenants

Different return expectations are a significant source of conflict between inside and outside shareholders. While outside investors strive for the maximisation of pecuniary returns, inside investors care about both pecuniary and non-pecuniary returns (human capital, work effort, etc.). Over the last 20 years aspects like this conflict have been used as a starting point to extend the question on the optimal financing mix to how to allocate decision (control) rights through **financial contracts**.[262] The basic idea here is that the relationship between principals and agents is more dynamic than static and that contracts between them cannot be designed such that all future contingencies are spelled out.[263] Given that eventualities are more or less impossible to anticipate, there must be at least a contractual agreement on the process of decision making in case an unforeseen event arises. As a result of this, equity and debt not only allocate cash flow rights but also control rights.[264]

Though a large body of theoretical work has been published on financial contracting, research still lacks empirical evidence. One of the most important empirical studies here is KAPLAN / STROMBERG (2001), who consider the venture capital industry to be a good field to study financial theory, as VCs most closely approximate the investors of theory.[265] One of the main findings is that all rights related to equity, mezzanine or debt instruments are contingent on a number of observable indicators, both of financial and non-financial nature.[266]

These observable indicators are frequently encountered in financial contracts and denoted as "**covenants**".[267] Empirical studies show that these covenants imply strong disciplinary effects for the management and shareholders.[268] In buyout financial contracts, covenants play a crucial role in defining managerial discretion. Among the most important covenants are:[269]

- *Cash sweep*: A certain percentage of the free cash flow after mandatory amortisation payments must be used to reduce further debt in order of seniority
- *Interest coverage*: Consolidated EBITDA over consolidated net interest expenses

---

[262] This incomplete contract approach has been presented in chapter 2.2.2 as the modern understanding of the transaction cost theory. In fact, without the existence of transaction costs, an ex-ante specification would be available for every future contingency.

[263] Hart, O. (2001), pp. 9-10.

[264] See e.g. Dewatripont, M./ Tirole, J. (1994).

[265] Kaplan, S.N./ Stromberg, P. (2001), p. 2.

[266] Kaplan, S.N./ Stromberg, P. (2001), p. 6.

[267] Covenants were first discussed intensively by Smith, C.W./ Warner, J.B. (1979).

[268] E.g. DeAngelo, H./ DeAngelo, L./ Wruck, K.H. (2002) illustrate the relevance of covenants by means of the L.A. Gear case.

- *Dynamic gearing*: Total net debt over net cash flows
- *Debt service cover ratio*: Cash flow before financing activities over mandatory amortisation and interest payments
- *Capital investments*: Investments undertaken by the target company must be broadly in line with the initial business plan, which constituted the decision basis for the banks

2.3.2.2.3. Seller's note, earnout, strip financing, and syndication

In the context of financial structuring further instruments beyond the mix of financing layers and the financial contract design are applied. The following four instruments are frequently encountered in IBO transactions and will be briefly explained:

A **Seller's note**[270] simply denotes a (conditioned) deferral of payment. Instead of receiving the full purchase price in cash, the seller receives a note that confirms a claim against the acquirer. However, the design of the claim may differ. It may range from an unconditioned deferral of payment of the residual purchase price, including interests, to a conditional deferral where the payback depends on the development of certain performance indicators. In this sense, it resembles an earnout contract.[271] Quite frequently, in return for the payment deferral, the seller is granted an equity kicker or other types of profit or value share.[272]

If a financing gap arises, an **earnout** may represent an elegant way of closing it by keeping the seller committed to the investment and reinforcing his confidence in the potential of the company he is selling. The earnout works in a similar way to a seller's note in that a certain portion of the purchase price is deferred to the years following the sale. In addition, whether the portion is actually paid out depends on the operating results of the target company. Hence, the seller will only commit himself to this price deferral if he really believes in the realisable value creation potential.[273]

In a **strip financing** arrangement, investors are invited to purchase a mix of all applicable financing layers in order to reduce the typical conflict between different investors which arises in the event that the target company gets into financial distress. Hence, the role of strip financing requires a

[269] Weitnauer, W. (2003), pp. 108-110.
[270] Alternatively "vendor note".
[271] Weitnauer, W. (2003), pp. 102-103.
[272] Hoffmann, P. / Ramke, R. (1992), p. 90.
[273] Tobler, S. (1998), p. 50.

positive probability of default in equilibrium.[274] It has not however proved to be a sustainable instrument. First of all, the central peril of the strip financing technique is still embodied in the different interests of equity, mezzanine and debt providers, albeit *within* the investing firm.[275] Furthermore, from an investor's perspective strip financing is difficult to assess as regards the fit with a given portfolio and thus rejected by many institutional investors. Finally, agency conflicts can be more efficiently mitigated by other instruments such as, e.g. sub-ordinated debt.[276]

PE firms are not always able or willing to carry the entire equity package besides alongside that of the management. In such cases, a lead arranger invites other PE firms to co-invest in the target company, resulting in a so-called **syndication**. Syndication is common practice in buyout transactions, particularly where deals are very large. Empirical studies have identified three perspectives that give rise to the syndication of private equity investments:[277] spreading financial risk through risk sharing theory, resource-based perspective, and access to future deal flow. Studies also show that financial aspects still dominate the decision on whether or not to syndicate a deal. Other aspects primarily determine the decision which companies to invite for the co-investment.[278]

2.3.3. Post-investment value generation

While the early years of buyouts (late 70s to mid-90s) witnessed a focus on deal structuring as a primary source of value generation (particularly financial structuring), this focus has since shifted to the holding period in which most of the equity value appreciation is generated. BERG / GOTTSCHALG (2003) were among the first to develop a consistent framework to capture different aspects of value generation in buyouts. They have developed the framework on a market multiple valuation rather than on the valuation techniques outlined in chapter 2.3.1.2. They decompose the equity value of a buyout into its integral components:[279]

Equity value = Valuation Multiple * Revenues * Margin % - Net Debt

[274] Arzac, E.R. (1992), p. 19.
[275] In fact, interviews with banks have confirmed that in the event of default the traditional bank perspective is likely to overrule interests associated with the equity or mezzanine providers.
[276] Arzac, E.R. (1992), p. 21.
[277] Theoretical and empirical studies do not yet differentiate between various stages of private equity invest-ments. Most articles focus on venture capital but their results shall – at least in part – be transferable to later stage investments as well.
[278] Manigart, S. et al. (2002), pp. 1-3.
[279] Berg, A./ Gottschalg, O. (2003), p. 7. Depending on the valuation method, different types of multiples and corresponding margins can be applied (EBIT, EBITDA, net profit, etc.). The multiple does not necessarily derive from comparable companies. Instead, a calculated DCF value can be divided by the current profitability figure to give the respective profitability multiple. This is a common method in practice.

Value creation, which is not rooted in changes of the buyout company's financial performance, is referred to as "*value capturing*" as opposed to value generated by an improved performance of the company, which will hereafter be called "*value creation*". While value capturing is reflected in the changes of the valuation multiple, changes in the performance of a company, value creation, result in revenue and margin increases, net debt reductions or combinations of these.[280] Figure 7 outlines the elements of post-investment value generation.

Figure 7: Post-investment value generation

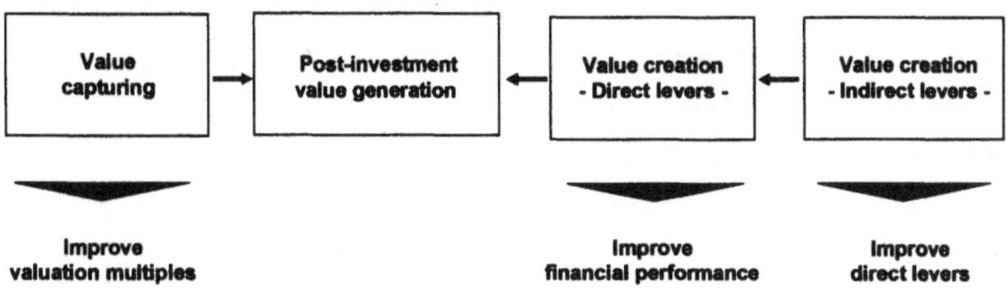

Source: Author, following Berg, A./ Gottschalg, O. (2003), p. 9.

2.3.3.1. Value capturing

Value capturing refers to any factors triggering an appreciation in the equity value without changes of the target company's performance. Four factors have received considerable attention in the academic literature. First of all, company insiders may be able to exploit their auspicious position in a way that they negotiate better valuation multiples.[281] Private information about the future development of the firm may also enable an opportunistic management to push down the purchase price.[282]

Second, besides private information about the target company, propriatory know-how about general market conditions also constitutes an advantage over other contractors. With their wide network of contacts and diverse experience, PE firms are able to better assess the industry environment.[283]

[280] Berg, A./ Gottschalg, O. (2003), pp. 7-8.
[281] DeAngelo, L. (1986), p. 44; Lowenstein, L. (1985), p. 731; DeAngelo, H./ DeAngelo, L./ Rice, E. (1984), p. 393.
[282] Ofek, E. (1994), p. 638.
[283] Anders, G. (1992), p. 82.

Third, value capturing can also be linked to superior dealmaking capabilities based on extensive transaction expertise which becomes obvious primarily during the negotiation and acquisition process.[284]

Finally, the general market valuation has a direct impact on the valuation multiples as they are usually computed based on the valuation of comparable companies, which in turn may be influenced by irrational behaviour. Thus, not only are the performance and expected development of comparable companies reflected in the multiples but also the general and partly opaque market movements which lead to changes in the valuation of a target firm.[285]Although these factors may still have a substantial influence on the valuation of buyouts, their significance has certainly diminished compared to the factors enhancing the financial performance of a company. The main reasons for this are the tightened disclosure requirements,[286] intensive deal screening activities, and professionalised processes with experienced parties on both sides of the table.[287]

2.3.3.2. Value creation

Value creation refers to an improvement of a company's financial performance. Some levers have a direct bottom-line impact and result in an immediate appreciation of the equity value, while others only lead to an indirect strengthening of the financial position. They enhance one or several direct levers, making it difficult to isolate the value impact of an indirect lever.

2.3.3.2.1. Direct levers

Levers that have a direct impact on a firm's value can be categorised as improvements in financial engineering, operational effectiveness or strategic distinctiveness.[288]

As regards **financial engineering** a distinction needs to be made between changes in the financial structure at the time of the acquisition ("financial structuring")[289] and changes after the acquisition. The direct effect of the acquisition structure must be seen in the counter-balancing influence of taxes and the cost of financial distress. Both are the subject of chapter 3 and will not be further discussed here. During the holding period, however, changes to the existing capital structure may

[284] Baker, G.P./ Smith, G.D. (1998), p. 3; Wright, M./ Robbie, K. (1996), pp. 699-700.
[285] Berg, A./ Gottschalg, O. (2003), pp. 11-12. To date, this factor has received surprisingly little attention although it is frequently mentioned by private equity professionals ("Multiple riding").
[286] Lee, D.S. (1992), p. 1062.
[287] Wright, M./ Robbie, K. (1996), pp. 700-701.
[288] Berg, A./ Gottschalg, O. (2003), p. 17.
[289] See chapter 2.3.2.2.

also have an impact on the value of the firm, since the cost of capital could potentially be reduced by specific actions. An example could be a case where the debt package is restructured in a way that the PE firm replaces an initial expensive bridge financing with a less expensive private loan or high-yield bond.[290] Moreover, depending on the type of business, a bunch of assets or revenue streams may be securitized to form asset-based loans, which also might lead to reduced cost of debt.[291] However, the potential to "squeeze out" further reductions in the cost of capital appears to be limited to specific businesses, since the recapitalisations bear cost that may offset the benefits of the cost of capital reductions.[292]

More importantly, improving **operating performance** has a direct impact on the left side of the balance sheet, margins and cash flows. A large number of articles have focused on the effect that buyouts have on the overall productivity and effectiveness of operations.[293] Measures that reduce operating cost and enhance the operating margin of a firm represent a major source of value creation. Immediately after the buyout the management starts to implement operating and overhead cost-reduction programs.[294] Furthermore, PE firms may initiate the replacement of inefficient management teams either at the time of the acquisition or post-acquisition as another way of improving operating performance.[295] In addition to reducing operating cost and removing inefficient management teams, another popular lever is to increase the productivity of the current assets. In particulary, an improved management of inventories, accounts receivables and payables helps to tighten the cash flow absorbed by working capital requirements.[296]

The third set of measures relates to the improvement of a company's **strategic distinctiveness**. While the management team takes nearly all decisions regarding the improvement of operational

290 Kraft, V. (2001), pp. 241-243. Actually, the change in the post-acquisition capital structure by itself only constitutes a value-enhancing strategy as long as investors cannot replicate the strategy by themselves, which, however, can be reasonably assumed. See chapter 3.1.4.1 for the irrelevance of the financial structure.

291 Gilbert, F.S. (1978), p.15. One popular example of an industry where asset-based recapitalisations are frequently encountered after acquisition is the pub business. In the UK several pub chains (e.g. Punch Taverns) have been refinanced so that either the pub estates or the claims against the pub lessees are bundled to constitute collaterals for note issues. Other industries are telecommunications and energy.

292 Another familiar example of a deal that is largely driven by the potential to reduce the cost of capital and increase debt capacity is that of Fred Meyer Inc., a US American retail company; for details see Baker, G.P./ Smith, G.D. (1998), p. 2.

293 Particularly Harris, R./ Siegel, D.S./ Wright, M. (2002); Long, W.F./ Ravenscraft, D.J. (1993a); Lichtenberg, F./ Siegel, D. (1990); Muscarella, C./ Vetsuypens, M. (1990); Palepu, K. (1990); Singh, H. (1990); Opler, T.C. (1992); Bull, I. (1989).

294 Baker, G.P. (1992), p.1110, Fox, I./ Marcus, A. (1992), p. 74. Interestingly, the development of R&D cost has attracted particular interest though the emprical results are not conclusive, see, e.g. Long, W.F./ Ravenscraft, D.J. (1993b), pp. 119-135.

295 Anders, G. (1992), pp. 81.

296 See, e.g. Kester, C.W./ Luehrmann, T.A. (1995), p. 123. Empirical studies have shown a substantial decrease in working capital levels of bought-out companies, e.g. Holthausen, R.W./ Larcker, D.F. (1996), p. 311.

performance, it is the strategic direction where the PE firm takes a substantial part in the decision-making process. These decisions comprise key considerations about the target market, product portfolio, degree of integration, price positioning, etc. However, the most common approach to improving strategic distinctiveness is to refocus on core activities in connection with an overall reduction of complexity.[297] After the removal of peripheral businesses, however, either internal or external growth must be accomplished in order to build a successful buyout story with an exit route via a trade sale or public offering.[298]

2.3.3.2.2. Indirect levers

As pointed out, indirect levers do not impose a direct impact on the value of a company, but may have a substantial indirect effect via their influence on one or more direct levers. BERG / GOTTSCHALG (2003) distinguish two categories of indirect levers, the reduction of agency cost and the parenting advantage that a PE firm may exert on its portfolio firms.[299]

The relevance of **agency cost** has been described in chapter 2.2.3. Three ways to reduce agency conflicts are frequently mentioned in the buyout literature: the reduction of managerial discretion, incentive alignment through an appropriate equity stake, and monitoring / controlling initiatives. The first two aspects are implemented through the appropriate financial structure in which the debt burden and equity share force the management to run the firm efficiently.[300] In the holding period tight monitoring and control of management activities is at the core of an amended governance structure.[301] The performance of the company and hence the management is continuously evaluated through a new corporate governance, where the investor holds seats on the supervisory board or even directly on the management board.[302] The level of involvement by the financial investor generally depends on the policy of the fund to pursue a hands-on strategy. Active investors strive for very tight monitoring of their portfolio companies through direct involvement (e.g. management board representation). Conversely, hands-off investors employ more indirect monitoring instruments (e.g. debt level).[303]

---

297 Easterwood, J./ Seth, A./ Singer, R.F. (1993), pp. 39-41.
298 Wright, M./ Hoskisson, R.E./ Busenitz, L.W. (2001), pp. 122-123; Markides, C. (1997), pp. 20.
299 Berg, A. / Gottschalg, O. (2003), p. 25.
300 These aspects are discussed in chapter 2.3.2.2.1.
301 Singh, H. (1990), pp. 121-122; Hite, G.L./ Vetsuypens, M.R. (1989), pp. 955-956.
302 Anders, G. (1992), p. 82.
303 Cotter, J.F./ Peck, S.W. (2001).

Finally, the PE firm may exert further influence on the portfolio firms, which can be subsumed under the term **parenting advantage** and which have consequences similar to those that are discussed in the research on multi- vs. single-business companies.[304] The first effect refers to the entrepreneurial spirit, which the buyout stimulates amongst managers and employees. Releasing the company from bureaucratic and organisational constraints and refocusing activities purely on the achievement of financial results should restore a climate of innovation and drive.[305] It may be particularly prevalent when a firm used to be a division or department of a large corporation, where a division's importance within a firm is often diluted by other factors, irrespective of its operating performance.[306] While the release of conglomerate constraints is different between divisional and whole-firm buyouts, the "once-in-a-lifetime opportunity" certainly provides additional momentum to the management and to the firm.[307]

In addition to triggering an entrepreneurial spirit, the often informal but constructive interaction between the financial investor and the portfolio company provides a comparative advantage over stand-alone firms.[308] In this respect, the PE firm takes on a role as active advisor to the management and the firm as such by selecting and replacing management teams.[309] Established PE firms have a track record of transactions in various industries under different circumstances. This knowledge is readily transferable to the portfolio firm and would not be available without the PE investor.[310]

Finally and helpful through the entire process, PE firms possess a wide and dense network of contacts in various industries, particularly in professional services. Not only during his or her time as investment manager but also in previous professions, a PE firm professional will have developed a network of valuable contacts.[311]

2.3.4. Exit

Whether all value-adding activities ultimately result in an appropriate return to the fund depends on the exit of the investment. Because a buyout is a priori intended to be sold off at the end of the

---

[304] Goold, M. et. al. (1994). For a thorough comparison of conglomerates vs. LBO associations regarding the value added by the holding company, see Baker, G.P./ Montgomery, C. (1994).

[305] Butler, P.A. (2001), p. 148; Lowenstein, L. (1985), p. 755.

[306] Wright, M./ Hoskisson, R.E./ Busenitz, L.W. (2001), p. 118.

[307] Lowenstein, L: (1985), pp. 755-756.

[308] Kester, C.W./ Luehrmann, T.A. (1995), p. 125.

[309] Anders, G. (1992), p. 80.

[310] Baker, G.P./ Smith, G.D. (1998), pp. 1-4.

[311] For example, the phenomenal success of KKR during the 1980s can be partly explained by the close ties to the financial community, in particular the affiliation with Drexel, Burnham & Lambert and advisory firms such as Deloitte, Haskins & Sells (today Deloitte & Touche). See Kaufman, A./ Englander, E. (1993), p. 75.

holding period in order to realise the value appreciation, the exit channel and the expected timing has to be considered early on at the time of the deal structuring, with a particular focus on the financial structure.[312]

There are several channels to exit the investment, the two most popular being the initial public offering (IPO) and trade sale.[313] Empirical studies show that the **initial public offering** (IPO) yields the highest return to the investors, which on average is five times the return generated by the second most profitable exit.[314] Another significant advantage consists in the direct access to further public financing[315] to cover liquidity needs arising from further firm growth.

Clear disadvantages of an IPO are the substantially higher direct and indirect cost. Direct cost include the transaction fees (e.g. banks), the cost of higher disclosure requirements (e.g. accounting principles, investor relations, rating), and the cost of investor attraction (e.g. roadshows).[316] Indirect cost relate mainly to the intense senior management involvement that absorbs much of the resources necessary for running the day-to-day business.[317] In addition, being a quoted company implies downsides resulting from external shareholder involvement; specifically, these are the need for continuous shareholder information (loss of "operating confidentiality"), exposure to stock price volatility, and lock-up[318] agreements.[319]

A **trade sale** usually represents the quickest way to divest the investment as potential investors are often identified and contacted during the holding period.[320] Moreover, it often constitutes the only channel available to small and medium-sized buyouts.[321] In a trade sale the new acquirer can either be a competitor, a company that is positioned forward or backward in the value chain, or an entirely unrelated business. A related business can often leverage substantial synergies. For this reason, too, a trade sale may yield high returns on the investment.[322]

312 Bader, H.P. (1996), pp. 136-137.
313 Further exit channels are the buyback, secondary buyout, investment swap, and liquidation, see Leschke, J. (2003), pp. 249-253.
314 In particular, a quoted company loses its value discount as a result of the private firm status such as the illiquidity discount, see chapter 2.3.1.2.1.
315 This can either be an additional equity offering (secondary offering) or publicly traded bonds, which have to meet rating and disclosure requirements similar to the ones a quoted company fulfills.
316 Bader, H.P. (1996), pp. 140-141. An IPO increases general investor awareness e.g. through analyst coverage which in turn improves the opportunities to raise liquidity at lower cost; e.g. Merton, R.C. (1987), p. 500 shows that the cost of capital are a decreasing function of the investor base.
317 Leschke, J. (2003), p. 250.
318 A lock-up bans the incumbent shareholders from selling off 100 per cent of their shares at the time of the IPO.
319 Bader, H.P. (1996), pp. 142-145.
320 Bader, H.P. (1996), p. 147.
321 Wall, J./ Smith, J. (1997), p. 37.
322 Bader, H.P. (1996), p. 147.

Moreover, in most cases the investor will be able to immediately realise 100 per cent in cash. The total cost are significantly lower than for an IPO, particularly given that only one investor needs to be found and persuaded. The main disadvantage, particularly from the perspective of the management, is the loss of independence as the bought-out company is reorganised as a subsidiary or division of a larger player.[323]

2.4. Implications for theory selection

The description of IBOs as the object of research has primarily served three objectives. First of all, explaining the financial structure of IBOs from a theoretical viewpoint requires selecting theories which best suit the specific nature of this type of buyout and which are best able to explain the financing behaviour. Second, in a subsequent step, the specific characteristics of IBOs will have an impact on the hypotheses development and particularly on the interpretation of the empirical results. Finally, the discussions put the capital structure in the context of the overall process of an IBO.

Some major findings from what has been discussed in the previous sections shall now be recapitulated to prepare the ground for the theoretical framework. The following aspects need to be kept in mind for the remainder of the study:

- IBOs exhibit substantial information asymmetries between the parties involved in the transactions. Problems of both hidden information and hidden action aggravate the transaction process and need to be addressed by the theory.

- The decision on the financial structure is taken by the major shareholder, the private equity investor; the better informed (incumbent) management has no substantial influence on the financial structure, particularly not on the leverage.

- Observability of the financing behaviour cannot be assumed given the opaque setting of private firms.

323 Leschke, J. (2003), p. 251.

3. Theoretical framework

Few topics in corporate management have been as controversially discussed as the question how managers choose the financial structure of the firms they preside over. The following section outlines the various approaches to answer the question and is divided into three sub-sections. After a brief overview of the main corporate finance theories developed in the past five decades, chapter 3.2 will be dedicated to provide an in-depth account of the static trade-off theory, while 3.3 discusses the impact of agency cost on the financial structure. These two theories constitute the theoretical background for the hypotheses on IBO capital structures.

3.1. Overview of corporate finance theories

The subsequent chapters provide a summary of major steps in the development of corporate finance theories. After outlining the traditional, neo-classic and neo-institutional views, this chapter will be rounded off by a review of these theories in light of their appropriateness for explaining capital structure decisions in IBOs.

3.1.1. Introduction

Corporate investments can be funded out of various sources. For example, funds can be generated internally on the basis of the company's existing assets. If the company is not able to raise the necessary amount, parts or the entire sum have to be injected by external parties.[324]

An IBO has to be classified as an event of external financing, as the NewCo. is founded exclusively for the purpose of taking over a target company without any initial cash endowment.[325] Unlike e.g. corporate M&A transactions, the NewCo. does not possess a cash pool and must receive the funding from external investors prior to the target acquisition.[326] When external parties provide funds for an IBO, they acquire claims over the cash flows generated by the bought-out company. However, these claims can vary in terms of seniority, maturity, and the structure of payments associated with these claims. The two generic forms of claims are fixed claims attached to debt capital and residual claims attached to equity capital. With regard to the nature of the claims, various intermediate types have been developed in the past, enabling financiers to perfectly match

[324] Franke, G. / Hax, H. (2003), p. 1; Wöhe, G. (2002), p. 670; Drukarczyk, J. (1993), p.15.
[325] See chapter 2.3.2.1.
[326] Weitnauer, W. (2003), p. 101.

varying financing needs and risk sensitivities.[327] The latter group can be summarised as sub-ordinated debt.[328]

It should be stressed that after the acquisition further financing of the business or a refinancing of the acquisition structure can be carried out using internal funds generated by the business.[329] In fact, the future *potential* to generate cash internally is inter alia an important determinant for the structure of the acquisition structure.[330]

However, the acquisition structure is exclusively financed through the three types of external funds, with the sub-ordinated capital dividing into debt- and equity-like instruments. Figure 8 depicts buyout financing as a case of external financing.

Figure 8: IBO financing as a case of external financing

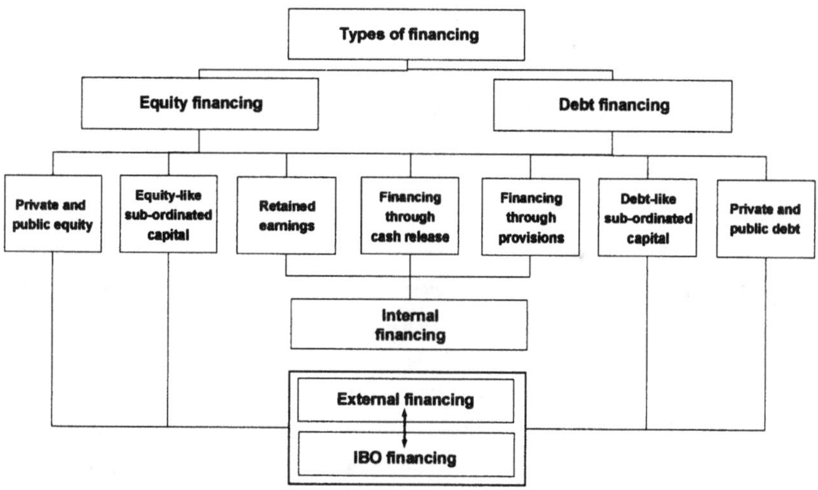

Source: Author, following Perridon, L./ Steiner, M. (2004), p. 354.

The composition of these different financing layers in clusters of more or less homogenous financial instruments constitutes the capital structure of a company.[331] How companies should design this structure and particularly what the optimal leverage, i.e. the amount of debt should be has been the

[327] Franke, G. / Hax, H. (2003), p. 31.
[328] See also chapter 4.3.
[329] Volkart, R. (1997), pp. 119-123.
[330] See Weitnauer, W. (2003), p. 70.
[331] Bitz, M. (2001), p. 1317.

subject of numerous academic discussions and articles. The starting point of the overview of corporate finance theories will be an outline of the leverage effect[332], which practice-oriented articles put in the forefront of discussions on LBOs.

3.1.2. The leverage effect

A first step towards understanding corporate financing behaviour is the leverage effect. This describes a mechanism encountered by *providers* of capital which emphasises the relationship between the return on equity and the cost of debt. A gradual substitution of equity capital (EC) by debt capital (DC) and hence an augmenting leverage (DC/EC) leads to an increase in the return on equity (r_e) as long as the return on assets (r_a) exceeds the cost of debt (r_d).[333]

$$r_e = r_a + \frac{DC}{EC} \times (r_a - r_d)$$

Of course, the mechanism also works in the opposite direction. Once the return on assets no longer exceeds the cost of debt, the return on equity will be leveraged downwards.[334]

In addition, it has been realised that with an increase in leverage the cost of debt are also likely to rise at some point, given the higher default risk.[335] Consequently, the positive effect of leveraging the return on equity will be reversed once the cost of debt exceeds the return on assets. In any case, the linear relationship requires adjustments regarding the shape of the function once a positive likelihood of a corporate default is assumed, which in turn depends on the actual leverage ratio.[336]

Providers of debt capital will consequently demand a higher price for the increasing likelihood of default. However, although the return on equity will only rise degressively, the basic mechanism still holds that it can be leveraged with more debt capital at a risk-dependent price. Figure 9 illustrates the relation between the return on equity (r_e) and the cost of debt (r_d) under the assumption of credit risk adjusted pricing.

---

332 See, e.g. Hug, J./ Ernst, D. (2003), p. 443.

333 See, e.g. Franke, G. / Hax, H. (2003), pp. 481-484; Coenenberg, A.G. (2003), p. 957; Perridon, L./ Steiner, M. (2004), pp. 488-489; Betsch, O./ Groh, A./ Lohmann, L. (2000), pp. 280.

334 Perridon, L./ Steiner, M. (2004), p. 491.

335 See, e.g. Solomon, E. (1963) or Gutenberg, E. (1987) for a comprehensive reading.

336 For a given level of business risk; see Perridon, L./ Steiner, M. (2004), pp. 490-491.

Figure 9: Leverage effect with credit risk-dependent cost of debt

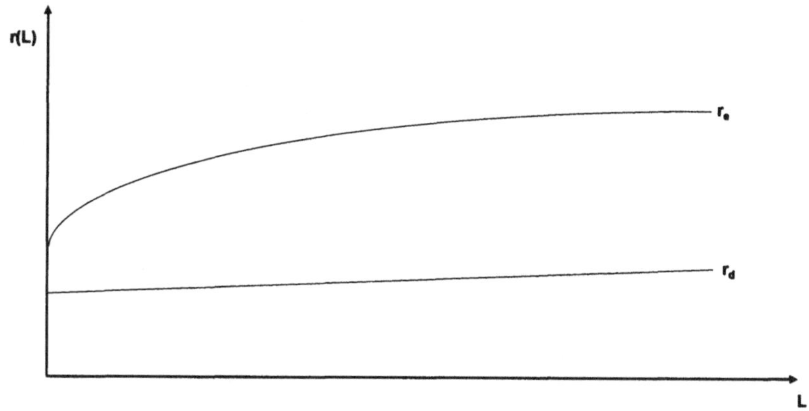

Source: Perridon, L./ Steiner, M. (2004), p. 490.

3.1.3. The traditional view

The traditional approach to financial decision making assumes the opposite view on the mechanism described for the leverage effect, hence the perspective of the *borrower* of capital.[337] The approach suggests that a firm can lower the cost of capital and therefore its value through leverage. Although investors will demand higher returns on their equity and for high debt levels also on the debt position, the penalty will be more than offset by the injection of the "cheaper" capital until an optimal leverage is achieved. Therefore, only the individual tolerance of the capital structure risk determines the optimal leverage and hence the maximum value of the firm.[338]

The more both debt and equity providers accept this risk and maintain the demanded cost the higher the optimal leverage ratio will be. It can be assumed that for low leverage ratios the risk of bankruptcy does not alter the cost of debt and equity significantly, but both will soar beyond a certain point, which in turn leads to a rise in the average cost of capital.[339]

Figure 10 depicts the cost of capital from a traditional viewpoint, where k_E denotes the cost of equity, k_D the cost of debt and k_T the total cost of capital as functions of the leverage L.

[337] Bitz, M. (2001), p. 1326.
[338] Perridon, L./ Steiner, M. (2004), p. 495.
[339] Breuer, W. (1998), p. 57.

Figure 10: Traditional view of the optimal leverage

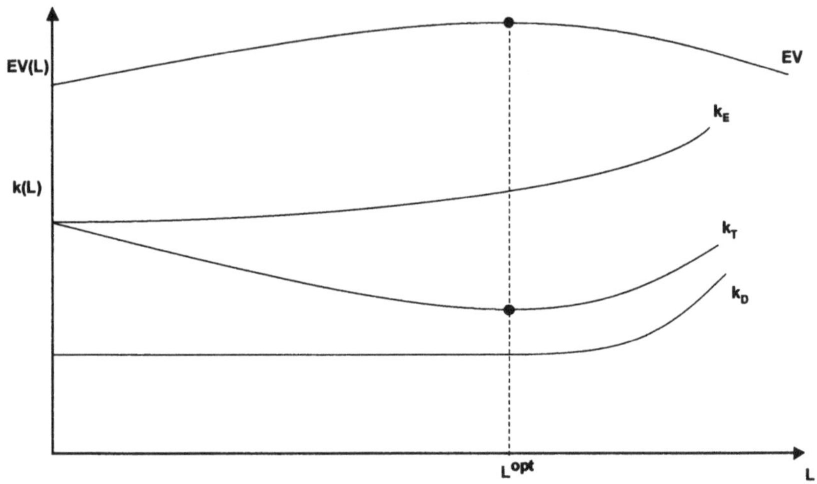

Source: Perridon, L./ Steiner, M. (2004), p. 496.

A central criticism of the traditional approach relates to the risk preferences of equity and debtholders, i.e. the risk position they would like to assume with regard to both the business and financial risk. Particularly, it neglects alternative ways to raise and invest capital and the general capital market conditions which the market participants face.[340]

Consequently, the discussion of how an increased leverage affects the return on equity and the capital structure risk does not give an answer to whether it increases stockholders' wealth.[341] An appropriate answer to that question requires an understanding of alternative investment opportunities for the equity being replaced by debt.[342] The following sections consider investing and borrowing on the personal level.

3.1.4. The neo-classic view

Basically, the neo-classic view on capital structure decisions starting with the seminal work of MODIGLIANI / MILLER explores the same question as the traditionalists.[343] Namely, whether by

[340] Breuer, W. (1998), pp. 58-59 or Bitz, M. (2001), p. 1328.
[341] Betsch, O./ Groh, A./ Lohmann, L. (2000), p. 279; Mittendorfer, R. (2001), p. 148.
[342] Franke, G. / Hax, H. (2003), p. 484.
[343] Modigliani, F./ Miller, M.H. (1958).

changing the leverage the total cost of capital and the firm value can be maximized for a given set of investments and gross profits.[344]

3.1.4.1. *The irrelevance theorem of MODIGLIANI / MILLER (1958)*

The MM world assumes a perfect capital market with no transaction cost (incl. taxes), no cost of distress, and the same access to capital markets for every market participant.[345] MM proved that the value of two homogenous firms must be equal irrespective of their capital structure (proposition I).[346]

The main difference to the traditional model – despite the strict assumptions – lies in the fact that market participants can take on every risk position they want just by perfectly replicating the firm's leverage on their own ("homemade leverage").[347] If this did not hold, investors could earn riskless profits based on arbitrage processes.[348]

Using MM's original notation,[349] proposition I can be stated as

$$V_j \equiv S_j + D_j = \frac{\overline{X_j}}{\rho_k}$$

where V_j is the market value of firm j, S_j and D_j the value of its outstanding shares and debt, respectively, and $\overline{X}$ the expected cash flow on the firm's assets, and ρ_k the expected return on assets of risk type k.

As an alternative to the argumentation via the arbitrage process, the irrelevance of leverage can be proved by means of the value additivity approach. The value of cash-ins from a given set of investments must be equal to the cash-outs to stock and debtholders. The way the firm is financed only determines the partition of the cash flows but not the total value of both streams together. Again, the reason is that investors can neutralise the consequences as a result of the partition by holding private counter-positions (an appropriately mixed portfolio of debt and equity claims). Hence, they can maintain the same position as before, regardless of how the cash streams are

344 Wöhe, G. (2002), p. 759.
345 For an overview of the assumptions of perfect capital markets, see Franke, G/ Hax, H. (2003), pp. 343-344; Betsch, O./ Groh, A./ Lohmann, L. (2000), p. 279.
346 Modigliani, F./ Miller, M.H. (1958), p. 266.
347 Modigliani, F./ Miller, M.H. (1958), p. 270.
348 Breuer, W. (1998), pp. 64-66.
349 Modigliani, F./ Miller, M.H. (1958), p. 268.

distributed.[350] Put differently, proposition I showed that if leverage has any benefits, then firms and investors are equally capable of producing them; so leverage does not impact the value of the firm.

In addition, MM's proposition II shows that leverage itself has no benefits for the cost of capital.[351] Proposition II derives directly from proposition I, as long as riskless debt is considered in the decision and hence requires little to prove except proposition I. Formally, proposition II can be formulated as follows:

$$i_j = \rho_k + (\rho_k - r)\frac{D_j}{S_j}$$

where i_j is the expected return on equity of the levered firm j and r the riskless rate for the firm's debt. The gains from using borrowed funds are offset exactly by the higher expected return which stockholders will require to compensate for the risk of a higher leverage. The linear relationship between the return on equity, the riskless rate[352], the expected return on assets and the firm's leverage is shown in figure 11.[353]

This closes the cycle to the traditional view, since the relationship would look the same in the traditional model if the providers of capital were to entirely neglect the risk position of the firm. The MM model allows any firm risk to be offset by holding a counter-balancing private portfolio. In other words, the irrelevance of a firm's capital structure for its value implies that individual investors do not prefer one risk position of the firm to the other. Only the individual risk preference (utility function) allows a judgement on whether one position is considered optimal from an individual investor's viewpoint. However, MM assume of course that investors have preferences and that individual optima exist. Specifically, they postulate that a firm's capital structure decisions may interfere with investor's optima but can be undone without further cost. Hence, investors still have the choice of taking the position they consider optimal, regardless of which capital structure decision the firm makes.[354]

[350] Franke, G/ Hax, H. (2003), pp. 343-346.
[351] Modigliani, F./ Miller, M.H. (1958), p. 271.
[352] MM's model assumed risk-neutral debt capital pricing. However, it has been proved by Stiglitz, J.E. (1969) and Rubinstein, M.E. (1973) that proposition I holds even if the cost of debt depend on the capital structure risk.
[353] Drukarczyk, J.(1993), p. 133.
[354] Drukarczyk, J. (1993), pp.147-149.

Figure 11: Cost of capital according to MM (1958)

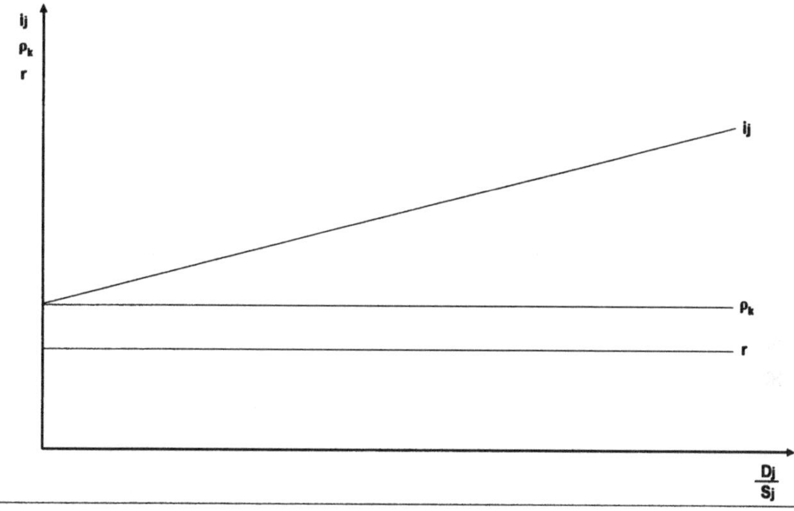

Source: Author, following Drukarczyk, J. (1993), p. 134.

From a theoretical viewpoint, MM's propositions have a tremendous impact on corporate finance decisions as they allow a capital market-based approach to valuing claims of different risk classes. However, in view of cross-sectional differences between capital structures and particularly leverage ratios, the MM propositions appear unable to explain reality.[355] In fact, MM themselves "corrected" their view, acknowledging the existence of corporate income taxes.

3.1.4.2. *The trade-off between taxes and financial distress*

Based on these considerations, MM extended their equilibrium model by proportional corporation taxes which the firm has to pay on its profits.[356] This represents the starting point for the gradual relaxation of the strict assumptions made in MM (1958).

[355] Bitz, M. (2001), p. 1329.

[356] Modigliani, F./ Miller, M.H. (1958), p. 272. Personal taxation is left out in the model of MM. Tax regulations relating to personal taxes vary particularly across countries. Statutes with lower taxes on capital gains were biased in favour of equity income over debt income. For a formal exposition on this aspect, see Modigliani, F./ Miller, M.H. (1963); Miller, M.H. (1977); DeAngelo, H./ Masulis, R. (1980) and Barnea, A./ Haugen, R./ Senbet, L. (1981).

Interest payments resulting from debt financing lower a firm's profit and hence reduce a firm's tax burden, a phenomenon which is called the "tax shield". As a consequence, taxes imply a permanent advantage of debt over equity, as private investors cannot replicate this effect through personal leveraging.[357] However, the theoretical optimum of close to 100% of debt appears to contradict reality, as some highly regarded firms such as Merck are financed virtually without debt.[358]

A number of other factors have a negative influence on the total share of debt. As a first counter-balancing effect, academics have elaborated on the probability of running into bankruptcy, producing direct and indirect cost for the firm. While the previous discussions on default risk as a reason to raise debt and equity prices focussed solely on the probability of losing money when the firm becomes financially distressed, the discussion here also covers the present value of potential cost associated with financial distress (e.g. process cost), representing an additional negative effect which in turn results in a lower optimal leverage. The trade-off between taxes and the cost of financial distress constitutes the static trade-off theory that remains a widely discussed model in the corporate finance literature.[359]

However, it has been frequently criticised over the years due to the lack of empirical support for the two aspects as exclusive determinants.[360] Particularly the relevance of the cost of financial distress has been questioned, based on both formal models[361] and empirical results.[362] However, despite the limited support from academics, pure economic reasoning suggests that the possibility of going bankrupt still plays a role among other determinants. Otherwise, changes in the regulatory environment (e.g. Basel II), which aim to better match debt prices with the risk taken by banks are not fully plausible.

3.1.5. The neo-institutional view

The assumption of perfect capital markets does not appear to reflect the real world. Market frictions are caused not only by taxes and the cost of financial distress, but also by the fact that participants

[357] Drukarczyk, J. (1993), pp.152-153.
[358] Brealey, R.A./ Myers, S.C. (2000), p.504.
[359] Important contributors to the trade-off theory include Kraus, A./ Litzenberger, R. (1973); Hirshleifer (1970), J. and Robichek, A.A./ Myers, S.C. (1965).
[360] See, e.g. Fama, E./ French, K. (2003), Titman, S./ Wessels, R. (1988) and Long, M./ Malitz, I. (1985). For theoretical considerations regarding the minor significance of the two aspects, see Breuer, W. (1998), pp. 109-112.
[361] See particularly Haugen, R.A./ Senbet, L.W. (1978) and (1988). The central criticism is based on the lack of a distinction between insolvency and bankruptcy.
[362] E.g. Frank, M./ Goyal, V. (2003).

in the market do not possess the same level of information.[363] The fact as such would not constitute a problem for less well-informed market participants as long as the better-informed players can credibly affirm that they will share all necessary information and act in the interest of non-insiders. However, both theory and practice assume that insiders will behave opportunistically and make decisions in their own best interest.[364] Relaxing the assumption of a symmetric distribution of information gives rise to a very fruitful field of research: the relevance of the capital structure for mitigating problems that result from information asymmetries. The following sections present a set of important theories, all rooted in the consideration of different levels of information among the contractors.[365]

3.1.5.1. Capital structure and hidden information

In their basic form, theories relating to hidden information argue that managers have more information about the firm than investors.[366] Two major lines of research follow this argumentation,[367] the first of which regards financial structure as a means of conveying information to external investors[368] and the second line postulates a pecking order of financing sources as a result of hidden information. However, the pecking order can be attributed to a signalling setting.[369]

In 1977, ROSS and LELAND / PYLE transferred knowledge developed for the labour market to the world of financial policy.[370] A management's financing behaviour conveys information about the quality of the firm which is usually referred to as **"signalling"**.[371] The model considers the management's incentives to choose a certain level of debt in light of the cost that would occur as a consequence of possible bankruptcy. These cost borne by the management (e.g. job loss) ensure the credibility of the decision that managers take, since more debt increases the likelihood of

---

363 Breuer, W. (1998), p. 119.
364 Franke, G./ Hax, H. (2003), pp. 421-422.
365 The discussions draw on the conflicts outlined in chapter 2.2.3.
366 Already in the generalisation of the MM framework Stiglitz, J. (1969) and (1974) noted that financial policies may convey information on firms' prospects.
367 A third line evolved under the term "screening", see, e.g. Rothschild, M./ Stiglitz, J. (1976). However, the only difference to the signalling approach by Ross, A. (1977) is that the information outsider willingly offers contracts on different terms. The information insider's choice reveals information about the firm. Hence, signalling and screening represent two sides of the same coin and shall thus not be discussed separately, although their modelling approach differs significantly. For basic discussions, see e.g. Wohlschieß, V. (1996), p. 20. In addition, credit rationing opens up another research area, see Stiglitz, J./ Weiss, A. (1981). Since the theory predicts banks' behaviour as a result of hidden information and the focus of this thesis lies on equity investors' behaviour, further discussions are forgone. For introductory reading, see Grinblatt, M./ Titman, S. (1998), pp. 557-560.
368 Ross, A. (1977) and Leland, H./ Pyle, D. (1977).
369 Myers, M.C./ Majluf, N.S. (1984) and Myers, S.C. (1984).
370 Advanced by Spence, A.M. (1973), the work is rooted in the work of Akerlof, G. (1970). An important subsequent contribution is Riley, J. (1975).
371 Ross, A. (1977), p. 27.

bankruptcy.[372] Whether a signal proves advantageous depends on the profits resulting from that signal and the cost of producing it. Only a positive difference between profit and cost can constitute a credible signal. Otherwise, it would make sense for firms of poor quality to convey a false signal.[373]

Similarly, the model of LELAND / PYLE regards the financial structure as a signal to outside investors. However, their focus is rather on the management's equity share as a reliable signal given their personal involvement.[374]

MYERS (1984) was motivated by MYERS / MAJLUF (1984) to describe the consequences of asymmetric information between managers and external investors as a **"pecking order"** of financing sources.[375] Investors, being aware of information asymmetries, conclude that managers are likely to issue equity when it is over-priced. As investors are only able to observe a medium quality, they tend to price equity issues at a discount. As a consequence, managers may be inclined to forgo positive NPV projects.[376]

However, the prohibitive cost of equity and the potential underinvestment problem can be circumvented by firms if they are able to use internal cash reserves or less risky debt. In this situation, managers will first use internal funds and then debt, which are less exposed to undervaluation.[377] Empirical tests predominantly support the relevance of the pecking order theory for corporates.[378]

3.1.5.2. Capital structure and agency conflicts

Theories based on agency conflicts address the problems dicussed in chapter 2.2.3. Because the investor cannot (fully) observe the agent's actions, he must assume that management will act opportunistically ("moral hazard").[379] Whether the cost associated with the harmful behaviour are denoted as agency cost of equity or debt depends on which investor they accrue to.

---

[372] Ross, A. (1977), pp. 27-34. A similar model, which uses debt as a signal, has been developed by Shah, S./ Thakor, A. (1987).
[373] Breuer, W. (1998), p. 122.
[374] Leland, H./ Pyle, D. (1977), pp. 372-377.
[375] The initial ideas of financing following a pecking order dates back to Donaldson, G. (1961) who found evidence for the existence of such financing behaviour. However, Myers, S.C. (1984) was the first to develop a clear theoretical underpinning of these observations.
[376] Myers, M.C. (1984), pp. 582-584.
[377] Harris, M./ Raviv, A. (1991), p. 306.
[378] E.g. Frank, M./ Goyal, V. (2003); Fama, E./ French, K. (2002) or Shyam-Sunder, L./ Myers, S.C. (1999).
[379] Franke, G./ Hax, H. (2003), pp. 428-429.

Debtholders and shareholders are likely to anticipate agency cost and put a risk premium on the required price which makes either equity or debt relatively more expensive. Therefore, the negative consequences ultimately accrue to those deciding on the financial structure and will hence be considered in the design of the financial structure.[380]

Potential risks associated with external equity financing can take on two different forms, excessive managerial consumption and the waste of free cash flow.[381] The risk of **managerial consumption** was described by JENSEN / MECKLING (1976).[382] They consider the case of an owner-manager who sells some of his equity to external investors. With the declining equity share they face a stronger incentive to spend company resources for private purposes, such as luxury cars or office furniture.[383]

The **waste of free cash flow** refers to the incentive for the management to invest in negative NPV projects, which only serve to make the firm bigger, as a size increase is paralleled by an enhancement of the management's reputation and, often, remuneration.[384] Debt may exert a disciplinary effect on the management, given the annual payments for interest and amortisation. Accordingly, the agency-oriented literature widely acknowledges debt to be a key instrument for disciplining and motivating the management to act in the interest of the equity investors.[385]

The conflicts can only be entirely avoided by a 100 per cent congruence of owner and manager.[386] However, as IBOs are characterised by small management stakes compared to typical management buyouts, these conflicts are probably highly relevant.

However, debt may also counter-balance its positive effect on the management's behaviour. Based on the model discussions of JENSEN (1986), STULZ (1990) emphasised that too much debt may force managers to skip positive NPV projects, given a lack of financial resources. Cost incurred by this underinvestment problem accrue likewise to shareholders and need to be traded against the benefits.[387]

---

380 Breuer, W. (1998), p. 155 and 179.
381 The two effects are also discussed under the terms perquisite consumption and overinvestment, respectively.
382 Jensen, M./ Meckling, W. (1976).
383 Jensen, M./ Meckling, W. (1976), pp. 312-313.
384 Jensen, M. (1986), p. 323.
385 See, e.g. the approaches discussed in Zwiebel, J. (1996) and Grossman, S./ Hart, O. (1982).
386 Fama, E.F. (1980), p. 295.
387 Stulz, R. (1990), p. 4.

Besides the principal-agent problems faced by external equity investors, similar problems arise from a viewpoint of external debt providers who act as agents vis-à-vis shareholders.[388] There are again two effects which academics have elaborated on: the risk of asset substitution and the problem of underinvestment.

Asset substitution also goes back to JENSEN / MECKLING'S 1976 article. Managers and other shareholders holding a certain part of the equity have an incentive to change their investment policy towards riskier projects. In doing so, they shift wealth from debtholders to shareholders, since debtholders were not a priori compensated for the increased level of risk.[389]

The decrease in the equity value due to the riskier investment programme can be more than compensated by the value gain at the cost of debtholders. However, debtholders are again likely to anticipate this behaviour for why shareholders will receive less for the debt than they would, e.g. in cases where managers did not hold equity shares.[390]

In 1977, MYERS pointed to the problem of **underinvestment**. When a firm is very close to bankruptcy, managers – with and without – an equity stake have a strong incentive to forgo profitable but risky projects because in the case of default they would bear the cost (job loss), and in the case of success the value would accrue largely to debtholders, thus securing their positions.[391]

3.1.5.3. Capital structure and product market interaction

Besides the two discussed problems above, a third line of research has evolved and has captured much (theoretical) attention. In particular, the interaction of the financial structure and the behaviour of market participants, specifically the interaction with the firm's competitors, has been a widely discussed issue in the neo-institutional finance literature. The idea was first elaborated by BRANDER / LEWIS (1986) in a formal model.[392] A large number of articles followed this work, all discussing effects of financial policies on product market participants.[393]

[388] See chapter 2.2.3.
[389] Jensen, M./ Meckling, W. (1976), pp. 334-347.
[390] Harris, M./ Raviv, A. (1991), p. 301.
[391] Myers, S.C. (1977), pp. 147-176.
[392] Brander, J.A./ Lewis, T.R. (1986), pp. 956-970.
[393] An overview of important studies is provided in Maksimovic, V. (1995) and Schumacher, F. (2001).

In a world where participants in a market cannot fully observe the behaviour of other firms, the financial structure conveys relevant information on the likely future strategy. More specifically, in markets with quantity competition firms can reliably commit themselves to behaving aggressively vis-à-vis competitors by increasing leverage as long as the financing behaviour itself can be observed by the market.[394]

However, the observability of financing behaviour is only one pre-condition. The incentive to trigger a reaction from competitors based on the firm's financial structure also depends on the firm's ability to influence the competitor's behaviour. Under atomistic competition, the actions of one market player may be observable but do not initiate actions by competitors. Hence, oligopolistic structures represent a necessary perequisite for this mechanism.[395]

3.1.5.4. Capital structure and the allocation of control rights

To provide a complete overview of the main lines of corporate finance research, the allocation of control rights will be briefly discussed again since valuable inputs have emerged from this research area. Chapter 2.3.2.2.2 has already covered this aspect in part under the heading financial contracting.

The discussion so far has covered functions of financing related to signals, preferences and incentives in the context of the economic characteristics of debt and equity. Besides understanding the effects triggered by equity or debt claims, the question of the allocation of state-dependent control rights over the firm can also be of some interest. Contracts can only cover those aspects that are observable by all contracting parties. Accordingly, they are not able to control for all future contingencies. This uncertainty arising from the incompleteness of the contract suggests an allocation of control rights to determine who decides what.[396]

Irrespective of the information distribution, the need for an allocation of control rights through equity and debt instruments arises. This is particularly the case when agreements cannot be fully verified, and future conflicts of interest seem likely. Usually, if contractor A disagrees with certain decisions to be taken by his contractor B he is able to purchase the decision right by making transfer

[394] Breuer, W. (2001), p. 152.
[395] Breuer, W. (1998), p. 201.
[396] Breuer, W. (1998), p. 212-214.

payments and thus block the decision. However, if these payments are economically unfavourable, then the allocation of rights in the financial contract becomes eminent.[397]

Two important fields of research have emerged in the financial contracting literature. The first of these discusses a state-contingent allocation of control rights, particularly the question of when to liquidate the firm and when to continue.[398] The second line pursues the question how the empirically observable "one share one vote" allocation can be explained. In resolving this question, academics consider the desired mechanism which supports efficient take-over attempts and retard inefficient attempts measured by the impact on total welfare.[399]

3.1.6. Discussion of theory choice

In chapter 2.4, some aspects have been emphasised which determine the appropriateness of the presented theories for the following empirical study. These aspects centred mainly upon the existence of information asymmetries and the fact that the poorly-informed PE investor structures the financial package and not the management.

As mentioned earlier, the trade-off theory lacks empirical support for usual corporates. Yet, the author believes that the inclusion of taxes and particularly the probability of becoming insolvent must be addressed in the empirical study for two reasons. On the one hand, strong information asymmetries limit the possibility of assessing the risk of default and thus have an indirect impact in the context of the trade-off theory.[400] Since IBOs exhibit substantial asymmetries, the cost of financial distress may be higher than for usual corporates. On the other hand, changes in the regulatory environment make a possible corporate default a relevant factor. With regard to the forthcoming introduction of Basel II, financial distress obviously has to be taken into consideration, particularly as the regulations will have an impact on the financing behaviour of banks vis-à-vis mid-sized companies.[401] Both these aspects may make the trade-off theory more relevant for IBOs than hitherto suggested in empirical studies.

---

397 Breuer, W. (1998), p. 214-216.

398 See, e.g. Aghion, P./ Bolton, P. (1992), pp. 473-494. For related work, see Bolton, P./ Scharfstein, D. (1990); Fluck, Z. (1998) and Hart, O./ Moore, J. (1998). These later works must be contrasted with earlier literature based on costly state verification, which discuss that profitability is private information but can be made public at a certain cost. However, these works do not emphasis contractual incompleteness and the allocation of decision/control rights. See Townsend, R. (1979) and Gale, D./ Hellwig, M. (1985).

399 Breuer, W. (1998), p. 216-217. Fundamental articles on this topic are Harris, M./ Raviv, A. (1988) and (1989) as well as Grossman, S./ Hart, O. (1988).

400 E.g. Ang, J.S. (1991) addresses this aspect in his frequently cited article on small business finance.

401 For the expected impact of Basle II on the financing of mid-sized companies and M&A activity in this segment, see, e.g. Brids, C. (2002) or Albach, H. (2001), pp. 553-554.

Clearly, information asymmetries are highly relevant to an IBO transaction. However, their relevance deviates slightly from the assumptions made in neo-institutional theories as regards their influence on the financing mix and hence makes some theories more suitable than others.[402] To illustrate this aspect, the following figure 12 contrasts the different information and decision structures as assumed by the neo-institutional context to those typical of IBOs. The IBO setting is based on the author's own experience and on interviews with various market participants.

Figure 12: Neo-institutional vs. IBO information and decision structures

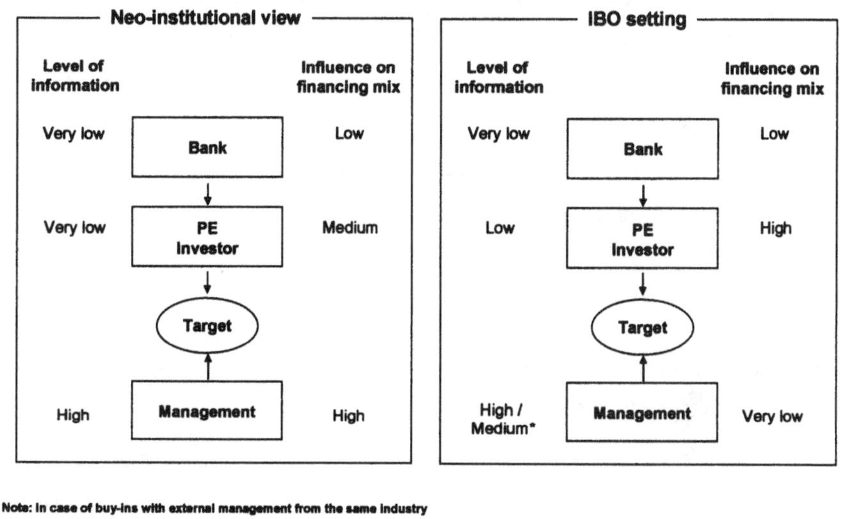

Source: Author.

In a neo-institutional setting the management structures the financial package and holds the relevant set of information. As a consequence of the hidden information, theory predicts that financing will follow a pecking-order or recommends that management should use the financial structure as a signalling tool.[403]

By contrast, an IBO setting does not provide a basis for discussing financial decisions from the perspective of hidden information problems. First of all, **signalling** does not constitute a workable approach as the poorly informed PE investor has the strongest influence on the financial structure and the management is only involved in determining the equity share. Even the final equity share of

[402] See also chapter 2.2.4.

the management is unlikely to deviate substantially from what the PE investors plans to assign. The signalling approach, however, requires that the information insider takes the decision to signal the quality of the firm to information outsiders. This does not hold for IBOs in general and especially not when an external management joins the team.[404]

A "shortened"[405] **pecking-order** shall also not be considered in the empirical study because the information asymmetries between PE investors and banks are minor at the time of the acquisition. The possible security undervaluation, which gives rise to the pecking-order theory does not occur in the same way as in a neo-institutional setting. In IBOs, the PE investor and the bank share much the same set of information since banks participate in the entire due diligence process and have access to all relevant sources of information.[406]

Problems arising from **hidden action**, however, are particularly pronounced in IBOs as long as the management does not hold all residual claims (although the principal-agent relation with the debtholders still holds). For theories based on moral hazard issues, it does not change the line of argumentation whether the PE investor or the management decides on the financial structure. In either setting, the management acts as an agent to the PE investor and jointly with the PE investor as agent to the banks. The interrelations determine agency cost at the expense of the majority shareholder or the debtholder. Therefore, all four lines of research may serve as explanations for capital structure decisions.

Finally, the interaction of the financial structure with product markets and financial contracting theory may also serve as theoretical framework. It can be said, however, that both approaches are insufficient for the purpose of this thesis. The former, **financial structure and product market interaction** lacks the necessary observability for company outsiders. While competitors may notice that a player in the industry is being bought out, they are unlikely to observe whether or not the buyout is financed with high proportions of debt capital. Moreover, from a practical viewpoint, it is virtually impossible for promoters of empirical studies like the present one to investigate the

403 See chapter 3.2.4.1.

404 Consequently, even the determination of the management equity stake would not really represent a signal in the sense of Leland / Pyle's argumentation. See Leland, H./ Pyle, D. (1977), pp. 371-387.

405 The pecking-order may be "shortened" since the PE investor cannot capitalise on internal funds as the buyout vehicle is usually not endowed with own funds. In addition, the target itself lacks the necessary cash because buyouts are mostly carried out on a debt- and cash-free basis.

406 The PE investor might be slightly better informed due to a closer contact with the internal management (as firm insider).

reaction of competitors to a buyout in the industry. An exception would be e.g. industries with very transparent pricing such as retailing.[407]

Financial contracting, however, has quite frequently been the subject of empirical tests and could well serve as a theoretical framework for this study. Yet, PE professionals have indicated in interviews that they are very unlikely to provide access to individual financial contracts owing to the strictness of the confidentiality agreements. Nevertheless, both theories would be interesting areas for further empirical studies given the usually oligopolistic structures of IBO industries and the complexity of the contracts.

Figure 13 summarises the results of the theory selection. The static trade-off theory and agency models appear to best serve the objective of the present thesis to test a small set of established corporate finance theories for their validity for IBOs. Other models display lack of fit with the nature of IBOs on one or more accounts. Therefore, the subsequent sections elaborate the two selected theories in depth.

Figure 13: Theory selection

Approach	Neo-Classic	Neo-Institutional				
Theory	Trade-off Theory	Pecking Order	Signalling	Agency conflicts	Product Market Interaction	Financial Contracting
Type of information asymmetry	N/A	Hidden Information	Hidden Information	Hidden Action	Hidden Action	Incomplete contracts
Applicable for this IBO study?	YES	NO	NO	YES	NO	NO
Rationale	• Relevance with regard to changing regulatory environment (Basel II) • Strong information asymmetries reinforce probability of company default or at least hampers its assessment	• At the time of the acquisition minor IA between PE investor and bank • PE investor decides on financing mix • No threat of undervaluation	• PE investor decides on financial structure • Informed mgmt. does not substantially influence the financing structure	• Threat of moral hazard incurs agency costs for both PE investor and bank	• Financing behaviour unobservable for company outsiders • Competitor reaction unobservable for promoter of empirical study	• Contract design unobservable within the empirical study

Source: Author.

[407] In fact, to the author's knowledge the only empirical studies which address competitors' reactions in the context of LBOs are Chevalier, S. (1995a) and (1995b), where retailers' pricing was examined as a consequence of a competitor's LBO. A well-known empirical study covering "usual" corporates is Phillips, G.M. (1995).

3.2. The trade-off between taxes and financial distress

The development of the trade-off between the benefits from tax-deductible interests and the probability of bankruptcy represents a milestone in the understanding of corporate financial behaviour. The remainder of this paragraph presents key studies on this theory. After an introductory discussion of the static trade-off theory, MILLER'S response from 1977 as a return to the irrelevance of capital structures shall be presented. Finally, DEANGELO / MASULIS' famous work in 1980, which builds on MILLER'S idea, rounds off the section.

3.2.1. The static trade-off theory

The development of the static trade-off theory was triggered by the works of MM in 1958. In their "correction article", MM introduced the effect of corporate taxation.[408] The implication of their model was an optimal debt level of 100 per cent, which contradicts reality and appeared so extreme that in the following years scholars focussed on the cost of financial distress as a counter-effect.

Particularly the work of ROBICHEK / MYERS (1965), HIRSHLEIFER (1970) and KRAUS / LITZENBERGER (1973) represented major steps towards understanding that firms have to trade the cost of potential financial distress against the benefits of taxes. The first two studies emphasised the need to incorporate the expected cost of financial distress,[409] which comprises both direct cost, such as the cost of the process, and indirect cost like reputation losses.[410] Prior to a likely default especially the cost of the various contracts with a firm's stakeholders (suppliers, customers, employees, etc.) begin to rise as a result of the increased default likelihood.[411]

KRAUS / LITZENBERGER were the first to establish a state-preference framework for the trade-off between taxes and the cost of financial distress, leading to an optimal debt level of less than 100 per cent.[412] Figure 14 illustrates the value of the firm (V) as a function of leverage (L) considering the present value of the tax shield and the present value of the expected cost of financial distress.

---

[408] Modigliani, F./ Miller, M.H. (1963).

[409] Robichek, A.A./ Myers, S.C. (1965), pp. 20-22 and Hirshleifer, J. (1970), p. 264.

[410] For the various possible direct and indirect costs, see Franke, G./ Hax, H. (2003), p. 11.

[411] Shapiro, A./ Titman, S. (1986), pp. 216-220.

[412] Kraus, A./ Litzenberger, R.H. (1973), pp. 911-922. This represents the static trade-off theory as referred to throughout the remainder of the thesis. However, some authors subsume other cost and benefits under the term trade-off such as even the discplination effect or agency costs, see, e.g. Frank, M./ Goyal, V. (2003), pp. 6-11.

Figure 14: The static trade-off theory of capital structure

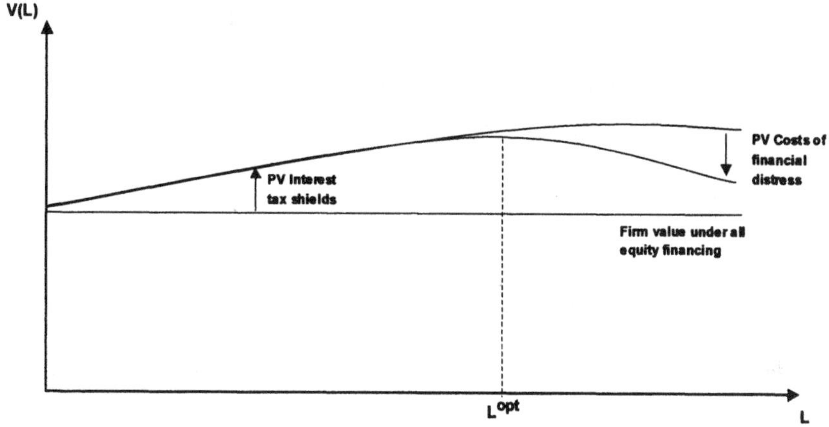

Source: Myers, S.C. (1984), p. 577.

MILLER (1977) notes that firms choose optimal debt levels by considering the ex-ante cost of financial distress and thus suggests that the mentioned cost of financial distress must be multiplied by the conditional probability of distress to measure ex-ante cost.[413] This implies that firms in which the cost of financial distress are high will have – irrespective of the likelihood of their bankruptcy – lower debt levels than firms with less substantial cost. In turn, debt levels in firms with the same cost of financial distress will differ in line with the likelihood of their defaulting.

Estimating the direct and indirect cost of financial distress is a particularly difficult task as it cannot be easily distinguished from other negative operating effects. Accordingly, empirical studies have come up with controversial findings.[414] The results of a fairly large number of empirical studies, which found the cost of financial distress to be substantial, might be overestimated, as they do not clearly discriminate between financial and economic distress or an interaction of the two.[415]

In addition, proponents of the theory point out that much of the existing empirical research has been misguided since growth in future profits, and hence future tax shields, are reflected in the equity

413 Miller, M. (1977), p. 263.

414 While some studies estimate them to be up to 20 per cent of firm value, see e.g. Andrade, G./ Kaplan, S. (1998), others put it at less than 5 per cent of market value, see e.g. Warner, J (1976). The latter article triggered Miller's doubts about the actual ex-ante relevance of bankruptcy costs, although indirect costs were not included in the study.

415 Andrade, G./ Kaplan, S. (1998), p. 1444. Examples of these empirical studies are Gilson, S. (1997); Hotchkiss, E. (1995); Asquith, P./ Gertner, R./ Scharfstein, D. (1994) or the frequently cited article by Altman, E. (1984).

value but not in the debt value.[416] This means debt increases to match future profits are not included in the leverage ratio. In other words, firms may have low leverage ratios but are yet fully tax-shielded. In short, debt ratios provide an inappropriate basis for testing the trade-off theory.[417]

The difficult task in estimating tax effects on corporate value, however, is to overcome data problems and complex tax codes as well as to comprehend taxation mechanism on the personal level.[418] Though substantial progress has been made to quantify tax benefits,[419] the same academics believe that for firms with low cost of financial distress the tax advantage should show up more powerfully and firms should be more levered than they actually are.[420]

3.2.2. The cost of financial distress: MILLER's (1977) criticism and capital market equilibrium

MILLER (1977) commented on the heated debates centring upon the discussion of bankruptcy cost that empirical research had up to that time not been able to identify a substantial influence on the firm value.[421] Instead, he postulated that the mere introduction of personal taxes could eliminate the "100 per cent debt" implication without considering bankruptcy cost or other effects. Considering the "classic US tax system"[422], he explicitly accounts for the existence of personal taxation of interests and dividends on the level of the firm's investors.[423] Central to the argumentation is the discrimination of interest income in comparison to dividend income, since taxes on interest income are significantly higher than taxes on dividend income.[424]

According to his argumentation, the marginal cost of debt and equity net of personal and corporate taxes should likewise be in equilibrium, so firms are indifferent between the two financing sources. Basically, the tax benefits of debt are offset by the debt disadvantage with regard to personal taxes. Depending on the personal tax rate, debt investors will demand higher pre-tax interest rates in order

---

[416] Renowned proponents of the static trade-off theory are Mackie-Mason, J. (1990); Smith, C.W./ Watts, R.L. (1992) and Long, M.S./ Malitz, E.B. (1985).

[417] Berens, J.L./ Cuny, C.J. (1995), p. 1186.

[418] Graham, J.R. (2000), p. 1901.

[419] Estimates on tax benefits range from 4.3 per cent of firm value net of personal taxation (see Graham, J.R. (2000)) to 10 per cent net of personal taxes (see, Kemsley, D./ Nissim, D. (2002)). However, in extreme situations the benefits can be much larger. The frequently discussed LBO of Safeway and RJR Nabisco achieved up to 20 per cent net of total asset value, see Graham, J.R. (2000), p. 1902.

[420] See, e.g. Graham, J.R. (2000).

[421] Miller, M. (1977), p. 262.

[422] The classic US corporate tax system treats corporate income as linear taxable, interest is fully deductible and equity payouts are not deductible. See Graham, J.R. (2000), pp. 1903-1904.

[423] Miller, M. (1977), pp. 268-273.

[424] The discrimination of any type of capital income was abolished with the introduction of the "tax reform act" in 1986. See Brealey, R./ Myers, S. (2000), p. 509.

to offset the discrimination of interest income. Hence, the returns on equity and debt will be in equilibrium after tax assuming that risk profiles are equal.[425]

On the basis of this mechanism MILLER derives an aggregate market equilibrium for the debt and equity volumes emitted by the market. What MILLER calls "clientele effect" refers to the different structure of debt-equity portfolios held by investors as a result of their varying income tax rates. Starting from fully equity-financed firms, an increase in debt can only be stimulated through an increase in pre-tax interest rates paid by corporates.[426]

Initial increases in market debt volumes without an increase in interest rates will only be accepted be tax-exempt investors. In order to attract tax-paying investors, interest rates must increase accordingly. That way, the "clientele effect" entails rising market debt volumes as a function of corporates' pre-tax interest rates. A system with progressively rising personal tax rates results in a convex function for debt, intercepting with a horizontal supply function at the market equilibrium quantity. Beyond this point, further debt increases do not make sense for firms, as the necessary interest rate increase is no longer offset by tax advantages.[427]

As a consequence of this model, an optimal debt volume only exists on the aggregate market level. Conversely, the firm's debt increase does not affect its value since the tax shield is exactly offset by the higher pre-tax interest payments.[428]

3.2.3. Capital structure optimum after DEANGELO/MASULIS (1980): The marginal tax rate

DEANGELO / MASULIS (1980) broaden the idea of MILLER to include other tax-deductible expenditures.[429] They, too, adopt the central assumption of a progressive personal taxation and a personal tax system which discriminates interest income against dividend income. However, they also include so-called "tax shield substitutes" or "non-debt tax shields", expenditures which are likewise deductible and reduce the tax burden. Among them are depreciation expenses, investment tax credits or tax-loss carry forwards.[430]

---

[425] Miller, M. (1977), p. 267.
[426] Miller, M. (1977), pp. 268-270.
[427] Miller, M. (1977), p. 269.
[428] Again, this implication only holds for tax systems distinguishing between interest income and dividend income on the level of the investor. The assumption has been frequently criticised in the literature, see, e.g. Brealey, R./ Myers, S. (2000), p. 509.
[429] DeAngelo, H./ Masulis, R. (1980).
[430] DeAngelo, H./ Masulis, R. (1980), pp. 7-10.

These non-debt tax shields reduce the marginal tax rate and thus the marginal benefit of higher debt volumes. On the basis of these considerations, DEANGELO / MASULIS derive a different market equilibrium which lies below that of MILLER.

As the tax advantage of debt decreases, companies will only accept further debt capital in case of adequately reduced interest payments.[431] Hence, a declining supply function follows. Figure 15 contrasts the market equilibrium of MILLER (1977) and DEANGELO / MASULIS (1980).

Figure 15: Capital market equilibria according to Miller (1977) and DeAngelo / Masulis (1980)

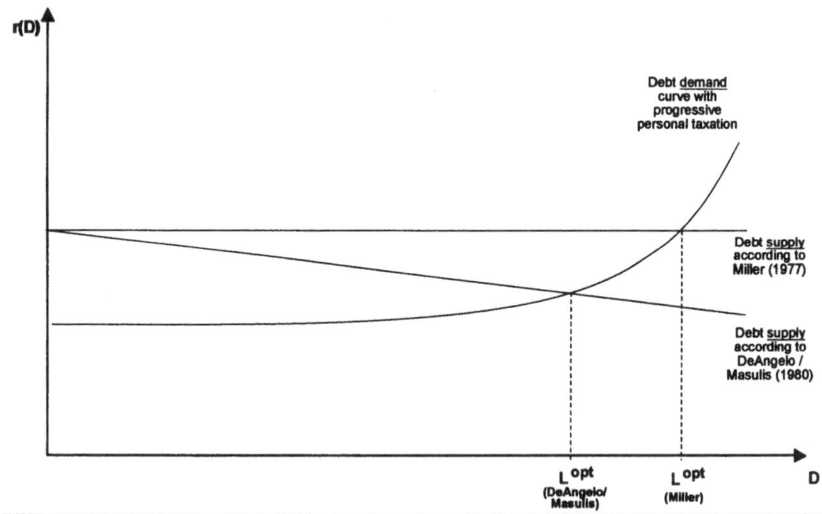

Source: Author, following Miller (1977) and DeAngelo / Masulis (1980).

The central implication of the model is that the irrelevance of capital structure decisions no longer holds from the individual firm's perspective as long as declining marginal tax rates are considered. Consequently, every firm has an optimal debt ratio, since different tax exposures exist, a fact which comes closer to the real world.[432]

However, the general validity of the model has been questioned following the results of empirical studies. For example, the regression test performed by BRADLEY / JARRELL / KIM (1984), an early

[431] DeAngelo, H./ Masulis, R. (1980), pp. 13-15.
[432] DeAngelo, H./ Masulis, R. (1980), pp. 13.

study on the marginal tax rate hypothesis was unable to confirm a predicted negative relation between leverage and non-debt tax shields. Instead, they found a significant positive relation.[433]

Explanations were advanced by DAMMON / SENBET (1988) and MACKIE-MASON (1990). The former emphasised the correlation of non-debt tax shields with other firm characteristics, which are predicted to correlate positively with leverage, in particular profitability and investments. If profitable firms invest heavily and borrow to fund these investments, this can induce a positive relation between debt and non-debt tax shield and render the tax substitution between interest and non-debt tax shields. In this context, the optimal level of non-debt tax shields is considered an endogenous variable.[434]

MACKIE-MASON,[435] however, pointed out that a large number of factors could invalidate the assessment of non-debt tax shields.[436] He specifically emphasised that non-debt tax shields are only relevant for moderately profitable firms. Unprofitable firms are likely to have a marginal tax rate of close to zero, irrespective of the level of non-debt tax shields, and highly profitable firms are usually not in a position to substantially reduce their taxable income – and hence the marginal tax rate – unless they carry large amounts of non-debt tax shield (e.g. loss carry forwards from an acquired company).[437]

3.3. Capital structure and agency conflicts

About the time when the discussion about the role of taxes in financing decisions peaked, a second assumption of MM propositions was relaxed by finance academics: the fact that contractors do not necessarily act in the same interest and that their behaviour is mutually unobservable. This constitutes one aspect of the neo-institutional view on capital structure decisions. In particular, it has been widely argued that agents do not always behave in the best interest of their principals. In their pioneering article JENSEN / MECKLING (1976) defined two fields of conflict, between the management and shareholders on the one hand and between debtholders and shareholders on the other.[438]

---

433 Bradley, M./ Jarrell, G./ Kim, E.H. (1984).
434 Dammon, R./ Senbet, L.W. (1988), pp. 358-359.
435 Later also Dhaliwal, D./ Trezevant, R. / Wang, S. (1992).
436 Mackie-Mason, J.K. (1990), pp. 1476-1478.
437 Mackie-Mason, J.K. (1990), pp. 1482-1483.
438 See chapter 2.2.3.

These conflicts trigger agency cost which are anticipated by investors and thus increase either debt or equity relative to the alternative financing source. The subsequent sections will discuss in more depth the implications of these two conflicts for financial decision making.

3.3.1. Principal-agent relation between debtholders and shareholders

Majority shareholders and managers who are entitled to hold parts of the residual claims take on an agent role vis-à-vis the providers of debt financing. Accordingly, in the post-investment phase the shareholders can behave to the disadvantage of debtholders, either leading to a problem of asset substitution after JENSEN / MECKLING (1976) or underinvestment as postulated by MYERS (1977).

3.3.1.1. Asset Substitution after JENSEN / MECKLING (1976)

Shareholders of a leveraged firm can make use of asset substitution to extract value from debtholders after debt has been put in place. The value of debtholders' claims is reduced by shifting risk from shareholders to debtholders for which the latter have not been compensated in advance.[439]

Within an options framework developed by BLACK / SCHOLES (1973),[440] asset substitution results from choosing higher-risk projects after debt has been issued under the condition that debtholders expect a less risky investment program. The basic considerations of JENSEN / MECKLING will now be summarised briefly.[441]

A manager-owned firm with no debt outstanding is assumed to face two mutually exclusive investment opportunities. Both investment opportunities I_1 and I_2 bear the same initial cost and yield random payoff streams with the same expected market value; they only differ by their variances $\sigma^2_1 < \sigma^2_2$. The risk-neutral owner-manager will be indifferent between the two investments in the event that he decides first on the investment program and then sells claims on the cash-ins from the investment. If, however, he decides first to issue debt and then on the investment programme the opportunity to extract value from debtholders arises. Using the BLACK / SCHOLES formula, the value of the debt and equity can be computed since the total value of the firm is independent of the investment choice.[442]

[439] Jensen, M.C./ Meckling, W.H. (1976), p. 335.
[440] Black, F./ Scholes, M. (1973).
[441] For the original argumentation, see Jensen, M.C./ Meckling, W.H. (1976), pp. 334-337.
[442] Jensen, M.C./ Meckling, W.H. (1976), p. 335.

The levered equity can be regarded as a European call option. Since its value increases with the variance of the outcome distribution, the equity (debt) value after the lower-risk investment I_1 has been undertaken is lower (higher) than the equity (debt) value for the higher-risk project I_2. Consequently, the owner-manager could benefit by pretending to exercise I_1, sell the debt at a higher price, and subsequently change the investment programme towards I_2.[443]

In order to avoid this behaviour,[444] debt investors may take appropriate counter-measures, summarised as agency cost of debt, and which make debt less valuable relative to equity. Specifically, they include the cost of monitoring and bonding the contract partner.[445] In addition, JENSEN / MECKLING also denote the cost associated with an increased probability of default as agency cost. They particularly point to the impact this would have on operating cost and revenues. An example would be the need to pay higher salaries to compensate for the increased risk or the threat of losing key customers who fear the potential collapse of a key supplier.[446]

3.3.1.2. Underinvestment after MYERS (1977)

A firm can be considered the sum of assets in place and opportunities to grow these assets. However, the value of the growth opportunities depends, at least in part, on future discretionary investments. Depending on the state of nature the investment is undertaken or not. Therefore, the growth opportunities can be viewed as call options to make future investments.[447] This represents the starting point for MYERS in determining how high-risk debt can impact the decision to actually pursue all growth opportunities. Firms that base their borrowing on future cash flows arising from real options (cash flow lending) tend to forgo these options and consume the debt funding instead. This disincentive is reinforced for higher debt levels as the owner increasingly serves the interest of the banks exclusively. The probability of benefiting from future earnings decreases.[448] Conversely, the less likely a firm is to become insolvent, the stronger is the incentive to actually exercise the given options.

In other words, the reinvestment of cash flows is undervalued relative to the alternative of distributing cash to shareholders, because the returns on investment accrue to debtholders with non-

---

443 Jensen, M.C./ Meckling, W.H. (1976), pp. 335-336.
444 Again, the debtholder will anticipate the behaviour and only pay a price that is consistent with the riskier project. See Jensen, M.C./ Meckling, W.H. (1976), p. 337.
445 See chapter 2.2.3.
446 Jensen, M.C./ Meckling, W.H. (1976), pp. 341-342.
447 Myers, S.C. (1977), p. 150.
448 Myers, S.C. (1977), pp. 156.

zero probability. Issuing risky debt hence weakens the incentive to undertake good future investments.[449]

3.3.2. Principal-agent relation between external shareholders and owner-managers

Similar to the agency cost of debt, outside equity likewise incurs cost which counter-balance the cost associated with debt financing and are borne by shareholders. Again, works particularly by JENSEN have paved the way to better understand the use of equity financing in a moral hazard framework.

With regard to the agency cost of debt, shareholders will also anticipate the risk associated with contractual relations with the management. Accordingly, they are likely to discount the value of their equity to match the expected value of the agency cost. In this way, equity capital trades lower in value than debt capital.[450]

3.3.2.1. Managerial consumption after JENSEN / MECKLING (1976)

When managers hold less than 100 per cent of the residual claims, they are inclined not to fully dedicate the company's resources to maximising the shareholder value, since they bear 100 per cent of the cost of their efforts but only a fraction of the benefits. Instead, where their share in the company decreases, managers are increasingly likely to appropriate perquisites out of the firm's resources for their own consumption. Hence, the owner-manager is inclined to turn the wealth effects upside down since he bears only a fraction of the negative effects but enjoys 100 per cent of the benefits.[451]

The most obvious cost which the owner-manager shoulders is the amount of work effort he devotes to the company.[452] If he reduces the level of effort, the benefits fully accrue to him, but the consequences are shared according to the diffusion of equity capital.[453]

The owner-manager will choose a level of consumption whose utility equals the fractional loss in firm value and wealth associated with his shareholdings. Figure 16 illustrates the mechanism of this trade-off as presented in JENSEN / MECKLING (1976).

[449] Myers, S.C. (1977), pp. 154-155.
[450] Breuer, W. (1998), p. 155; Smith, C.W./ Warner, J.B. (1979), p. 119.
[451] Jensen, M.C./ Meckling, W.H. (1976), pp. 312-313.
[452] Breuer, W. (1998), p. 155.

Figure 16: The trade-off between managerial consumption and the reduction in firm value from an owner-manager's perspective

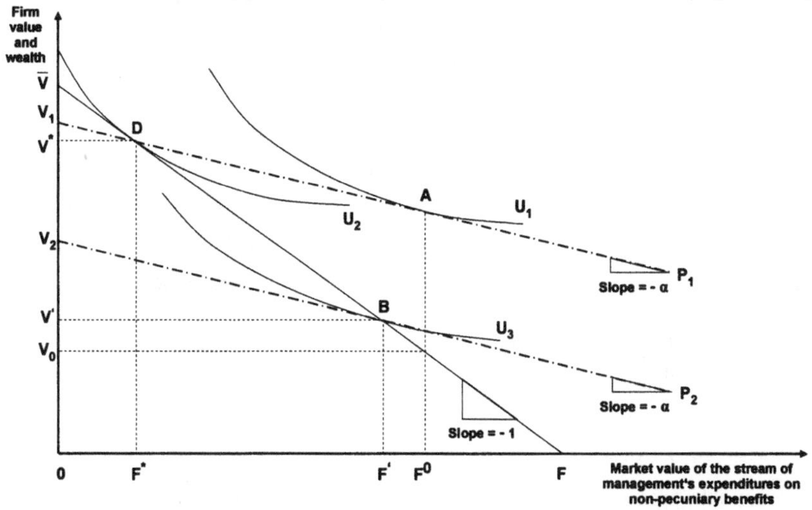

Source: Jensen, M.C./ Meckling, W.H. (1976), p. 316.

F denotes the value of the stream of the manager's expenditures accrued to the firm as a result from non-pecuniary benefits (managerial consumption) and *V* is the value of the firm and shareholder wealth. In figure 16, $\overline{V}$ represents the maximum firm value for zero managerial consumption. For a manager holding 100 per cent of the equity capital, an increase of $1 in *F* reduces the firm value *V* by $1. Hence the slope of this trade-off (the budget line) equals –1. All else being equal, his wealth, e.g. the share in the firm value αV (for the moment α = 100 per cent) and the managerial consumption *F* generate a utility *U* for the owner-manager. As long as the marginal substitution between the two factors decreases with increasing levels of managerial consumption, the utility function will be convex. Assuming the level of benefits consumed to be F^*, the resulting firm value will be V^* and the appropriate utility function is tangent to $\overline{V}F$ at point *D*. If the owner-manager sells portions of the equity he holds, the cost of the non-pecuniary benefits no longer accrue exclusively to him, only at αF. Conversely, the outside shareholder bears $(1-\alpha)F$. The outside shareholder is likely to pay the price V^* for an observed level of managerial consumption F^*. However, if the new shareholder cannot force the owner-manager to commit himself to F^*, he is free to choose any level of benefit *F*, if his behaviour cannot be observed. Receiving the full

[453] Debtholders are also affected by the reduced level of effort where this behaviour jeopardises the existence of the company and therefore the viability of the debt capital.

purchase price $(1-\alpha)V^*$, his utility can be maximised by moving towards the highest utility level, which is tangent to a new budget line V_1P_1. This utility function U_1 is touched at point A and has a slope = $-\alpha$, which reflects the fact that an increase in F will have a smaller impact on his wealth than before. Consequently, the firm value drops to V_0 as a result of the higher expenditures F_0.[454]

These considerations describe the moral hazard faced by outside shareholders. The incentive not to go for these non-pecuniary benefits depends on the equity share α. It can be shown, however, that information asymmetries result in a lower than optimal α, which yields a loss in welfare. If behaviour was observable, both inside and outside shareholders would strive in a concerted action to bring the owner-manager's non-pecuniary benefits to a welfare-maximising level.[455]

3.3.2.2. *Free Cash Flow waste after JENSEN (1986) and the underinvestment hypothesis after STULZ (1990)*

Besides managerial consumption, outside shareholders face another potential threat which was advanced by JENSEN some 10 years later. The management of a firm, even if it holds a small equity share, has an incentive to invest in projects with a negative NPV but which increase the size of the company ("overinvestment"), usually coming along with a strengthening of the management's power.[456] Free cash flow, which is "cash flow in excess of that required to fund all projects that have positive net present values when discounted at the relevant cost of capital"[457], is wasted on unprofitable projects instead of being cashed out to all shareholders.[458] To a large extent, these problems affect the shareholders, as the negative value of the projects undertaken is borne by the residual claimants – relative to their equity share. As for managerial consumption, the problems fully accrue to shareholders but may also impact debtholders if the company is on the brink of insolvency.[459]

Related to the incentive to increase firm size and thus underpin their power, managers may undertake negative NPV projects in order to pursue a strategy of diversification.[460] Risk-averse

---

[454] Jensen, M.C./ Meckling, W.H. (1976), pp. 313-317.
[455] Breuer, W. (1998), pp. 159-160.
[456] The underinvestment problem ('managerial consumption') as described by Jensen / Meckling (1976) only differs from the overinvestment of free cash flow in a marginal way since, e.g. even luxury office furniture or company cars can be viewed as very small low-return projects. The difference relates only to the fact that in the case of overinvestment, the volume of the project already exhibits a certain utility for the management. See Breuer, W. (1998), p. 165 FN 10.
[457] Jensen, M. (1986), p. 323.
[458] Jensen, M. (1986), p. 323.
[459] Breuer, W. (1998), p. 188.
[460] Shleifer, A./ Vishny, R. (1991), pp. 51-59.

managers have an incentive to strive for a diversified company in order to reduce the probability of a company default.[461]

On the basis of JENSEN'S considerations, STULZ (1990) developed ideas regarding the downside effects of too much debt beyond the agency cost of debt outlined in the previous section. Depending on the financial situation of the firm, debt-related payments can lead to a cash flow that is too low to fund all existing positive NPV projects and therefore results in an underinvested firm. The cost of the underinvestment equal the NPV of the profitable projects that were not realised.[462]

STULZ reckons that the volatility of the cash flows largely determines the existence of underinvestment cost, since a highly unstable business is more likely to face periods of underinvestment.[463] He further stresses four substantial implications arising from the negative relation between cash flow volatility and the usefulness of debt to reduce managerial discretion:[464]

- *Value of diversification:* Shareholders can gain from – no-cost – mergers between identical firms with non-correlated cash flows, as they will benefit from reduced volatility and thus lower cost of underinvestment.
- *Value of hedging*: Reducing cash volatility through hedging instruments also reduces the cost of volatility.
- *Period-by-period volatility:* It is the volatility of cash flows for each period that counts and not the volatility of the present value of future cash flows.
- *Value of financial engineering:* Through a combination or contractual design of various capital instruments, management shall be given resources when the cash flow in one period is lower than the amount of profitable investments; resources shall be withdrawn when the cash flow is higher.

Overall, advances that have been made in understanding agency conflicts take us a major step forward in understanding financial policies. Under moral hazard considerations, the optimal capital structure results from a balancing of debt-related cost as described by JENSEN / MECKLING (1976), MYERS (1977) and STULZ (1990) and the cost of using outside equity as formulated by JENSEN / MECKLING (1976) and JENSEN (1986). Figure 17 summarises these relationships.

---

[461] Amihud, Y./ Lev, B. (1981), p. 606.
[462] Stulz, R.M. (1990), p. 9.
[463] Stulz, R.M. (1990), p. 16-18. However, Stulz does not discuss why debt prevents firms from raising new capital. To the author's knowledge, this issue has not been addressed at all to date.
[464] Stulz, R.M. (1990), p. 18.

Figure 17: Optimal capital structure under agency considerations

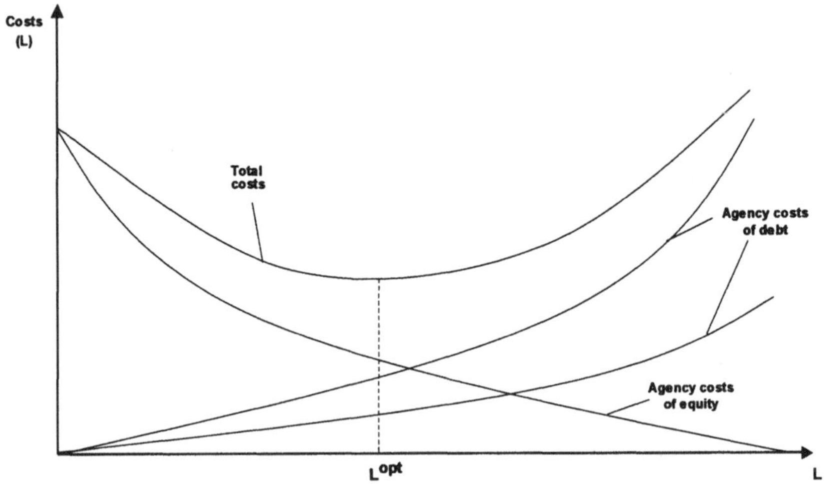

Source: Author, following Jensen, M.C./ Meckling, W.H. (1976), Myers, S.C. (1977), Jensen, M.C. (1986), and Stulz, R. (1990).

3.3.3. Alternative ways to eliminate agency conflicts

Each theory that explains the effects of moral hazard on the capital structure decision implies that changes in the leverage influence the degree of agency cost borne by claimholders. Depending on the exogenous factors, the significance of each type of agency cost differs with each firm. Consequently, different leverage ratios constitute the appropriate value-maximising amount of debt capital. A feature which the presented models have in common is that the financial structure (partly) overcomes the effects of moral hazard. However, along with the development of these considerations, scholars have derived other means to mitigate the threat of moral hazard for claimholders. These approaches can be distinguished by whether they limit managerial discretion directly or indirectly.[465]

Direct approaches include actions or instruments which have a direct influence on the owner-manager's behaviour. First and foremost it was JENSEN (1986) who emphasised the advantage of

[465] Hartmann-Wendels, T. (1990), p. 231.

debt for restricting managerial discretion.[466] The (annual) payments for interests and debt amortisation absorb much of the free cash flow which could otherwise be misused for unprofitable projects.[467] Therefore, increasing the leverage cannot just be considered a result of the existence of agency cost of equity, but also a means to mitigate them by restricting managerial discretion. This describes two sides of the same coin. Much empirical evidence has been found for this disciplination hypothesis[468] as a main source of gains in private transactions.[469]

A similar idea has been advanced by EASTERBROOK (1984), who emphasised the disciplining effect of dividends in two ways. Like debt payments, the cash outflow demands a more efficient management of the company. In addition, for high contractually fixed dividends, the management must approach the capital market to raise new liquidity either from equity investors or banks. This process, in turn, requires the management to reliably signal the profitability of the projects.[470] However, the effect of dividends on disciplinary is probably weaker than the effect of debt since failure to pay debt obligations leads to insolvency and hence to management job losses, while dividends have a less far-reaching implication.[471] Another important direct influence on the discretion of managers vis-à-vis their debtholders was introduced into the literature by SMITH / WARNER (1979), namely the implementation of covenants regulating managerial behaviour.[472] All cost incurred by the introduction of covenants into financing contracts are viewed as monitoring cost.[473]

Indirect measures, on the other hand, aim at setting incentives such that conflicts of interest are mitigated without directly limiting the management's discretion. A number of important studies have been made, focussing primarily on the role of non-capital markets with regard to their impact on the behaviour of owner-managers. For instance, FAMA (1980) outlines how efficient labour markets may sanction an agent's misbehaviour.[474] Furthermore, JENSEN / RUBACK (1983) have advanced the idea that the market for corporate takeovers act as an instrument of disciplination

---

466 Zwiebel, J. (1996) extends Jensen's model (1986) by assuming that managers act according to the degree of entrenchment. They are likely to avoid the diciplining role of debt and therefore issue equity. However, as the financing mix is decided upon by the private equity firm and not by the managers, this theoretical aspect shall not be deepened.

467 Jensen, M.C. (1986), p. 324. For the significance of distinguishing the effects of long-term and short-term debt, see e.g. Hart, O./ Moore, J. (1995).

468 Jensen, M.C. (1986), p. 324.

469 See, e.g. Muscarella, C.J./ Vetsuypens, M.R. (1990); Lehn, K./ Poulsen, A. (1989); Kaplan, S. (1989), and Bull, I. (1988).

470 Easterbrook, F. (1984).

471 Jensen, M.C. (1986), p. 324.

472 See also chapter 2.3.2.2.2.

473 Jensen, M.C./ Meckling, W.H. (1976), p. 338.

474 Fama, E.F. (1980).

since managerial slack leads to undervaluation and the threat of takeover.[475] Finally, HART (1983) pointed to a similar impact by product markets.[476]

Both direct and indirect instruments have attracted substantial interest on the part of academics. However, since none of these measures point to the discussion of an optimal capital structure – with the exception of the disciplination hypothesis by JENSEN (1986) – they will not be considered in detail in this thesis, but only to the extent that they are relevant for the interpretation of the empirical results.

3.4. Summary

Over the last 50 years a number of effects have been identified as substantial endogenous factors in a market that was once described by MM as frictionless and for which the irrelevance of the capital structure was proclaimed.

These effects represent actual frictions of the market. They are the starting point for various theoretical approaches explaining certain financial policies. Given the different benefits and cost, capital structure theories suggest how financial policy should react to the existence of these market frictions in order to maximise firm value. However, the actual relevance of each market friction changes with different characteristics of the transaction, which makes financial structuring very much contingent upon the specific deal. Therefore, to test the validity of the models, the theoretically predicted influence on leverage must be compared with the observed capital structures in an IBO sample.

The first section of the previous chapter presented the various corporate finance theories that root in the identified market frictions. Since the theoretical approaches cannot contribute equally to the understanding of IBO financing, a well-reasoned selection had to be carried out. Based primarily on a small set of selection criteria two theories, the trade-off theory and agency models, were selected as the basis for the study.

The second section of the chapter then provided an in-depth discussion of the two approaches. Figure 18 summarises the selection process.

---

[475] Jensen, M.C./ Ruback, R.S. (1983). For empirical evidence, see Jarrell, G.A./ Brickley, A./ Netter, J.M. (1988). An interesting discussion on the impact of anti-takeover regulations on managerial behaviour and capital structure can be found in Garvey, G.T./ Hanka, G. (1999).

[476] Hart, O. (1983).

Figure 18: Theory selection process

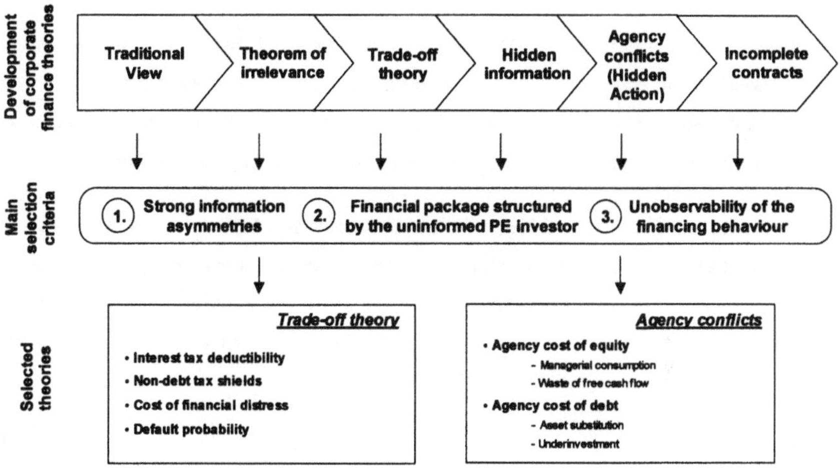

Source: Author.

4. Discussion of IBO financing layers

So far, the discussions have covered the specific characteristics of IBOs and the capital structure theories which try to explain actual financing behaviour. In the first place, these theories make predictions on the leverage of a firm. Accordingly, most empirical studies have focussed on the choice between senior debt and equity as the two poles of the range of possible instruments.

However, this range comprises a far larger set of instruments, both between senior debt and equity, in the form of sub-ordinated debt, and within each class. In any case, each financing layer reflects a specific combination of risk and return for the holder of the security. Though the leverage represents the key variable for the present study,[477] other instruments will also be the subject of tests and therefore need to be presented as well.[478]

The remainder of this section will discuss each layer of capital, senior debt, equity and sub-ordinated debt as the mezzanine form. For each class, an introduction to the economic characteristics that are typical of that class will be followed by brief descriptions of the various instruments that characterize IBOs.

4.1. Senior debt

Usually, senior-ranked debt accounts for the largest share of funds in IBOs. The defining criterion is the prioritisation in the event of liquidation. Proceeds from the liquidation are distributed first to senior lenders, then to sub-ordinated lenders and, finally, to shareholders. Senior debt is usually borrowed from banks, insurances, or other financial institutions.[479]

4.1.1. Economic characteristics of senior debt

Senior debt holds a fixed claim on the cash flows generated by a firm. Usually, these claims have a very deterministic character in a way that they are not conditional on certain firm-specific or

---

[477] Ratio of senior debt to total capitalisation. See chapter 5.3.2. for an elaborate discussion of the dependent variables of the study.

[478] In fact, since the early 90s, some empirical studies have incorporated other instruments beyond senior debt capital and will be mentioned in the respective paragraphs. However, as IBOs have almost not been covered at all, leverage should first be at the center of interest.

[479] Downes, J./ Goodman, J.E. (2003), p. 633. See also chapter 2.1.3.3. Leasing can also take the position of a senior-ranked liability but shall not discussed here as it is not part of an IBO financing package. A comprehensive overview of leasing is provided in Feinen, K. (2001).

macroeconomic factors.[480] However, what makes fixed claims fixed is the fact that the holder does not benefit from the appreciation of the firm value and has an unrestrained claim on the repayment of the capital.[481]

Clearly, the value D of a claim depends on the amount of cash flows available when repayments are due, i.e. when the debt matures. Assuming a firm with debt of a face value d and a time to maturity T. Besides amortisation no further payments are to be made. The value of the fixed claim equals $D(V_T)$ where V_T is the total value of the assets. A shareholder will only realise proceeds from the firm if V_T exceeds d, i.e. he receives dividends for $V_T>d$ and realises a loss for $V_T<d$. In this case the debtholder receives V_T and not d. At the time of maturity the value of the fixed claim $D(V_T)$ equals [482]

$$D(V_T) = \min[d, V_T]$$

Applying an option theoretical approach, the debt claim $D(V_T)$ can be split into a fixed (riskless) part reflecting the face value of the claim and the risk to realise it. This risk component can be viewed as a put option $P(d)$ with P being a long put and $-P$ a short put with a strike price d in T. The value of the short put will be zero or $V_T - d$ conditional on which value is lower. Formally, the value of the risk component equals [483]

$$-P(d) = \min[V_T - d, 0]$$

Both functions together determine the value of the senior fixed claim as they are used in buyout transactions. Figure 19 illustrates the economic characteristics of risky debt, where the degree of risk is exclusively reflected in the value of the put option.

[480] Exceptions are, e.g. floating rate notes, whose interests fluctuate according to changes in market interest levels (e.g. LIBOR or EURIBOR), see Frank. G./ Hax, H. (2004), p. 33.
[481] However, debt of a firm that is on the brink of insolvency will certainly benefit from an increase in firm value and have a higher market price than before.
[482] Müller, O. (2003), p. 36-38.
[483] Müller, O. (2003), p. 38.

Figure 19: Liquidation value of fixed claims

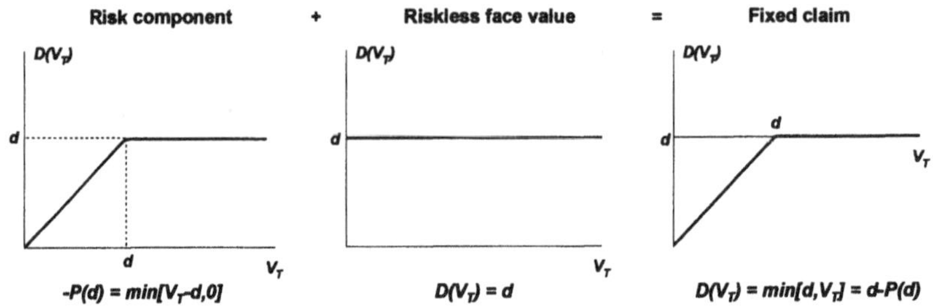

Source: Müller, O. (2003), p. 37.

Understanding the economic characteristics of debt has been an important step forward in the valuation of liabilities, particularly which factors determine the value of the put option and how interest structures reflect the continuous stochastic process.[484]

4.1.2. Types of senior debt

Senior debt comprises different types of notes, loans, and debentures, which are not specifically denoted as junior or sub-ordinated debt.[485] In buyouts, mainly three types of senior debt are applied, senior A, B, and C tranches,[486] which differ regarding payment schedules and maturity.[487] It has to be noted that these descriptions refer to acquisition debt. However, in IBOs the operating units can of course assume further loans to finance their investments.[488]

[484] A fundamental article is Merton, R.C. (1974).

[485] These denominations shall be used synonymously as their characteristics do not differ. See Downes, J./ Goodman, J.E. (2003), p. 633. However, the term bonds shall only be used for publicly traded debentures.

[486] Beyond these three, individual buyouts may carry more tranches (D,E, ...) in order to achieve a cost-effective risk allocation. See Golland, F. (2003a), p. 179.

[487] Here, maturity does not refer to the distinction between long-term and short-term notes but the nuances of long-term maturities (between 5 and 10 years). IBOs are structured in a way that only long-term liabilities are used to finance the acquisition, since no PE investor is willing to take the risk of being left with a financing gap after a short-term tranche has expired (source: interviews). However, the maturity structure in general has attracted considerable attention in the corporate finance literature and is certainly a research field which should not be neglected relative to other aspects of financial policy. For example, Hart, O./ Moore, J. (1995) emphasised the impact of different maturities for controlling management's behaviour. A well-known empirical article on the relevance is Barclay, M.J./ Smith, C.W. (1995a). See also Guedes, J./ Opler, T. (1996) and Diamond, D. (1993).

[488] In contrast to acquisition loans they can carry maturities of up to 15 years. See Drill, M./ Böhmert, S. (2003) p. 117.

4.1.2.1. Senior debt (Senior A)

The bulk share of financing needs is usually provided in the form of senior A tranches. These tranches comprise loans with yearly amortisation and interest payments. Their lending is based solely on the potential to generate cash flows. For that reason IBO financing is generally referred to as cash flow lending, although banks take collaterals, whenever possible, particularly share pledges in the target company. However, their value depends in turn on the future cash flows of the target company. Not in every case will the acquisition finance bank be able to collateralise parts of the operating assets.[489] In a share deal, the shares themselves may be pledged to the lender (hence secured senior debt), while in an asset deal the assets are sometimes still under collateralisation of the house banks.[490] However, even if they are able to take pledges on operating assets, they will not adjust the debt level beyond the level that is justified by the firm's cash flows.[491] Senior A tranches usually have maturities of 5-7 years, with most loans being at the upper end of the range.[492]

In addition, revolving credit facilities which have a short-term character, as they are deemed to finance the day-to-day business, are also guaranteed for the same time horizon (thus actually viewed as long-term loan) and frequently subsumed under a senior debt position. Furthermore, banks grant so-called bridge loans which serve to finance time gaps between the time when the acquisition price is paid out and the eventual financing.[493] Other committed facilities can be e.g. Capex loans[494] for further envisaged acquisitions or capital investments using the target firm as a platform (buy and build).[495]

Given the shortest maturity, interest rates for senior A tranches are lower than for any other financing source of IBOs.[496] Currently, margins in Germany range between 200 and 225 basis points (bps) above EURIBOR.[497]

---

489 Peters, H.P. (1988), pp. 173-174.
490 See also chapter 2.1.3. This only reflects a typical structure. Of course, deals may also involve senior debt that is fully secured through the operational assets.
491 In fact the more assets are collateralised, the higher will be the bank's ex-ante return since less equity capital must be put up according to Basel II regulations.
492 Fromman, H. (1992), p. 124.
493 Arbeitskreis Finanzierung der Schmalenbach-Gesellschaft Deutsche Gesellschaft für Betriebswirtschaft e.V. (1990), p. 841. Bridge loans are the only true short-term loans (3-12 months). In the survey, however, respondents were asked to replace bridge loans with the ultimate financing instrument.
494 Denotes a facility specifically determined to finance an upcoming acquisition.
495 Mittendorfer, R. (2001), p. 169.
496 Hug, J./Ernst, D. (2003), p. 445.
497 KPMG Leveraged Finance Study (2003), p. 5. GBP-based loans are linked to the LIBOR. To the author's knowledge similar studies for the whole of Europe have not yet been published.

Banks usually require yearly, half-yearly or quarterly amortisation payments so that 50 per cent of the debt is paid back half way to maturity.[498] For theoretical considerations, the amount of senior A loans has priority over total debt figures since it is the annual payment obligation which disciplines the management in the sense of JENSEN (1986). Consequently, in recent years empirical studies have focussed on the differences between the effects of straight senior A loans and other forms of debt.[499]

4.1.2.2. Cash flow-reduced debt (Senior B/C)

Senior A debt has been primarily characterised by regular payments, both interest and amortisation payments. However, the structure of the cash flows from operations and investment or simply the size of the deal may force the PE investor to make use of debentures, which do not require frequent payments.[500] In buyouts free cash flows are sometimes scarce in the early years after the acquisition, since growth has to be financed. Here, instruments with payments due upon maturity are in need, which senior B/C tranches frequently represent in buyouts.[501]

Senior B/C tranches are so-called bullet payment notes, i.e. to be amortised at maturity or at least in later years. They allow firms with "back-loaded" cash flows to increase the total debt capacity.[502] Compared to senior A, senior B/C tranches enjoy longer periods to maturity of 7-10 years.[503] As regards the prioritization in the event of bankruptcy senior A and B/C share the same ranking. However, as senior B/C tranches can only be redeemed after A tranches had been paid off, they are more risky. This explains the higher coupon rate relative to senior A tranches.[504] Currently, the margins for senior B debt range between 200 and 275 bps above EURIBOR though most transactions will be around 260 bps. Given the longest tenors, senior C notes were found to carry margins of 250-350 bps, with 325 bps as the most frequently named indication.[505]

Another factor which differentiates senior B/C tranches from A tranches is the syndication of the position. In large transactions the lead-arranging bank may only assume a fraction from the original

[498] Fromman, H. (1992), p. 124.
[499] E.g. Barclay, M.J./ Smith, C.W. (1995b).
[500] Mittendorfer, R. (2001), p. 169.
[501] Diem, A. (2005), p. 21.
[502] Kaplan, S./ Stein, J. (1993), p. 327.
[503] Source: interviews.
[504] Diem, A. (2005), p. 21.
[505] KPMG Leveraged Finance Study (2003), p. 5.

position ("final take"). The remaining debt is syndicated with other banks in the case of A tranches, while B/C tranches are often – at least in lage deals - syndicated with institutional investors.[506]

4.2. Equity capital

Holders of equity capital are the owners of a firm. In buyout transactions equity financing is primarily obtained from three sources: financial investors, the management of the acquired company, and the vendor of the company.[507]

4.2.1. Economic characteristics of equity

Considering the same example as in chapter 4.1.1, the value of the equity claim $E(V_T)$ at maturity T depends on the value of the firm V in T as well as d representing the face value of d due in T. Shareholders receive whatever assets or earnings are left in the business after all its debts are repaid. The residual value of the firm equals zero until d is amortised. After that, $E(V_T)$ increases linearly with the increase in the firm value V_T.[508] Therefore $E(V_T)$ equals

$$E(V_T) = \max[V_T - d, 0] \text{ ,}$$

Figure 20 illustrates the straightforward relationship of the equity's residual value and the value of the firm with equity and senior debt financing.

Figure 20: Liquidation value of equity claims

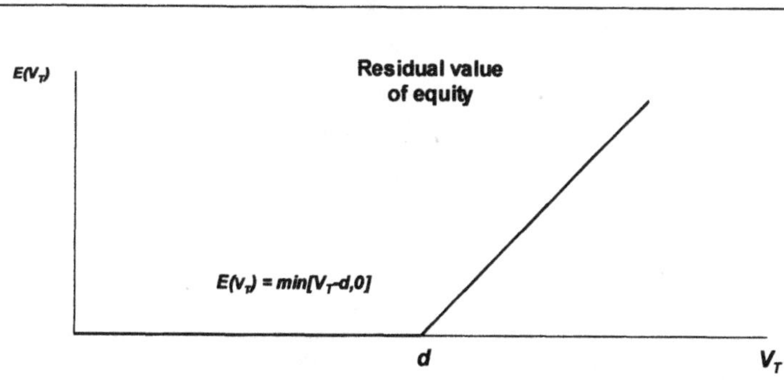

Source: Culp, C.L. (2002), p. 14.

[506] Source: interviews.
[507] Mittendorfer, R. (2001), p. 161.
[508] Müller, O. (2003), p. 39.

4.2.2. Types of equity capital

In classifying equity claims, focus will be on the two main types, preferred and common equity, both of which are components of a typical IBO capital structure.[509] In addition, the shareholder loans will be presented since from a PE investor's perspective it also represents an equity claim. Finally, the capital reserve also constitutes a part of the equity capital. However, given it is the agio paid on the common and preferred shares, they are not treated as a different financial instrument.[510]

4.2.2.1. Common and preference shares

PE investors and the firm's management jointly own the company after the IBO by usually acquiring 100 per cent of the outstanding equity claims, which derive primarily from common and preference shares.[511] Unlike other instruments, common and preferred stock do not have a maturity and are at the firm's disposal for an infinite period of time.[512]

In their basic form, common shares have two constituting features, the conditional right to participate in the company's earnings, and the authorisation to take a number of central decisions such as the right to liquidate the firm or to appoint members of the management board.[513] In contrast, particularly in Anglo-Saxon countries, preference shares carry limited voting rights, but offer higher dividends with priority over dividends to common shareholders. They also enjoy precedence over common shareholders in the case of liquidation.[514]

Dividends on preferred equity can often be granted in the form of PIKs, hence not in cash but in even more preferred shares.[515] However, unlike publicly traded preference shares, private preference shares (as used in IBOs) do not grant higher dividends but often no dividends at all since the holders are mainly interested in the value appreciation and not in dividend income. Instead, they enjoy certain control, information, or participation rights.[516]

---

509 Equity capital may consist of a far larger set of instruments. For an overview and further references, see Breuer, W./ Hartmann, N./ Kleefisch, A. (2003). However, as the differences cannot be grasped in the empirical part, a detailed discussion shall be forgone.

510 Cullom, P./ Stein, C. (2001), p. 138.

511 The US terminology uses common and preferred stock.

512 Brealey, R.C./Myers, S.C. (2000), p. 393.

513 Breuer, W./ Hartmann, N./ Kleefisch, A. (2003), p. 328.

514 Sutton, T. (2000), pp. 366-367.

515 Brealey, R.C./Myers, S.C. (2000), p. 979.

516 Achleitner, A.-K./ Wahl, S. (2004), p. 70.

In order to allow the management to participate with a share of about 10-15 per cent without exceeding 1-3 times their annual salary, PE investors provide additional equity capital in the form of shareholder loans. Management receives share capital at better conditions than the PE investor (ex-ante incentives through sweet equity). Since in most cases the management holds the common share capital exclusively, the value appreciation accrues primarily to them.[517] On the flipside, shareholder loans like preference shares are superior to common shares in default, and therefore PE investors enjoy some downside protection for their investment.[518]

To further incentivise the management, it is frequently entitled to underwrite additional equity capital, depending on the achievement of certain milestones (equity ratchets).[519] If the management holds preference shares, a right to convert them into common shares is usually attached with a conversion price again conditional on certain performance indicators.[520]

Preference shares in the sense they are used in buyouts enjoy characteristics of both common shares and debt claims, such as the right to participate in the value appreciation and voting rights on the one hand and a slightly lower risk on the other. For that reason, they are often subsumed under sub-ordinated debt.[521]

4.2.2.2. Shareholder loans

It might be surprising for the reader to see shareholder loans[522] presented within the equity position, because academics usually consider them to be part of sub-ordinated debt.[523] However, as previously indicated, shareholder loans are provided by PE investors to make the financing feasible without the need to put in too much straight equity capital.[524] In this sense, the classification here merely reflects the practioner's perspective. As shareholder loans are granted out of the managed private equity fund, they calculate the internal rate of return on this position in the same way as on the common and preference share capital.[525] In fact, following international accounting standards, shareholder loans have to be classified as an equity position under certain conditions.[526]

---

517 Krebs, A. (1998), p. 19.
518 Mittendorfer, R. (2001), p. 177.
519 Mittendorfer, R. (2001), p. 178.
520 Sahlmann, W.A. (1990), p. 510.
521 Kraft, V. (2001), pp. 217-218.
522 In some publications, they are also referred to as 'loan stock', see, e.g. Mittendorfer, R. (2001), p. 177.
523 E.g. Drukarczyk, J. (1993), pp. 611-617.
524 Cullom, P./ Stein, C. (2001), p. 138; Fromman, H. (1992), p. 127.
525 Source: interviews.
526 However, these conditions vary across countries and shall not be further discussed as the classification is not relevant for the present study.

In their basic structure, shareholder loans carry fixed interest rates that are payable in cash or accumulate as PIK loans. While they enjoy the main advantages of debt capital, particularly the deductibility of interest payments, they also have some specific benefits. For example, any detail regarding interest payments, amortisation schedules, etc. can be incorporated in the contract to meet the requirements of the PE firm. Also, any cost that would typically accrue to banks do not occur in the transaction.[527]

4.3. Sub-ordinated debt

All senior debt notes have the same priority rank in the case of bankruptcy. Debt instruments that rank behind senior debt are called sub-ordinated debt[528] and can be of various types which do not share the characteristics of either first-ranked senior debt or of straight equity capital. Theoretical considerations suggest that in many cases it is preferable to issue a diverse set of classes of debt rather than just straight senior debt, with covenants allowing limited dilution of each class.[529] In any case, given their increasing popularity sub-ordinated debt can be presumed to offer advantages which the generic forms equity and senior debt do not.[530]

4.3.1. Economic characteristics of sub-ordinated debt

Regarding economic characteristics, sub-ordinated debt takes an intermediate position between the two extremes, senior debt and equity. It facilitates a smooth transition from fixed to residual claims.[531] Given the wide range of possible designs, there is no one unique set of characteristics. Rather, the economic nature can be very close both to that of senior debt and that of equity. However, in order to understand the general construction, the characteristics of junior debt[532] and convertible debt shall be illustrated as an example.[533]

Junior debt represents straight fixed claims, which are junior to first-ranked debt in the priority order in the event of bankruptcy.[534] Amortisation and interest payments are made when obligations

---

[527] E.g. Drukarczyk, J. (1993), pp. 610.
[528] The academic literature (particularly in Germany) has not yet developed a consensus denomination. While in many papers, this segment is referred to as mezzanine capital, practitioners prefer sub-ordinated debt since definitions in the literature are highly inconsistent. For a more detailed discussion, see, e.g. Müller-Trimbusch, J. (1999), pp. 22-23.
[529] Hart, O. / Moore, J. (1985), p. 569.
[530] Drukarczyk, J. (1993), p. 581.
[531] Frank. G./ Hax, H. (2004), p. 31.
[532] In some publications, junior debt is generally used synonymously with sub-ordinated debt.
[533] Müller, O. (2003), pp. 41-44.
[534] The priority order in insolvency is settled in an intercreditor agreement.

related to senior debt claims are satisfied.[535] Junior debt constitutes the tightest interpretation of privately placed mezzanine.[536] A firm with a total asset value V_T, which has issued two zero-coupon loans to finance its assets, one senior-ranked and one junior-ranked, will earn a face value d (market value D) for the senior tranche and j for the junior tranche (market value J). While the value of the senior tranche $D(V_T)$ equals min[d, V_T],[537] the value of the junior tranche $J(V_T)$ is a function of the firm value, the face value and the face value of the senior tranche.[538]

$$J(V_T) = \begin{cases} j, & d + j \leq V_T \\ V_T - d, & d < V_T < d + j \\ 0, & V_T \leq d \end{cases}$$

Figure 21 illustrates the "pecking order" of the different claims on the firm value V_T with junior debt between senior debt and equity.

Figure 21: Value of junior debt in contrast to senior debt and equity

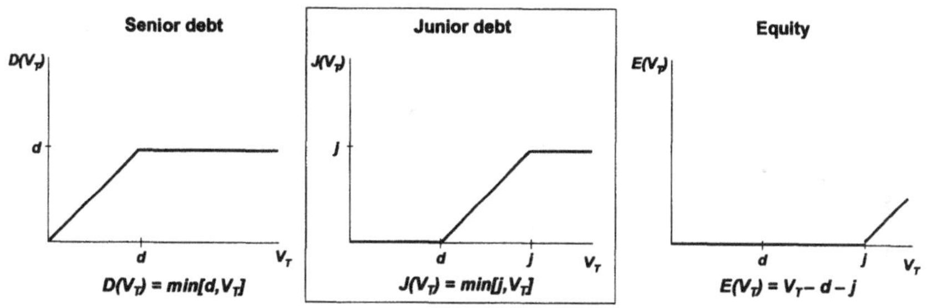

Source: Müller, O. (2003), p. 43.

Convertible loans represent another typical instrument of sub-ordinated debt, which allow the holder to convert the debt claim into residual claims. This means that the holder receives the right to either earn fixed payments or residual payments but never both types of claims at the same time.[539]

Again, we assume that a firm finances its assets with sub-ordinated debt and equity. However, instead of junior debt the owner decides to issue convertible debt with a market value $C(V_T)$ incorporating both equity and senior debt characteristics. At the time T the holder of the convertible

[535] Möller, K. (1996), p. 7.
[536] Betsch, O./ Groh, A./ Lohmann, L. (2000), p. 301.
[537] See chapter 4.1.1.
[538] Müller, O. (2003), pp. 42.

debt is entitled to receive the face value of the *senior* claim d with the same priority as other senior debtholders in the case of liquidation. Alternatively, the debt can be converted into n new shares in the firm having an equity capital with N ordinary shares. The fraction γ of the firm that can be converted equals $\gamma \equiv n/(N+n)$. Depending on the firm value V_T the value $C(V_T)$ equals [540]

$$H(V_T) = \begin{cases} \gamma V_T & d \le \gamma V_T \\ d & d \le V_T < d/\gamma \\ V_T & V_T < d \end{cases}$$

Alternatively, the relation can be expressed as

$$H(V_T) = \min(V_T, d) + \max(\gamma V_T - d, 0)$$

Clearly, the value of the convertible $C(V_T)$ after the conversion equals the value of the equity. At the same time, it must at least equal the value of the senior claim $D(V_T)$. Since the chance to benefit from increases in the firm value constitutes a value itself and equals the "out-of-the-money" value of a call option[541], $C(V_T)$ should be higher than $D(V_T)$. Figure 22 illustrates the relation without incorporating the options premium.[542]

Figure 22: Value of convertible debt in contrast to senior debt and equity

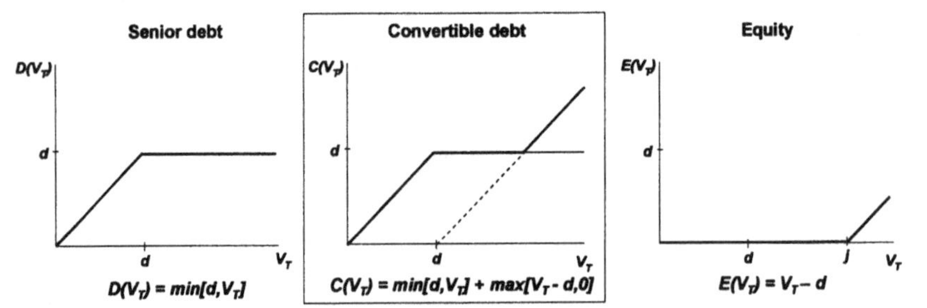

Source: Müller, O. (2003), p. 51.

539 As opposed to warrant-linked debt. See, Drukarczyk, J. (1993), p. 600.
540 Müller, O. (2003), pp. 49-50.
541 For the valuation of options see, e.g. Brealey, R.A./ Myers, S.C. (2000), pp. 596-644.
542 See also Brealey, R.A./ Myers, S.C. (2000), pp. 656.

4.3.2. Types of sub-ordinated debt

To date, neither practical nor theoretical contributions have been able to develop a widely accepted systematisation of sub-ordinated debt. Subsequently, the author follows the understanding of most practitioners in primarily distinguishing mezzanine capital and high-yield bonds.[543] It allows a clear distinction without knowledge of specific contractual details. In the empirical study, further distinctions within the class of mezzanine (in the sense of a privately placed instrument) are not made as it can take on numerous forms and the eventual nature of the instrument is determined by contractual specifications.[544]

4.3.2.1. Mezzanine capital

In the practical and theoretical literature several criteria to systematise mezzanine instruments have been applied. One unambiguous way is to distinguish private and public mezzanine.[545] Within the latter group, high-yield bonds represent the most relevant instrument.[546] Given the specific characteristics and prominent role in financing large buyouts, this type of financing shall be described separately in the next chapter. Private mezzanine, however, comprises all privately placed types.[547] Over the years, this understanding of mezzanine instruments has been adopted by practitioners.[548] Along with private placement, they are particularly characterised by a large number of contractual clauses regarding the achievement of certain performance indicators or limitations on future investment or financing activities.[549]

Another way would be to separate equity and debt mezzanine depending on the actual characteristics. For debt-like mezzanine instruments the interest payments are key, while for mezzanine instruments that are closer to equity participation in the value increase of the firm prevails.[550] However, the deductibility of potential interest payments represents a constituting

[543] Structuring sub-ordinated debt that way shall not constitute a good, bad or just appropriate way. Rather, the motivation derives from the fact that practitioners must have a common understanding of what instruments are recorded in the questionnaire for the empirical study. For theoretical considerations, any other commonly reported systematisation could also be applied.

[544] A similar approach has been applied by other authors, e.g. Mittendorfer, R. (2001), Willis, J.R./ Clark, D.A. (1993), Perille, R.F. (1996) and Zombanakis, A./ Ball, M. (1997).

[545] E.g. Müller, O. (2003).

[546] Besides high-yield bonds, any kind of publicly traded bond with an attached right to convert or exercise an option into equity capital can be subsumed under sub-ordinated debt. However, they are not further discussed given their limited relevance for buyout financing. See Müller-Trimbusch, J. (1999), p. 23.

[547] Müller, O. (2003), p. 211.

[548] Müller-Trimbusch, J. (1999), p. 23.

[549] Brewis, J. (1998), p. 21.

[550] Link, G. (2001), pp. 15-16.

feature of mezzanine instruments apart from their subordination and a high degree of flexibility.[551] While the use of unsecured mezzanine is probably the usual case, in some instances the lenders of mezzanine may nevertheless demand first-priority interests in the company's assets.[552] Depending on whether the mezzanine enjoys collateral attached to the security, some authors distinguish junior mezzanine and senior mezzanine as another delineation criterion.[553] Some common instruments of mezzanine will be presented below.[554]

First and foremost is the previously mentioned **junior debt** (also "junior sub-ordinated debt"), a usual debt claim which according to the intercreditor agreement ranks behind senior claims in case the firm becomes insolvent. The sub-ordinated position justifies a risk premium relative to senior debt.[555]

The distinction between debt and equity in buyouts is often muddied by equity conversion rights or warrants attached to the various classes of debt. **Convertible debt** represents one way of offering upside potential to the debtholder. This incentive was discussed early on in the light of the so-called "debt sweetener" hypothesis, indicating that the upside potential just serves to make the senior tranche more attractive and not to issue equity on a delayed basis.[556] As regards research coverage, convertible bonds are the most frequently discussed type of sub-ordinated instruments.[557]

Besides convertible debt, **warrant-linked debt** is also a frequently encountered instrument that allows the lender to benefit from equity appreciation and therefore justifies a low nominal interest coupon. As opposed to convertibles, the fixed claim on the firm's cash flow remains untouched when the holder exercises the warrant, the right to purchase shares from the firm.[558] They are not to be confused with options since warrants are granted on *new* shares while options carry the right to buy *existing* stock. In addition, warrants have a longer maturity of several years, while options only have 6-9 months.[559] It can be shown that warrant-linked debt does not yield lower cost of capital for

---

551 Gereth, B./ Schulte, K.W. (1992), p. 1.

552 See Harris, T.J. (2002), p. 61.

553 E.g. Achleitner, A.K./ Wahl, S. (2004), p. 65.

554 Particularly the German market has developed a variety of country-specific mezzanine instruments, which shall not be further discussed given the specificity. For an overview, see e.g. Betsch, O./ Groh, A./ Lohmann, L. (2000), p. 303.

555 Achleitner, A.K./ Wahl, S. (2004), p. 67.

556 See Pilcher, C.J. (1955); Broman, K.L. (1963); Bringham, E. (1966) and later Brennan, M./ Schwartz, E. (1988). The latter argument was raised again under the term "back door equity financing" by Stein, C. (1992). However, the rejection of the delayed equity financing hypothesis was later confirmed by several authors, see e.g. Billingsley, R.S./ Smith, D.M. (1996).

557 They are often discussed in the context of VC financing. Examples are Cornelli, F./ Yosha, O. (2003), Schmidt, K.M. (2003), Isagawa, N. (2000), and Lee, H.W./ Figlewicz, R.E. (1999).

558 Brealey, R.A./ Myers, S.C. (2000), pp. 645.

559 Müller, O. (2003), p. 47.

the firm. Rather, the main advantage appears to be the flexibility for the investor to adapt to the state of the firm. High-risk firms are otherwise likely to obtain debt only under very restrictive conditions. Warrant-linked debt proves to be a stable instrument in terms of value as it comprises counter-balancing effects, i.e. the increasing uncertainty reduces the value of the debt claim, while the value of the warrant rises at the same time.[560] In addition, they may help to mitigate moral hazard problems because they allow allocating control rights depending on the state of the firm.[561] Particularly a simultaneous solution of over- and underinvestment problems can be achieved.[562]

Other types of **debt with an equity kicker** can also be used in buyouts. They are frequently granted in the form of back-ended payments which represent one-off payments at maturity, usually as a percentage of earnings, value increases or similar key performance indicators.[563] Having mostly a deferred-cash character, mezzanine instruments often defer not only the amortisation payments but also all or parts of the interest payments in the form of PIK notes.[564] Besides providing a flexible tool to match cash-in flows with cash-out flows, the firm can take advantage of the interest-induced tax advantages without directly incurring cost of financial distress.[565]

Given the variety of mezzanine instruments, the cash compensation for the increased risk assumption ranges widely from 400bps to 800bps above EURIBOR, with most financing arrangements fluctuating around 600pbs.[566] Typically, in addition to the cash reward, a PIK margin of 300-500 bps or an equity kicker of 4-8 per cent can be assumed so that the total yield for the mezzanine instrument may vary between 12 and 18 per cent[567] According to market experts, the European market for mezzanine capital reached €4bn in 2003, an increase of one-third compared to 2002, and replaced the dominance of high-yield bonds.[568] The reason for the recent rise in mezzanine cost despite generally stagnating financing cost is seen in the fact that mezzanine lenders increasingly carry equity risks.[569]

560 Drukarczyk, J. (1993), pp. 594-600.
561 Bascha, A./ Walz, U. (2000), p. 417.
562 Isagawa, N. (2000), p.15
563 Barthold, B. (2000), p. 226.
564 Goodman, L.S./ Cohen, A.H. (1989), p. 9. A related agreement to the PIK structure is the pay-if-you-can (PIYC) clause, which offers an even higher degree of flexibility. For further readings, see Golland, F. (2003a), p. 180.
565 Hart, O./ Moore, J. (1995), pp. 567-568.
566 KPMG Leveraged Finance Study (2003), p. 5.
567 Einem, C.v./ Tränkle, C. (2004), p. 170.
568 Becker, W. (2003), p. 52.
569 Golland, F./ Gehlhaar, L. (2003), p. 447.

4.3.2.2. *High-yield bonds*

High-yield bonds (HYB) are publicly-traded bonds issued by firms to raise long-term capital. Given the sub-ordination, they are often considered as publicly traded mezzanine. Today, however, HYBs are considered to represent not only a financial instrument in a high-risk financing segment. Rather, they form an asset class of their own.[570] This understanding is based mainly on the distinction between investment grade and sub-investment grade securities. Investors in these bonds are offered risk premiums given the low solvency of the issuing firms.[571] The Anglo-American literature has reached consensus on HYBs as a sub-investment grade bond regarding the ability to meet future obligations (long-term rating).[572] HYBs were very popular instruments for financing take-overs in the 1980s.

Compared to other sub-ordinated instruments, HYBs usually enjoy higher seniority. This refers to the so-called contractual subordination. One can distinguish a partial or total contractual subordination depending on whether all claims or just parts are subordinated to other instruments.[573] In practice, however, HYBs may suffer from subordination due to the legal structure of the entire transaction ("structural subordination"). Because an extra legal unit has to be founded to issue HYBs, claims on the operating unit may be prioritised over HYB claims despite the contractual superiority.[574] Given the vulnerability of HYBs to changes in the operating performance of the financed firms, the yields on HYBs reflect the overall condition of the economy quite well. Accordingly, the sensitivity of HYB yields to economic cycles often serves as a macroeconomic indicator and has been the subject of academic discussions.[575] Currently, yields for HYBs range between 7.5 per cent and 11 per cent. In addition, as issuing HYBs is a particularly costly process, minimum volumes should be around €100m.[576] Besides the high cost, another disadvantage consists in the low degree of flexibility as regards recapitalisations. Since it often involves prohibitively high cost for the issuer, the financial structure must be tightened for the foreseeable future until the exit.[577] In addition, the structure itself does not allow HYBs to be closely tailored to the needs of the firm as regards the pay-off structure and other contractual details. They tend to be very much

[570] Yoga, G. (1991), p. 4.
[571] Müller-Trimbusch, J. (1999), pp. 15.
[572] Fabozzi, F.J./ Modigliani, F. (1996), p. 491.
[573] Mittendorfer, R. (2001), p. 159.
[574] Müller. O. (2003), pp. 161-164.
[575] E.g. Collin-Dufresne, P./ Goldstein, R.S.; Spencer, M. (2001) and Gertler, M. (2000). Reset clauses may be attached to the bonds by which interests are adjusted at fixed dates if the market value of the bond falls below a certain threshold. For a practical example of reset bonds, see Breuer, W. (2000).
[576] For an overview of the cost of raising HYB capital, see Müller-Trimbusch, J. (1999), pp. 197-203.
[577] Mittendorfer, R. (2001), p. 174.

standardised to facilitate allocation to several institutional investors.[578] Given that the firm has to reach capital market maturity, HYBs are often issued later during the holding period to replace an initial bridge loan facility.[579] Table 1 provides further details regarding HYBs and mezzanine capital.

Table 1: Comparison of high-yield bonds and mezzanine instruments.

Criteria	Mezzanine	High-Yield Bonds
Minimum volumes	No	ca. €100 Mio.
Tenure	5 – 10 years	7 – 10 years
Interest	EURIBOR + 400-800bps cash 300-500bps PIK spread	7.5% - 11%
Equity component	Warrants and performance-based payments	No
Investment rationale	Capital gains	High interest payments
Funding	Ensured	Depends on market condition
Pricing	Ensured	Depends on market condition and liquidity
Investors	Small investor basis	Very large investor basis
Liquidity	Low	High
Rating	No	Recommended
Contractual flexibility	High	Low
Seniority	Subordinated	Subordinated
Amortisation structure	Bullet payment	Bullet Payment
Unscheduled repayments	Always possible	Limited; usually only in the second of half of the tenure with decreasing redemption premium
Financial covenants	Various	No
Issuing cost	Fairly low	Very high
Selling procedure	Bank meetings (information memorandum as basis)	Road show (prospectus as information basis)

Source: Mittendorfer, R. (2001), p. 175 with modifications.

578 Allen, J.R. (1996), p. 713.
579 Hug, J./ Ernst, D. (2003), p. 445.

4.4. Summary

This section has provided an overview of the instruments that are usually applied in IBOs. Besides the general delineation of senior debt, equity and sub-ordinated debt, the main types of instrument within each class have been discussed. Implicitly, the descriptions have referred to various characteristics of the instruments which ultimately determine the position on the risk/return scale as described in figure 23. Research has dedicated substantial effort to understanding the different characteristics and their role in financial policy. However, it is not fully recognised whether or not the various characteristics (non-contingent claim, seniority, securing) of debt are equally important and whether they necessarily have to go together.[580]

In buyout transactions, a general approach is to use debt with longer-term maturity, which is matched to the investment horizon of between 5-10 years, although the timely pay-down represents an explicit objective in the early years following the acquisition. This means that the bulk of the deal is financed with long-term debt, although credit facilities with a short-term character are also applied (e.g. working capital facility). PE investors will always demand a guarantee for these credit lines covering the period until the exit. In this sense, even short-term credit lines gain a long-term character. Instead of only one block of senior debt, buyouts usually include tranches of A-C, sometimes even more tranches. They differ in the tenor, amortisation schedules, interest rates and the market in which they can be syndicated. Upon liquidation, sub-ordinated debt only receives proceeds from the sale of a firm's assets when all senior debt has been paid down, hence the sub-ordinated nature. Holders of equity claims have lowest seniority and receive the residual of the proceeds.

Furthermore, instruments can be differentiated according to the pay-off structure they carry, which in turn refers to the compensation on one hand and the amortisation structure on the other. In general, compensation can take on three forms, cash interest payments, accumulating interest payments (PIK), and a possible equity kicker in order to incorporate potential upsides. As regards the amortisation schedule, debt payments can be due on a frequent basis with equal amounts or at maturity of the claim ("bullet payment loans"). In practice, however, the contractors often agree on intermediate solutions depending on the cash-flow structure of the target.[581] Finally, instruments can differ as to whether they are publicly traded or only the subject of a private transaction. In IBOs

580 Hart, O./ Moore, J. (1998), p. 1.
581 Achleitner, A.K./ Wahl, S. (2004), p. 67.

most of the instruments have a private character. The only instrument of relevance for large transactions appears to be the high-yield bond.

In practice, the different combinations of these characteristics can result in such a diverse set of instruments that an empirical study cannot grasp the differences appropriately without access to individual financial contracts. However, within the main classes the instruments share most of the constituent features as elaborated, so that they should be sufficiently homogenous to strike an appropriate balance between general validity of their findings and individual detail. Figure 23 summarises the various characteristics a financial instrument may exhibit and the resulting range of instruments available to IBOs.

Figure 23: Overview of financial instruments and its characteristics

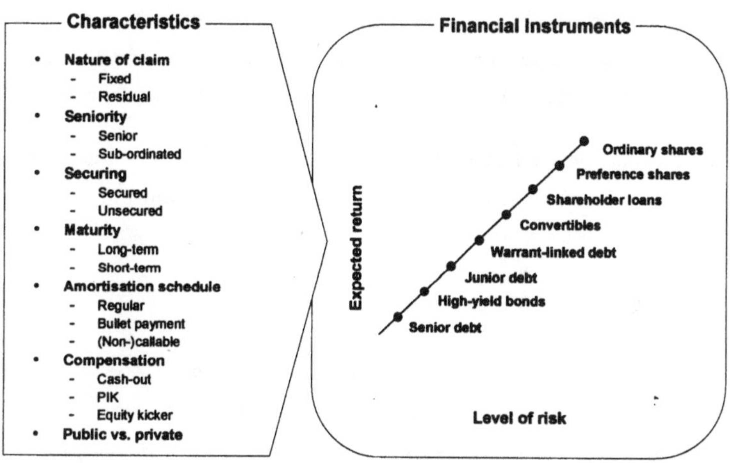

Source: Author.

5. Hypotheses on IBO capital structures and operationalisation of variables

On the basis of the previous chapters, the present one develops hypotheses on IBO capital structures and operationalises the selected explanatory and dependent variables. After a brief description of the research model, the theoretically expected influence on leverage will be derived for each characteristic from the perspective of the static trade-off theory and agency considerations. It has to be emphasised that the hypotheses focus solely on leverage in order to test the validity of capital structure theories as the main objective of the thesis.[582] In total, this will result in 14 hypotheses, seven for each theory. For each characteristic an extensive review of prior empirical studies on corporate capital structures will be provided. Though the research designs and methodologies differ among the studies, the purposes are the same in the way that they test the influence of certain variables on the capital structure for a given setting. While the review primarily underpins the relevance of the characteristics, it also helps to contrast the results with those of this study.[583]

The second part of the chapter is devoted to the operationalisation of both the explanatory and the dependent variables. To a large extent, the operationalisation rests on the use of these variables in previous studies to ensure the comparability of results.

5.1. Description of the research model

Theoretical models and most existing empirical studies focus on the choice between senior debt and equity since it is the leverage that should most clearly reflect the various aspects raised in theory. This thesis ties up to the same rationale by focussing predominantly on the debt-equity choice.[584]

Two common approaches are suggested by existing research to consider the leverage, the application of the actual share of senior debt in the capital structure [585] or the consideration of a

[582] As stated in the discussion of the research questions, testing the determinants of other financial instruments will not be subject to a hypothesis-driven approach.

[583] However, the theories underlying these results are not necessarily the same as in this study. In some cases the empirical results are based on the pecking-order theory. Discussions will take these differences into consideration.

[584] In addition, leverage is the key indicator for the capital structure expressed by practitioners, see, e.g. Mittendorfer, R. (2001). In fact, PE professionals first explore how much senior debt they need to raise and how much they are able to raise from banks. It represents the first and main decision variable. See also chapter 2.3.2.2.1.

[585] Practitioners do not speak about leverage in the form of debt as a percentage of total capitalisation but in multiples of EBITDA (or EBIT alternatively). See, e.g. Cullom, P./ Stein, C. (2001), p. 138.

binary variable of $x=1$ if the transaction is highly leveraged and $x=0$ if that is not the case. Both approaches bundle equity and sub-ordinated debt together to form the equity capital.[586]

The decision to opt for the latter solution is driven by three reasons. First, studying *highly* leveraged transactions (HLT) applies the terminology of the US supervisory authorities[587] and conforms to the general linguistic use in the research, although the definition of a HLT differs across studies.[588] Second, quite a number of empirical studies examine the *likelihood* that a certain financing need or discrete event is financed with debt or equity capital (or specific instruments) rather than how the change of an independent variable impacts the value of the dependent variable.[589]

Examining the probability of a certain financing behaviour leads to the application of logistic regression models. Their nature to model the relationship as a logistic function represents the third reason. While classic multiple regression models assume linear relations between independent and dependent variables,[590] so-called logit models assume logistic relations which better describe reality.[591] Without knowing the exact scatter plot of the variables, pure economic reasoning would suggest an s-curved logistic function for some of the determinants. For example, an incremental increase in a firm's profitability is likely to have a low impact on its creditworthiness when the firm exhibits EBIT margins of 0 per cent and very high margins of 30-40 per cent. However, for EBIT margins in the range of say 5-15 per cent, incremental increases are likely to have a higher impact. Without studying actual behaviour in more detail or applying theoretical reasonings, one would expect an s-curve relation as used in many economic models (e.g. product market saturation). These reasons have made logit models the generally preferred econometric technique in empirical research on financing decisions.[592]

As discussed in chapter 3, the level of the cost and benefits associated with different classes of capital changes with specific firm characteristics. These characteristics represent the explanatory variables within the research model.

---

586 In the view of banks both represent parts of the liable equity capital which influences the lending behaviour of senior debt providers. Other authors follow that rationale, see, e.g. Andrade, G./ Kaplan, S.N. (1998), p. 1451.

587 See Borio, C. (1990), p. 5 with reference to the Federal Reserve Board, Federal Deposit Insurance Corporation and Comptroller of Currency: Highly Leveraged Transactions Interpretation, 6th February 1990, Washington.

588 See, e.g. Andrade, G./ Kaplan, S. (1998); Arzac, E. (1996); Denis, D.J. (1994); Schmid, H. (1994) and Kaplan, S./ Stein, J. (1990). The operationalisation of an HLT will be provided in chapter 5.3.2.1.

589 See, e.g. Cumming, D.J. (2002); Hovakimian, A./ Opler, T./ Titman, S. (2001); Schwenhold, F. (2001); Jung, K./ Kim, Y./ Stulz, R. (1996).

590 Backhaus, K. et al. (2003), p. 60.

591 Chapter 6.3. discusses the background and use of logit models in detail.

592 For an overview of corporate finance studies and the applied econometric techniques, see appendix 5. As can be seen, logit models represent the most popular technique in corporate finance studies.

The theoretical framework consisting of the static trade-off theory and agency considerations suggests how leverage is likely to be influenced by changes in these variables. These two theories represent the foundation on which to debate the influence of the transaction characteristics. If the "reaction" is not reflected in the empirical results, it either leads to doubts about the validity of the theoretical framework, doubts about the efficiency of the capital structure decisions or the adequacy of the empirical study methodology.

As will be outlined in each section the next chapter, empirical corporate finance studies have focussed on the following seven characteristics most frequently and are therefore included in the present research model:

- Risk class
- Transaction size
- Tangibility
- Growth
- Profitability
- Uniqueness
- Free cash flow

These characteristics may be incorporated in the research model in two ways. First, they may directly reflect the relevance of certain market frictions (e.g. available free cash flow as an indicator of agency cost of equity)[593]. Second, their impact may be more indirect in a way that ceteris paribus the respective cost or benefits are likely to show up more clearly. Here, the lines of argumentation include two or more elements (e.g. firms with growth opportunities have c.p. less free cash flow and should consequently have lower agency cost of equity).

This study pursues the latter rationale. Instead of controlling for direct indicators, an indirect argumentation is preferred as measures are very difficult to record in a questionnaire-based study.[594] Put differently, characteristics not only have a direct influence on the cost elements but are also interrelated and hence impose an indirect influence on the capital structure. The following graphic represents an attempt to sum up the relationships between the elements of the research model as

[593] See chapter 3.3.2.2.

[594] An example would be the cost of financial distress that is sometimes directly estimated using Altman's Z, which can be computed from annual report data but hardly from a questionnaire. See, e.g. Frank, M./ Goyal, V. (2003), p. 19 for an application of Altman's Z.

claimed by theory.[595] The elements comprise three for the trade-off theory (default probability, cost of financial distress and taxes), two for the agency theory (agency cost of debt and equity) and the seven characteristics.

Figure 24: Theoretical relations between transaction characteristics and the cost elements in a trade-off and agency context (not IBO-specific)

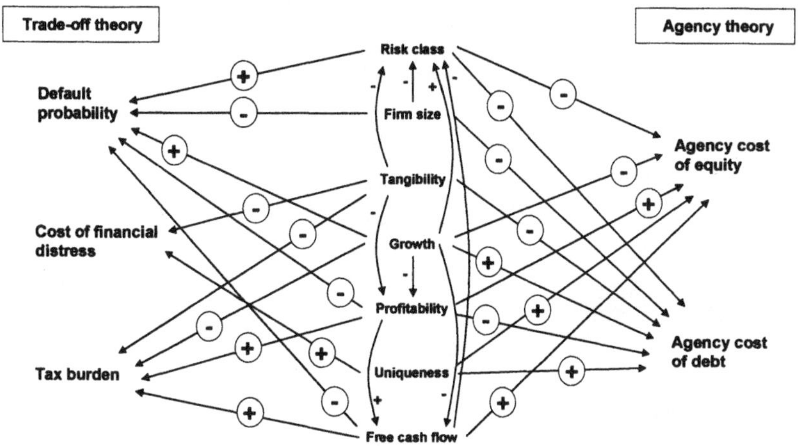

Source: Author.

The subsequent paragraphs discuss the exact lines of argumentation for each characteristics in light of an IBO's specific character. On the basis of the various articles put forward in the context of the two theories, the influence of the transaction characteristics will be elaborated. Figure 25 illustrates the research model with its explanatory and dependent variables and the theoretical interlink.

[595] It is foregone at this point to explain how the influence is derived given the extensive explanations within the hypotheses development.

Figure 25: Overview of the research model

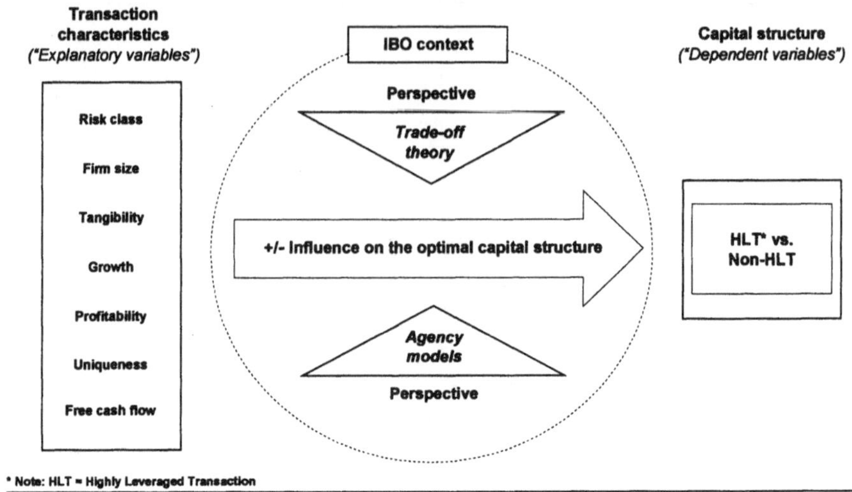

Source: Author.

5.2. Development of hypotheses

A specific IBO characteristic must be reflected in the development of the hypotheses when it clearly opposes the validity of an original theoretical argumentation. Otherwise, the hypothesis would not meet the condition of adequately considering the nature of the research object.[596]

The subsequent set of hypotheses will be based entirely on the theoretical models presented in chapters 3.2 and 3.3. Two hypotheses will be developed for each characteristic, one for the influence from the perspective of the trade-off theory and one for the agency models. A hypothesis states how an incremental increase of one determinant, assuming that the other determinants remain constant, will influence the likelihood that a transaction is structured as an HLT. If a theoretical approach is indeterminate or altogether silent about the influence of one characteristic, no significant relationship will be hypothesised. Likewise, if different argumentations underlying a theory (e.g. taxes and financial distress) result in inconclusive or contradicting predictions, a non-significant relationship will be hypothesised either.

[596] See Bortz, J./ Döring, N. (2002), p. 7 for general discussions of hypothesis development, including the conditions to be fullfilled.

5.2.1. Risk class

A firm's specific risk has been one of the most widely discussed explanatory variables in corporate finance literature. KALE / NOE / RAMIREZ (1991) assert that academics have reached a consensus for business risk as a key determinant.[597] The main line of argumentation follows the trade-off theory, determining a firm's capital structure as a result of the increased default probability among few other determinants.[598] The reason for an inverse relation between business risk and leverage lies primarily in an increased earnings volatility as a measure for risk, which results in a higher probability of bankruptcy for a given level of debt and thus a lower debt capacity.[599] This reasoning should also apply for IBOs.

> *H1a: Considering the trade-off theory, IBOs of a higher risk class are less likely to be structured as an HLT.*

Within an agency context the agency cost of debt in the sense of MYERS (1977) seem to play a vital role in determining the optimum leverage.[600] According to him, owner-managers are more inclined to forgo profitable growth opportunities if the business was risky than if not, because the benefits are more likely to accrue to debtholders only.[601] Consequently, cashing the money out to shareholders seems beneficial. Or on the flipside, if a firm did not suffer from volatility at all, debtholders would get their money back anyway and the owner-manager would fully benefit from the profitable projects. In this respect, risk leads to higher agency cost of debt, which in turn decreases the optimum level of senior debt. In addition to the threat of underinvestment, potential asset substitution should aggravate the problem faced by debtholders since the owner-manager has an increased incentive to realise more risky projects ex post. If the firm is in a good state, they would benefit from that choice while, conversely, if they chose less risky projects, they would fall short of cash-ins whether the firm is in a good or bad state.[602] This increases the associated agency cost of debt.

> *H1b: Considering an agency context, IBOs of a higher risk class are less likely to be structured as an HLT.*

---

[597] Kale, J./ Noe, T/ Ramirez, G. (1991), p. 1693.
[598] Castanias, R. (1983), p. 1621.
[599] Johnson, S.A. (1997), p. 54.
[600] Kim, W.S./ Sorenson, E.H. (1986), p. 136.
[601] Myers, S.C. (1977), p. 167.
[602] Jensen, M.C/ Meckling, W.H. (1976), pp. 334-337.

Early empirical studies draw a rather inconclusive picture. Most studies found significant relationships between risk and leverage, with a slight prevalence of negative outcomes. In this sense, the statement of KALE / NOE / RAMIREZ (1991) can only be accepted to the extent that risk represents a key determinant but not as regards a clear direction of influence. Table 2 provides an overview of the empirical studies

Table 2: Influence of risk on firm leverage in prior empirical studies

Positive		*Negative*		*Insignificant*	
Dessi / Robertson	1999	Frank / Goyal	2003	Opler / Titman	1993
Shenoy / Koch	1996	Fan / Titman / Twite	2003	Billingsley / Lamy / Thompson	1988
Lowe / Naughton / Taylor	1994	Brailsford / Oliver / Pua	2002	Titman / Wessels	1988
Thies / Klock	1992	De Jong / Veld	2001	Kester	1986
Gardner / Trzcinka	1992	Hirota	1999	Marsh	1982
Kale / Noe / Ramirez	1991	Wald	1999	Ferri / Jones	1979
Crutchley / Hansen	1989	Boyle / Eckhold	1997		
Barton / Gordon	1988	Downs	1993		
Kim / Sorenson	1986	Bayless / Chaplinsky	1991		
		MacKie-Mason	1990		
		Chowdhury / Miles	1989		
		Friend / Lang	1988		
		Bradley / Jarrell / Kim	1984		
		Taub	1975		

5.2.2. Transaction size

Considering the trade-off theory, bankruptcy considerations suggest that larger firms are more diversified than small ones with less volatile profits and therefore less prone to collapse.[603] With a reduced default probability large firms should have higher optimal debt levels.

> *H2a: Considering the trade-off theory, large IBOs are more likely to be structured as an HLT.*

Accordingly, larger firms with a longer business history are thought to incur lower monitoring cost owing to a higher level of lender informedness, an argument which was first advanced by FAMA (1985). Therefore, large IBOs should have a reduced level of agency cost of debt in the sense of JENSEN (1976) and consequently a higher ratio of debt to total capitalisation.[604]

[603] Titman, S./ Wessels, R. (1988), p. 6.
[604] Johnson, S.A. (1997), p. 54.

H2b: Considering an agency context, large IBOs are more likely to be structured as an HLT.

An analysis of empirical studies on usual corporates shows a positive relationship between firm size and leverage in two-thirds of all cases. The findings of the remaining studies were divided almost evenly between insignificant and negative.

Table 3: Influence of size on firm leverage in prior empirical studies

Positive		***Negative***		***Insignificant***	
Frank / Goyal	2003	Jung / Kim / Stulz	1996	Rajan / Zingales[3]	1995
MacKay / Phillips	2002	Lee / Gentry	1995	Lowe / Naughton / Taylor	1994
Goyal / Lehn / Racic	2002	Rajan / Zingales[2]	1995	Chung[4]	1993
Hovakimian / Opler / Titman	2001	Kale / Noe / Ramirez.	1991	Chaplinsky / Niehaus	1993
Ozkan	2001	Billingsley / Lamy / Thompson	1988	De Jong / Veld	1988
Dessi / Robertson	1999			Friend / Lang	1988
Wald	1999			Kim / Sorenson	1986
Hirota	1999			Marsh	1982
Jordan / Lowe / Taylor	1998				
Cornelli et. al.	1996				
Shenoy / Koch	1996				
Rajan / Zingales[1]	1995				
Homaifa / Zietz / Benkato	1994				
Klein / Belt	1994				
Downs	1993				
MacKie-Mason	1990				
Crutchley / Hansen	1989				
Titman / Wessels[4]	1988				
Barton / Gordon	1988				
Ferri / Jones	1979				
Taub	1975				

Note: [1] for UK
[2] for Germany
[3] ifor France and Italy
[4] influence on long-term debt

5.2.3. Tangibility

With regard to the structure of a firm's assets, specifically the share of fixed tangible assets, the a priori direction of influence is debatable. Among the arguments related to the trade-off theory, the most obvious one refers to fixed tangible assets as collaterals for debt financing, which suggests a positive relationship. This reduces the uncertainty of future debt service for the lender and should thus lead to higher debt levels.[605] Furthermore, tangible assets maintain higher liquidation values in default, which in turn lowers the cost of financial distress.[606] However, the argument is not relevant for an IBO's leverage, because, as outlined in chapter 4.1.2.1, IBO financing is not related to the amount of assets that can be collaterlized but to the expected future cash flows.

A factor that goes hand in hand with the structure of the asset side has been stressed by KIM / SORENSON (1986), notably the negative influence of depreciation cost on leverage. They argue that depreciation cost reduce the benefit of interests through their tax deductibility.[607] The same reasoning has been discussed by other authors under the aspect of non-debt tax shield (NDTS) on the basis of DEANGELO / MASULIS' (1980) arguments.[608] Since depreciation cost should be c.p. higher for firms with large shares of tangible assets (unless 100 per cent of the intangible assets are depreciable), they should result in lower debt levels for these IBOs.

> *H3a: Considering the trade-off theory, IBOs with more tangible assets are less likely to be structured as an HLT.*

A reason for a positive relationship between tangibility and leverage roots in the agency cost of debt as discussed by JENSEN / MECKLING (1976) and MYERS (1977). The straightforward yet striking argument here is that the threat of both asset substitution and underinvestment will be lower the more assets are in place relative to the firm's growth options. Owner-managers' discretion increases with the number of envisaged growth projects ahead.[609] This increases the optimal debt level for IBOs from an agency perspective.

> *H3b: Considering an agency context, IBOs with more tangible assets are more likely to be structured as an HLT.*

To date, empirical studies for corporates have drawn a clear picture about the influence of tangibility. By far the majority of studies have found a positive relationship and most authors attribute the effect to the collateralisation of fixed tangible assets. Only few studies have found

605 Titman, S./ Wessels, R. (1988), p. 3; Bradley, M./ Jarrell, G./ Kim, E. (1984), p. 874.

606 Rajan, R./ Zingales, L. (1995), p. 1459; Harris, M./ Raviv, A. (1990), p. 323; Williamson, O.E. (1988), p. 581. Cays, S.E. (2001) provides empirical evidence for this assertion as regards indirect costs (p. 8).

607 Kim, W.S./ Sorenson, E.H. (1986), p. 137.

608 See also chapter 3.3.3. Empirical studies that specifically address the relevance of NDTS include Frank, M./ Goyal, V. (2003); MacKie-Mason, J. (1990); Bradley, M./ Jarrell, G./ Kim, E. (1984). To the author's knowledge no European articles have focussed on non-debt tax shields to date. However, the basic mechanism as assumed by DeAngelo / Masulis hold for European tax systems as well.

609 MacKie-Mason, J. (1990), p. 1477.

either a significantly negative or insignificant relationship. Table 4 shows the results of selected empirical studies on the influence of tangibility.

Table 4: Influence of tangibility on firm leverage in prior empirical studies

Positive		*Negative*		*Insignificant*	
Fan / Titman / Twite	2003	Frank / Goyal	2003	Titman / Wessels	1988
MacKay / Phillips	2002	Barton / Gordon	1988	Brailsford / Oliver / Pua	2002
Dittmar	2002	Ferri / Jones	1979	Rajan / Zingales[2]	1995
Goyal / Lehn / Racic	2002	Baker	1973		
Hovakimian / Opler / Titman	2001				
Dessi / Robertson	1999				
Hirota	1999				
Wald	1999				
Johnson	1997				
Berger / Ofek / Yermack	1997				
Shenoy / Koch	1996				
Rajan / Zingales[1]	1995				
Downs	1993				
Chung[3]	1993				
Jensen / Solberg / Zorn	1992				
Thies / Klock	1992				
Bayless / Chaplinsky	1991				
MacKie-Mason	1990				
Friend / Lang	1988				
Friend / Hasborouck	1988				
Long / Malitz	1985				
Bradley / Jarrell / Kim	1984				
Marsh	1982				
Taub	1975				

Note: [1] for Germany, France, and UK
[2] for Italy
[3] influence on long-term debt

5.2.4. Growth

A company's growth was discussed early on in the context of corporate finance. Before most of the ground-breaking articles on corporate financial policy were published, BAXTER / CRAGG (1970) had already listed a number of textbooks whose authors suggested keeping leverage low since growth is primarily associated with risk.[610] However, no matter how pioneering these works may be, a theory-based justification for postulating a systematic relationship between growth and leverage has grounded on other research.

[610] Baxter, N./ Cragg, J. (1970), p. 229.

TITMAN / WESSELS (1988) appear to best summarise the thoughts of most articles that suggest a negative relation between growth and firm leverage. First of all, since growth options represent firm value, which instantly depreciates in the event of financial distress, growth tends to be better financed with equity.[611] In addition, IBOs with significant growth opportunities require above-average dedication to business-building activities such as R&D, marketing and sales. Hence, interest deductibility has a less beneficial effect on the IBO.

H4a: Considering the trade-off theory, IBOs with more growth opportunities are less likely to be structured as an HLT.

From an agency perspective, the presence of growth options appears to increase agency cost of debt the higher the leverage of the firm is. Higher debt levels give an incentive to pass up many of the profitable investments, as the benefits accrue largely to debtholders.[612] Accordingly, growth requires banks to impose more costly monitoring and tighter covenants. This follows the frequently cited "costly contracting hypothesis" advanced by SMITH / WARNER (1979).[613] Claimholders must account for the higher flexibility of the management to choose among a given set of projects.[614] Moreover, as regards the agency cost of equity, firms with more profitable investments should have lower levels of FCF available for the management to be invested in low-return projects, which in turn mitigates the agency cost of equity as discussed by JENSEN (1986) and JENSEN/ MECKLING (1976) and reduces disciplination benefits of debt.[615] Overall, agency theory predicts lower optimal debt levels for IBOs in the presence of considerable growth options.

H4b: Considering an agency context, IBOs with more growth opportunities are less likely to be structured as an HLT.

Amongst the various firm characteristics, growth is probably one of the empirically best-covered determinants. To date, evidence for the influence of growth on firm leverage largely confirms the theoretical prediction that debt is less appropriate for high-growth firms than for low-growth firms. Indeed, most of the studies found negative relationships, although quite a number of tests also found either positive or no significant result. See table 5 for the summary of the results.

---

[611] Titman, S./ Wessels, R. (1988), p. 4.
[612] Myers, S.C. (1977), p. 149.
[613] Kale, J./ Noe, T/ Ramirez, G. (1991), p. 1706.
[614] Titman, S./ Wessels, R. (1988), p. 4.
[615] See Jensen, M.C. (1986), p. 325.

Table 5: Influence of growth on firm leverage in prior empirical studies

Positive		*Negative*		*Insignificant*	
Wald	1999	Frank / Goyal	2003	Brailsford / Oliver / Pua	2002
Dessi / Robertson	1999	Goyal / Lehn / Racic	2002	Munro	1996
Jordan / Lowe / Taylor	1998	Dittmar	2002	Jung / Kim / Stulz	1996
Boyle / Eckhold	1997	MacKay / Phillips[1]	2002	Lee / Gentry	1995
Homaifa / Zietz / Benkato	1994	Hovakimian / Opler / Titman	2001	Klein / Belt	1994
Thies / Klock	1992	Ozkan	2001	Downs	1993
Chowdhury / Miles	1989	Gul	1999	Opler / Titman	1993
		Hirota	1999	Chaplinsky / Niehaus	1993
		Lang / Ofek / Stulz	1996	Titman / Wessels	1988
		McConnell / Servaes	1995		
		Rajan / Zingales	1995		
		Barclay / Smith	1995		
		Lasfer	1995		
		Lowe / Naughton / Taylor	1994		
		Chung[2]	1993		
		Smith / Watts	1992		
		Kale / Noe / Ramirez	1991		
		Barton / Gordon	1988		
		Kim / Sorenson	1986		

Note: [1] for OLS regression
[2] influence on long-term debt

5.2.5. Profitability

As far as the profitability of a firm is concerned, the most common expectation in the literature on capital structure is for a negative relationship between profitability and financial leverage. The argumentation of most authors points to the ability of profitable firms to finance themselves with internal funds, following a pecking order of finance.[616] However, as outlined in chapter 3.1.6., the pecking order does not apply to the characteristics of IBOs, since they are not financed with internal funds and the information and decision setting does not provide a signalling framework based on hidden information requirements.

Therefore, other factors must also be taken into account. BARTON / HILL / SUNDARAM (1989) emphasise that pure economic reasoning would suggest higher debt levels for profitable firms as they are better able to provide the debt service.[617] Similarly, GALE (1972) recalls the traditional

[616] See e.g. Frank, M./ Goyal, V. (2003), p. 23; Titman, S./ Wessels, R. (1988), p. 6; Friend, I./ Lang, L. (1988), p. 277.
[617] Barton, S.L./ Hill, N./ Sundaram, S. (1989), p. 42.

understanding of financial decision making before MODIGLIANI / MILLER. Leveraging the company was simply considered a means to increase return on equity.[618]

However, in the context of the static trade-off theory, high profitability at a given volatility first of all reduces the likelihood of a corporate default. In addition, firms with higher profits benefit from the increased tax shelter of debt interests. Therefore, more profitable IBOs should exhibit higher leverage ratios.[619]

> *H5a: Considering the trade-off theory, very profitable IBOs are more likely to be structured as an HLT.*

For a given amount of growth options, profitable firms generate high cash inflows leading to higher levels of free cash flow, which again give rise to an increase in the agency cost of equity that can be controlled by higher debt levels.[620] In addition, the lower threat of corporate default mitigates the incentive to underinvest the company, as the return on the projects is more likely to benefit the management.[621] Hence, both arguments result in an higher expected leverage of an IBO.

> *H5b: Considering an agency context, very profitable IBOs are more likely to be structured as an HLT.*

As regards the empirical evidence, most studies attempt to test the pecking-order theory in contrast to alternative theories. The majority of these studies found significant negative relationships, which in turn confirms the predictions of the pecking-order theory for the world of normal corporates. However, a fair number of studies could not confirm the pecking-order theory. See table 6 for the results of the most relevant studies.

---

[618] Gale, B.T. (1972), p. 418. See also chapter 3.1.2.
[619] Fama, E./ French, K. (2002), p. 6.
[620] Harris, M./ Raviv, A. (1991), pp. 301-302.
[621] Myers, S.C. (1977), p. 171.

Table 6: Influence of profitability on firm leverage in prior empirical studies

Positive		*Negative*		*Insignificant*	
Dessi / Robertson	1999	Frank / Goyal	2003	Brailsford / Oliver / Pua	2002
Boyle / Eckhold	1997	Goyal / Lehn / Racic	2002	Dittmar	2002
Cornelli et. al.	1996	MacKay / Phillips	2002	Jung / Kim / Stulz	1996
Downs	1993	Hovakimian / Opler / Titman	2001	Opler / Titman	1993
Bacless / Chaplinsky	1991	Ozkan	2001	Billingsley / Lamy / Thompson	1988
Barton / Gordon	1988	Wald	1999	Titman / Wessels	1988
Taub	1975	Hirota	1999	Long / Malitz	1985
		Jordan / Lowe / Taylor	1998		
		Berger / Ofek / Yermack	1997		
		Lee / Gentry	1995		
		Rajan / Zingales	1995		
		Lowe / Naughton / Taylor	1994		
		Thies / Kock	1992		
		Allen / Mizuno	1989		
		Chowdhury / Miles	1989		
		Friend / Lang	1988		
		Kester	1986		
		Toy et. al.	1974		

5.2.6. Uniqueness

A firm's uniqueness or, alternatively, the specificity of its assets, has triggered less controversial discussions than other determinants. From the perspective of the trade-off theory, the anticipated cost of financial distress are higher, since unique assets are difficult to liquidate given fewer potential buyers. Conversely, liquid assets are first candidates for debt financing because they are more marketable in the case of corporate default.[622]

Likewise, in a firm group context, specific assets exhibit low degrees of redeployability and can hardly be used alternatively. An example of an easily deployable asset would be commercial land that could be used for different commercial activities.[623]

In addition to the direct effects on the firm itself, a default is particularly costly for its employees and customers facing higher direct expenditures to overcome the consequences (particularly the search for new employment and source of supply).[624]

622 Shleifer, A./ Vishny, R. (1992), p. 1358.
623 Williamson, O.E. (1988), p. 589.
624 Titman, S. (1984), p. 150.

This has an indirect impact on the firm given that employees will demand higher salaries and/or longer periods of notice to counterbalance for the downsides. Uniqueness should therefore have a clear negative influence on the optimal debt level.

H6a: Considering the trade-off theory, unique IBOs are less likely to be structured as an HLT.

In an agency context, one can argue that specific assets impose a higher degree of outcome uncertainty with regard to an agent's actions. The higher the asset specificity, the lower should be the optimal leverage.[625] WALD (1999) points out that agency cost of debt as a result of potential underinvestment are higher the less capital is entrenched in homogenous liquid assets, such as plant and machinery.[626] However, the outcome uncertainty should hold for shareholders as well, i.e. in the presence of highly specific assets the associated agency cost of equity should also rise, which leads to an indeterminate net influence of uniqueness on a firm's leverage.

H6b: Considering an agency context, the influence of an IBO's uniqueness on the likelihood of being structured as an HLT cannot be predicted.

Although uniqueness has not been covered as intensely by empirical studies as other determinants, the results suggest a negative relationship. With the exception of BRAILSFORD / OLIVER / PUA (2002), all studies have found negative relationships, irrespective of how uniqueness was operationalised. See table 7 for the results.

Table 7: Influence of uniqueness on firm leverage in prior empirical studies

Positive		*Negative*		*Insignificant*	
		Frank / Goyal	2003	Brailsford / Oliver / Pua	2002
		Hovakimian / Opler / Titman	2001		
		Wald	1999		
		Berger / Ofek / Yermack	1996		
		Chaplinsky / Niehaus	1993		
		MacKie-Mason	1990		
		Titman / Wessels[1]	1988		
		Long / Malitz	1985		
		Bradley / Jarrell / Kim[1]	1984		

Note: [1] jointly determined with sales expenditures

[625] Breuer, W. (1995), pp. 624-625.

[626] Wald, K. (1999), p. 170.

5.2.7. Free cash flow

As regards the cost of financial distress, the presence of high levels of cash flows for a given volatility should alleviate the bank's uncertainty about retaining borrowings since the likelihood of bankruptcy is reduced and the loans can be amortized more quickly. Likewise, a strong free cash flow could be an indicator of an above-average level of profitability, which in turn requires the debt shelter from taxes. Hence, IBOs with strong free cash flows should carry more debt.

> *H7a: Considering the trade-off theory, IBOs with high levels of free cash flow are more likely to be structured as an HLT.*

A large number of studies are based on the seminal article by JENSEN (1986) regarding the severeness of agency cost of equity associated with high levels of free cash flows. Most of these articles discuss free cash flow in connection with the gains from LBOs. Clearly, high levels of free cash flow reinforce the management's incentive to waste cash flows for negative NPV projects. This is anticipated by equity investors and only accepted at disadvantageous conditions, which in turn lowers the attractiveness of equity even further.[627] Conversely, debt may serve as a means of disciplination because of the regular cash outflows and lower available cash flow.[628] Therefore, IBOs are likely to show a positive relation between free cash flow and leverage.

> *H7b: Considering the trade-off theory, IBOs with high levels of free cash flow are more likely to be structured as an HLT.*

Only surprisingly few empirical articles have examined this question. A reason why free cash flow is rarely specified in empirical tests could be that other determinants implicitly control for the level of cash flow.[629]

The few existing empirical studies have produced mixed results. While only OSKAN (2001) and SHUETRIM / LOWE / MORLING (1993) have found a significant positive relationship, others have identified either a negative one or were not able to find significant relationships at all.

---

627 See chapter 3.4.2.2.

628 E.g. Phan, P./ Hill, C. (1995); Frankfurter, G./ Gunay, E. (1992); Muscarella, C.J./ Vetsuypens, M.R. (1990); Bull, I. (1989); Kaplan, S. (1989).

629 For example, growth companies usually need cash flow to realise their growth options, i.e. all else being equal, the firm should exhibit lower cash flow levels.

To some extent this result is surprising given the clear positive impact of debt on cash flow-generative businesses. Table 8 depicts the results of the few studies.

Table 8: Influence of free cash flow on firm leverage in prior empirical studies

Positive		*Negative*		*Insignificant*	
Lang / Ofek / Stulz	1996	Ozkan	2001	Brailsford / Oliver / Pua	2002
Opler / Titman	1993	Shuetrim / Lowe / Morling	1993	De Jong / Veld	2001
		Chaplinsky / Niehaus	1993	Jung / Kim / Stulz	1996
				Lasfer	1995
				Lehn / Poulsen	1989

5.3. Operationalisation of variables

The following section operationalises the variables on both sides of the research model. First, the explanatory variables will be discussed in light of earlier studies. The subsequent paragraphs operationalise the dependent variables, with the focus on the discussion of how a HLT can be defined.

5.3.1. Explanatory variables

In order to establish a link to prior corporate finance research, the explanatory variables used here are the same as those applied in a number of earlier studies. However, given that unlike most corporate finance studies the data was not received from databases, a practice perspective had to be taken into account.

In particular, some metrics are inappropriate for this survey, since they are not recorded by PE funds or they are difficult to calculate. Therefore, operationalisation also includes parameters as used in practice but nonetheless remain clear indicators for the respective determinant. Like other surveys, the present study includes more than one indicator for each determinant in order to account for the threat of poor return rates for certain variables.[630] Except for 'uniqueness', all determinants are non-latent variables, i.e. their metrics are quantifiable. In contrast, uniqueness represents a typical latent variable; it is likely to have an impact on the dependent variable but cannot be expressed in numbers directly. Only indicators for unique or non-unique firms can be quantified (e.g. the share of R&D). Conversely, e.g. profitability, free cash flow and size can be measured

630 E.g. Brailsford, T./ Oliver, B./ Pua, S. (2002); Titman, S./ Wessels, R. (1988); Marsh, P. (1982); Ferri, M./ Jones, W. (1979).

directly.[631] As will be discussed later, the nature of the variables largely determines the appropriateness of an econometric model.[632]

5.3.1.1. *Risk class*

Regarding the operationalisation of a firm's risk class, these studies have relied mostly on the volatility of an income measure before interest to reflect the unlevered risk of the firm.[633] Frequently, the standard deviation of operating income (EBIT) over a period of 5-20 years has been applied since it can be easily computed and best reflects the original understanding of risk as volatility in the operating performance.[634] Sometimes, it has been scaled by assets to exclude size effects[635] or its mean.[636] A less robust measure is the absolute value of the change in profitability from period *t-1* to *t* as recently used by FAN / TITMAN / TWITE (2003).[637] Finally, the type of industry can be considered as an indicator for business risk, given different levels of cyclicality faced by firms.[638]

In accordance with most studies, this survey captures the degree of risk that the firm faces by means of the volatility of an income measure. However, instead of using EBIT as operating measure, EBITDA is applied due to its higher practical relevance to express a firm's operating cash flow potential.[639]

To be calculated over a period of 7 years, EBITDA volatility captures short-term fluctuations in the operating performance. As a complementary long-term perspective, the survey also records the respective industry cyclicality.

---

631 One could argue that neither growth nor risk class is directly measurable. However, for both variables proxies can be found that are well-accepted as a constituent characteristic and therefore should be regarded as more than just an indicator.

632 In fact, a large share of latent variables requires structural equation models such as PLS or LISREL. See chapter 6.3.1.

633 For a possible definition of volatility as one measure of risk as well as other measures, see Betsch, O./ Groh, A./ Lohmann, L. (2000), pp. 61-68.

634 E.g. Kim, W.S./ Sorenson, E.H. (1986), p. 136; Ferri, M./ Jones, W. (1979); Taub, A.J. (1975), p. 412.

635 E.g. MacKay, P./ Phillips, G. (2002), p. 10; Wald, K. (1999), p. 170; Bradley, M./ Jarrell, G./ Kim, E. (1984), p. 873.

636 E.g. Dessi, R./ Robertson, D. (1999), p. 6.

637 Fan, J./ Titman, S./ Twite, G.(2003), p. 16.

638 E.g. Brailsford, T./ Oliver, B./ Pua, S. (2002), p. 11.

639 See Schiereck, D./ Klab, A./ Kitzmann, J. (2004), pp. 330-331 for an example of how EBITDA is incorporated as an indicator for the success of an IBO. The only shortcoming could be the less pronounced relative volatility based on EBITDA compared to an EBIT-based volatility, as the EBITDA exhibits higher values for positive depreciation and amortisation cost.

However, instead of a numerical taxonomy, the deal record sheet simply includes a 7-category scale with values ranging from 'None' to 'Very high'.

5.3.1.2. Transaction size

Two different measures are generally applied to account for the size of the firm, either a sales measure or the total assets of the firm. In fact, most studies use total sales[640] or a (natural) logarithm of total sales as a proxy for the company's size.[641] Others use total assets at book values in their regressions.[642] MARSH (1982) ran the regressions with a set of three different variables, the logarithm of total sales, the logarithm of capital employed, and the market capitalisation of the firm. All measures proved to be highly correlated with leverage and generated almost identical results.[643]

By analogy with the market capitalisation parameter used by MARSH, the value of the transaction (enterprise value plus transaction cost) will be used in the present study. In addition, the level of sales at the time of the acquisition shall be surveyed, since it is an readily available figure with no further computations.

5.3.1.3. Tangibility

All previously mentioned studies use the same metric to operationalise the tangibility of a firm, namely the share of fixed tangible assets in total book value assets.[644] Under fixed tangible assets they subsume property, plant and equipment assets.[645] The methodology employed in this study follows these authors by including fixed assets divided by total assets as the sole variable on asset structure.

Irrespective of their beneficial nature, tangible assets also feature a shortcoming that was emphasised by FERRI / JONES (1979) and BAKER (1973). They pointed out that along with more tangible assets the firm has to cope with an increased level of fixed cost leading to a higher

640 E.g. Ferri, M./ Jones, W. (1979), p. 633; Remmers et. al. (1974), p. 30.

641 E.g. Frank, M./ Goyal, V. (2003), p. 17; Ozkan, A. (2001), p. 180; Rajan, R./ Zingales, L. (1995), p. 1452; Titman, S./ Wessels, R. (1988), p. 6.

642 For example, Chung, K.H. (1993) uses a 4-year average of total assets (p. 89). Brailsford, T./ Oliver, B./ Pua, S. (2002), p. 25 and Hovakimian, A./ Opler, T./ Titman, S. (2001), p. 7 include the ln (log) of total assets.

643 Marsh, P. (1982), p. 132, FN 37.

644 E.g. Fan, J./ Titman, S./ Twite, G. (2003), p. 37; Chung, K. (2001), p. 89; Hovakimian, A./ Opler, T./ Titman, S. (2001), p. 8; Rajan, R./ Zingales, L. (1995), p. 1453; Friend, I./ Lang, L. (1988), p. 275; Ferri, M./ Jones, W. (1979), p. 642.

645 E.g. Hovakimian, A./ Opler, T./ Titman, S. (2001), p. 8; Wald, K. (1999), p. 171.

operating leverage.[646] FERRI / JONES (1979) specifically elaborates on this aspect by including a measure of operating leverage beyond the balance sheet-based tangibility ratio. In accordance with common definitions, they included the percentage change in EBIT as a proportion of the percentage change in sales as elasticity metric.[647] However, they pointed to operational limitations of this elegant measure with the consequence that the balance sheet-based parameter generated the best results. Firms with high tangible assets fell predominately into the low-leverage group.[648]

5.3.1.4. Growth

Given the wide range of empirical studies, it is not surprising to see how many measures have been employed to approximate the growth of a firm. The various metrics can be sub-divided into forward and backward-oriented metrics. Although theories are based on the consideration of the presence of *future* growth and not realised growth, backward-oriented measures are jointly employed with forward-oriented measures. This is because past growth may well serve as a reliable indicator of future growth and forward-looking measures are not necessarily of a more reliable quality to guarantee that future growth options will actually arise.

The most frequently used backward-oriented measures are year-on-year changes in earnings[649], total assets[650], total sales[651] and employment[652]. Another common past measure is the amount of CapEx invested, usually scaled by the book value of assets.[653] In contrast, a measure that is reflected in past numbers but whose impact on firm growth becomes effective in the future includes R&D expenditures.[654] However, as will be seen in the section on firm 'uniqueness', R&D spending should be better used to approximate the specificity of assets.

Measures that directly account for the presence of future growth options include the market-to-book ratio, commonly known as Tobin's Q.[655] It measures the ratio of the market value of a firm's assets

---

646 Ferri, M./ Jones, W. (1979), pp. 642-643 and Baker, S.H. (1973), p. 504. Operating leverage denotes the elasticity how a firm's operating income changes relative to a given change in sales. For a discussion see e.g. Betsch, O./ Groh, A./ Lohmann, L. (2000), p. 283.

647 Ferri, M./ Jones, W. (1979), p. 634.

648 Ferri, M./ Jones, W. (1979), p. 643.

649 E.g. Kim, W.S./ Sorenson, E.H. (1986), p. 138.

650 E.g. Frank, M./ Goyal, V. (2003), p. 17 and Titman, S./ Wessels, R. (1988), p. 4.

651 E.g. K. (1999), p. 172; Dessi, R./ Robertson, D. (1999), p. 17; Lehn, K./ Poulsen, A. (1989), p. 777.

652 E.g. Lang, L./ Ofek, E./ Stulz, R. (1996), p. 7.

653 E.g. Frank, M./ Goyal, V. (2003), p. 17; Lang, L./ Ofek, E./ Stulz, R. (1996), p. 7; Goyal, V./ Lehn, K./ Racic, S. (2002), p. 40; Kale, J./ Noe, T/ Ramirez, G. (1991), p. 1704; Titman, S./ Wessels, R. (1988), p. 4.

654 E.g. Titman, S./ Wessels, R. (1988), p. 4.

655 E.g. Hovakimian, A./ Opler, T./ Titman, S. (2001), p. 8; Rajan, R./ Zingales, L. (1995), p. 1453;

to the book value of its assets, hence the growth options are reflected in the enumerator.[656] There is a considerable number of metrics which capture the equity appreciation deriving from future projects (e.g. price-earnings-ratio).[657]

In light of the different possible metrics, this empirical study employs three measures, the enterprise value divided by the firm's EBITDA, CapEx to operating cash flow and the average sales growth. The first measure directly picks up the idea of Tobin's Q. However, since the book value of assets is an uncommon measure in practice, it has been replaced by EBITDA, a measure of current profitability. It can be expected that high-growth firms realise higher EV/EBITDA multiples than low-growth firms. In addition, practitioners frequently employ this variable so that the metric should be readily available. Applying the CapEx to operating cash flow ratio directly points to the existence of presumably profitable investments. The last measure identifies the compound annual growth rate of sales[658], a commonly used figure in practice.

5.3.1.5. Profitability

In contrast to other determinants, the different studies measure a firm's profitability in a very similar way, usually as the operating income divided by a measure of scale. Therefore the EBIT or operating income is mostly scaled by total assets[659] or, in some cases, total sales[660]. Alternatively, instead of the operating income the EBITDA may be used.[661] Measures based on the net income also exhibit the causality problem with capital structure.[662] In the subsequent tests the firm's EBITDA divided by sales shall be used since many practitioners refer to this measure as the profitability margin.

5.3.1.6. Uniqueness

Quite intuitively one would expect the share of intangible assets to best reflect the uniqueness of a firm. However, taking intangibles as a proxy is a highly inadequate measure, since tangible assets

---

656 See Goyal, V./ Lehn, K./ Racic, S. (2002), p. 40.

657 Hoever, it is important to use metrics that are gross of financing effects. For example, the price/earnings ratio is dependent on the actual leverage and hence might be biased, given the reverse causality.

658 The CAGR of a series is calculated using $CAGR = \left(\frac{Y_n}{Y_1}\right)^{\frac{1}{n}} - 1$: Y_1 denotes the value in year 1 and Y_n the value in year n.

659 E.g. Brailsford, T./ Oliver, B./ Pua, S. (2002), p. 12; Dessi, R./ Robertson, D. (1999), p. 17; Wald, K. (1999), p. 172; Titman, S./ Wessels, R. (1988), p. 6.

660 E.g. Titman, S./ Wessels, R. (1988), p. 6.

661 E.g. Rajan, R./ Zingales, L. (1995), p. 1453.

662 E.g. Fan, J./ Titman, S./ Twite, G. (2003), p. 37; Hovakimian, A./ Opler, T./ Titman, S. (2001), p. 8.

can be very specific and intangible assets can be unspecific and highly marketable.[663] Instead, most authors prefer to see R&D expenditures as the main driver behind the level of asset specificity and apply measures such as R&D spending divided by sales.[664] In addition, TITMAN / WESSELS (1988) and BRADLEY / JARRELL / KIM (1984) suggest including selling expenditures over total sales, as specific assets require above-average efforts to promote and sell their products.[665] Furthermore, to take into account the considerations of TITMAN (1984), the former authors also employ a third measure of uniqueness, the quit rate, i.e. the percentage of an industry's total work force that quits the industry in any given year, as the churn rate proxies for the specificity of an industry.[666] Finally, FRANK / GOYAL (2003) directly include the type of industry under examination. By means of a binary dummy, they distinguish between more and less knowledge-driven industries on the basis of an industry code classification.[667]

Following most authors, this empirical study will employ R&D expenses over total sales as the main measure of a firm's uniqueness. In addition, the market share of the firm will be recorded, since a very large market share is also an indication of a very specific product offered by few firms.

5.3.1.7. Free cash flow

LEHN / POULSEN (1989) suggest to measure free cash flow as operating income minus taxes, interest expenses and dividends paid.[668] DE JONG / VELD (2001) apply this measure together with two alternatives having total sales and total assets respectively as denominator. All three measures give similar results.[669]

Other authors employ the same metric, with operating cash flow divided by book value of assets representing a very popular measure.[670] OZKAN (2001) uses a measure that relates to the level of available liquidity, the ratio of current assets and current liabilities (incl. cash and cash equivalents).[671] However, in light of the argument that JENSEN (1986) advanced, none of these measures appears to really approximate the agency cost of equity, since the critical argument is that management invests in negative NPV projects after *all* positive NPV projects have been realised.

663 Williamson, O.E. (1988), p. 588.
664 E.g. Hovakimian, A./ Opler, T./ Titman, S. (2001), p. 7; Wald, K. (1999), p. 170; Titman, S./ Wessels, R. (1988), p. 5.
665 Titman, S./ Wessels, R. (1988), p. 5 and Bradley, M./ Jarrell, G./ Kim, E. (1984), p. 873.
666 Titman, S./ Wessels, R. (1988), p. 5.
667 Frank / Goyal (2003), pp. 34-35.
668 Lehn, K./ Poulsen, A. (1989), p. 777.
669 De Jong, A./ Veld, C. (2001), p. 1873.
670 E.g. Brailsford, T./ Oliver, B./ Pua, S. (2002), p. 22 and Opler, T./ Titman, S. (1996), p. 1995.

This means that only the (unlevered)[672] cash flow after capital expenditures, hence what is commonly denoted as free cash flow before financing activities, allows these effects to be captured. To the author's knowledge the only empirical test employing this measure is provided by CHAPLINSKY / NIEHAUS (1993).[673]

In addition to the free cash flow scaled by total sales, a practitioners' indicator shall be included as well, namely net financial liabilities (NFL)[674] divided by FCF since it represents a proxy for the time it takes to fully deleverage the firm.

5.3.2. Dependent variables

Two sets of dependent variables will be subsequently operationalised, first, the key measure of an HLT and second, the measures of the different financial instruments, notably equity, sub-ordinated debt, high-yield bonds and senior A loans.

5.3.2.1. HLT vs. Non-HLT

For theoretical discussions, a firm's leverage represents the key dependent variable. However, it only represents the starting point for determining what a highly leveraged transaction is. As discussed in chapter 5.1, the dependent variable used in this research model has a dichotomous character, taking the value of *y=1* if the transaction falls into the HLT category and *y=0* if not. The cut-off value to delineate the two classes has to be determined based on the leverage ratio.

Different approaches have been advanced by academics as to how to measure the leverage in an empirical study. Particularly the early academic literature tends to consider leverage ratios in book values (book value of debt / book value of total assets). In contrast, more recent studies record the leverage based on market values (market or book value of debt / enterprise value).[675] Moreover, some authors advocate an interest coverage ratio (interest expense / EBIT or cash flow) instead of

---

671 Ozkan, A. (2001), p. 182.

672 'Unlevered' constitutes an important limitation, as a free cash flow net of interest expenses depends on the level of debt, which distorts the empirical results. Some practitioners refer to a measure like this as EBITDAC (EBITDA after CapEx), source: interviews.

673 Chaplinsky, S./ Niehaus, G. (1993), p. 57.

674 NFL are defined as total (long and short-term) financial liabilities less cash and cash equivalents.

675 Examplary articles measuring the leverage based on book values include Barclay, M./ Morellec, E./ Smith, C.W. (2001); Wald, J.K. (1999); Lang, L./ Ofek, E./ Stulz, R. (1996); Rajan, R./ Zingales, L. (1995); Titman, S./ Wessels, R. (1988); Bradley, M./ Jarrell, G./ Kim, E. (1984). Articles applying market values are Fan, J./ Titman, S./ Twite, G. (2003); Brailsford, T./ Oliver, B./ Pua, S. (2002); Goyal, V./ Lehn, K./ Racic, S. (2002).

looking at debt ratios.[676] Given that PE professionals and company valuations focus on market (transaction) values, the leverage metric should account for this in order to ensure a common understanding. The leverage ratio L_i of the transaction i recorded in this study shall thus be defined as

$$L_i = \frac{Market\ value\ of\ senior\ debt\ D_i}{Enterprise\ value\ EV_i + transaction\ fees\ T_i}$$

where senior debt comprises all facilities as described in chapter 4.1.2, enterprise value constitutes the market value of all outstanding claims, and transaction fees are the capitalised cost of the transaction.

However, a major shortcoming of market values needs to be stressed: The value of the equity capital reflects the expected future development of the firm. This means that in the case of growth opportunities as a determinant of the capital structure, a high growth potential will c.p. lead to a lower leverage solely as a result of the measure applied. Nonetheless, it has been commonly reported and confirmed in notable empirical studies[677] that the results are generally robust to the choice of different measures.[678] BOWMAN (1980) already demonstrated that the cross-sectional correlation between leverage ratios in terms of book value and market value is very high.[679] Accordingly, the model is not likely to be misspecified as a result of using market values.

As a next step, the cut-off value, i.e. the value beyond which a firm is viewed as highly leveraged, has to be defined, although a "right" value does not exist.[680] Prior corporate finance studies do not provide helpful indications for a cut-off point. ANDRADE / KAPLAN'S sample of HLTs have a mean leverage ratio of 89 per cent based on book values.[681] This appears very high even for book value ratios.[682] However, two studies exist that discuss taxonomies of leverage classes, one by KAPLAN / STEIN (1993) and one by FERRI / JONES (1979). The former study gives an indication of what they consider to be a HLT. In order to specifically assess HLTs, they exclude those recapitalisations and buyouts that exhibit market value debt levels of less than 60 per cent.[683] By using a special

676 E.g. Welch, I. (2002), p. 32; Kale, J./ Noe, T./ Ramirez, G. (1991), p. 1705.
677 E.g. Hovakimian, A./ Opler, T./ Titman, S. (2001).
678 MacKay, P./ Phillips, G. (2002), p. 10.
679 Bowman, J. (1980).
680 Similar problems arose in studies using logit regressions to analyse the issuance of *significant* amounts of debt or equity. What constitutes *significant* has usually been randomly selected. A threshold for a *significant* amount could, e.g. be if the amount of the issue divided by the book value of assets exceeds 5 per cent, see Hovakimian, A./ Opler, T./ Titman, S. (2001), p. 12.
681 Andrade, G./ Kaplan, N.S (1998), p. 1451.
682 For comparative numbers, see Kaplan, N.S./ Stein, J. (1993). Moreover, since book values are not recorded in the study, the operationalisation cannot be applied.
683 Kaplan, N.S./ Stein, J. (1993), p. 219.

algorithm, the latter study derives a classification for different leverage groups. Though only the mean for each of seven groups is provided, it allows the approximate cut-off value for a highly-leveraged firm to be estimated at around 65 per cent.[684] Finally, the definition of the US supervisory authorities may be applicable as discussed in chapter 2.1.2.1. However, the discussed 75 per cent is also based on book values and therefore inappropriate for this study.

Given the controversial operationalisations, the median of the sample IBOs shall be applied rather than draw a fixed cut-off value in advance. This gives equal groups of HLTs and Non-HLTs, which in turn provides a better basis for robust econometric results than do unequal groups.[685] It is common procedure to translate values below and above the cut-off value into dummy numbers indicating the group affiliation. A number of studies employ binary dummy numbers for certain firm characteristics, e.g. to determine whether the firm is a high-growth or low-growth enterprise.[686] Another example would be a dummy to denote firms with high cash flows or low cash flows.[687] These studies apply the median for each characteristic as a cut-off value. Given their similar context, the same proceeding will be applied for the following tests.

5.3.2.2. Detailed financial instruments

The analysis of other financial instruments beyond the debt/equity choice completes the picture on capital structure decisions. The models will examine the use of equity, sub-ordinated debt, high-yield bonds and senior A loans.[688] To ensure the same econometric methodology as for the operationalisation of HLTs, the test will also employ binary dummy variables. In a first step, the use of equity will be examined. The dummy variable takes 0/1 values, depending on whether or not the transaction has more equity capital than the median value of the sample.[689] In contrast, the dummy variable on the use of sub-ordinated debt takes the value $y=1$ if sub-ordinated debt is used and $y=0$ if not. Finally, the different instruments within the senior debt (senior A vs. senior B/C) and sub-ordinated debt class (mezzanine vs. HYB) are subject to regressions, introducing dummy variables again. Similarly, when the transaction carries senior A tranches exceeding the median of the sample, the dummy for senior A use takes the value $y=1$. As regards the application of HYBs, the dummy variable takes a value of 1 if this type of financing is used.

---

684 Ferri, M./ Jones, W. (1979), pp. 635-636.
685 For a discussion of the impact of sub-sample distribution on the validity of results, see Hosmer, D.W./ Lemeshow, S. (2000), p. 339-345.
686 Opler, T./ Titman, S. (1996), p. 1997.
687 E.g. Lasfer, A. (1995), p. 277.
688 See chapter 7.5.

5.4. Summary

Based on the discussions in previous chapters, the first part of this section covered the development of hypotheses on capital structure decisions for IBOs. For each of the seven characteristics, the expected influence on the likelihood that an IBO will be structured as an HLT has been derived from the static trade-off theory and agency models. In addition, results from earlier empirical studies on usual, mainly quoted corporates have been provided to enrich later discussions of potential differences between IBOs and other firms. See table 9 for an overview of the hypotheses and the results of prior empirical studies.

Table 9: Summary of hypotheses on IBO financing

	Prior empirical results	Trade-off theory		Agency context	
Risk class	-	-	H1a	-	H1b
Transaction size	+	+	H2a	+	H2b
Tangibility	+	-	H3a	+	H3b
Growth	-	-	H4a	-	H4b
Profitability	-	+	H5a	+	H5b
Uniqueness	-	-	H6a	o	H6b
Free Cash Flow	o	+	H7a	+	H7b

Note: + = significantly positive relationship; - = significantly negative relationship;
o = not significant or indeterminate relationship

In the second part of the section, the variables to be applied in the research model, both dependent and explanatory, have been operationalized based on their use in prior empirical studies. While most of the operationalisations have also been included in other studies, some had to be supplemented by indicators with which practitioners are familiar in order to ensure their suitability for a questionnaire-based study. See table 10 for a summary of the dependent and explanatory variables.

---

[689] Please note that equity capital alone does not constitute the counter-position to senior debt since equity and sub-ordinated debt jointly form the counterpart.

Table 10: Operationalisation of dependent and explanatory variables

DEPENDENT VARIABLES

Variable name	Values	Description
HLT	0/1	Dummy variable with value y = 1 if SENIOR DEBT > Median; (Senior vs.Equity + Sub)
EQUITY	0/1	Dummy variable with value y = 1 if equity capital > Median; (Equity vs. Sub + Senior)
SUB	0/1	Dummy variable with value y = 1 if subordinated debt is used; (Sub vs.Equity + Senior)
HYB	0/1	Dummy variable with value y = 1 if HYB are used (HYB vs.Mezzanine)
SENIOR A	0/1	Dummy variable with value y = 1 if SENIOR A > Median; (Senior A vs. Senior B/C)

EXPLANATORY VARIABLES

Characteristics	Variable name	Description
Risk class	EBITDA_VOL	Estimated average standard deviation of EBITDA over the last 7 years
	IND_CYCL	Medium- to long-term cyclicality of the target company industry
Transaction size	TRANS_VALUE	Market value of equity and debt capital incl. additional cost (e.g. banking fees)
	SALES	Total sales of the target company in the year prior to the IBO
Tangibility	TANG	Share of tangible assets (PPE) in % of total assets
Growth	EV_EBITDA	Transaction size divided by last year's EBITDA (Transaction multiple)
	CAPEX	Share of capital expenditures* in % of operating cash flow (3-year Ø)
	CAGR_SALES	Compound average growth rate of total sales over the last 5 years
Profitability	EBITDA_SALES	EBITDA in % of total sales in the year prior to the IBO
Uniqueness	R_D	R&D expenditures in % of total sales in the year prior to the IBO
	MARKET_SH	Market share based on sales of the target company in the year prior to the IBO
Free Cash Flow	FCF_SALES	Free cash flow before financing activities in % of sales
	NFL_FCF	Net financial liabilities in % of free cash flow before financing activities

* Note: Without acquisitions

Source: Author.

6. Methodology of the empirical study

So far, the discussions have focussed on IBOs and the question how their characteristics may influence the capital structure. A survey among PE professionals forms the basis for answering this question. The following section presents the methodology of the survey, particularly the design and analysis tools.

6.1. Survey design

The survey was conducted between August and November 2004 by means of a standardised questionnaire. It was designed to gather relevant information on both the financial structures and buyout characteristics.

6.1.1. Survey process

The objective of the thesis would suggest deploying specialised databases[690], publications[691] and market intermediaries such as banks that have access to the relevant data.[692] However, after initial tests it became evident that none of the sources offers sufficiently detailed information. Only a survey among PE firms appeared to be a feasible way of collecting data for a sufficiently large sample of deals to test the empirical hypotheses.[693]

For the primary research, the single key challenge was to overcome confidentiality issues. Given the level of detail required, a sufficient return rate could only be achieved by leveraging existing contacts, thorough research and a consequent survey process with follow-up emails and calls.

In the light of existing buyout research, a minimum number of 80-100 transactions had to be aspired in order to achieve meaningful results. To obtain this threshold number, a significant amount of resources had to be dedicated since only 436 European IBOs have been reported over the last 7 years.[694] The survey comprised four stages

690 Examples of dedicated M&A databases are Zephyr, Mergerstat, Thomson Financial's M&A database, etc.

691 E.g. Unquote, FINANCE, etc.

692 Another way would have been to contact commercial registers. However, given the difficulty of finding the relevant registers across Europe and that these often have outdated figures, this appeared to be a highly uncertain method. Vest arrived at a similar conclusion when he attempted to gather financial data for his study of spin-off MBOs, see Vest, P. (1995), p. 31.

693 For a general overview of questionnaires and other methods of quantitative data collection, see Bortz, J./ Döring, N. (2002), pp. 137-294.

694 See figure 1 on page 2.

- **Explorative interviews**: In order to assess the practical relevance, identify key considerations in the decision process and inquire about willingness to co-operate, 20 interviews were conducted over a period of about one year. Among the interviewees were representatives of PE funds in Germany, France, UK, and Switzerland as well as banks engaged in acquisition financing.
- **Pre-tests**: Once an initial version of the questionnaire had been developed, pre-tests with 6 PE professionals were implemented to assess its practicability and final adjustments were made.
- **Written survey**: The finalised questionnaire was then sent out to 215 European PE funds that have engaged in institutional buyouts over the last 7 years. Names and addresses were drawn from private contacts, the EVCA and internet research.
- **Follow-up iteration**: Following up on the first survey round, emails were sent out to PE funds that had not responded within a period of 3 weeks. Finally, addressees who still did not respond were contacted by phone.

The core step in the survey process was the written survey mailed to 215 PE professionals. Each professional was a representative of one PE fund.[695] As the required number of 80-100 deals ruled out an interview-based discussion of each transaction, it was decided to use a standardised questionnaire on the lines of a closed-ended questionnaire, given that the aim was to record deal characteristics.[696] The main advantages of a standardised questionnaire are:[697]

- Relatively low time consumption and high cost efficiency
- Anonymity as regards individual transactions
- Higher acceptance rate given the flexibility to choose the time and degree of completion of the questionnaire

A written survey based on a standardised questionnaire exhibits, however, some disadvantages. The most relevant ones are a potential informant bias, which will be briefly addressed in chapter 7.1.3.2, and the lack of a common understanding of the surveyed information.[698] Two ways of overcoming the latter disadvantage have been pursued. First of all, pre-tests and discussions with PE

[695] For 12 PE funds, representatives from different offices were chosen. In order to avoid double consideration of a transaction in which more than one European office was involved, returns from these offices were cross-checked. In the event of strong similarities between two returns from the same firm, the representative was contacted and asked to confirm that data did not relate to identical deals.

[696] For a delineation of standardised questionnaires, closed-ended questionnaires and structured interviews, see Atteslander, P. (1995), pp. 179-180.

[697] Atteslander, P. (1995), p. 167, Rogge, H.J. (1992), p. 85.

[698] See, e.g. Stier, W. (1999), pp. 198-199 and Atteslander, P. (1995), p. 168 for a discussion of the main shortcomings.

professionals ensured that most practitioners would understand the requested information as it was intended by the author. Second, a sheet with additional notes was included in the mailing. Besides general information, most variables used in the survey, both dependent and independent, were defined explicitly.[699]

Together with a cover letter, three questionnaires and the additional notes sheet were sent out to PE professionals on the top (managing director) or second level (investment director), because it is they who are usually in a position to decide whether the requested data may be disclosed or not. Quite often, they forwarded the questionnaires to the respective investment managers, who had most transaction characteristics and financial data at their fingertips. Every addressee was asked to complete one deal record sheet for three transactions of their choice, leading to a maximum number of 132 transactions, assuming an expected return rate of 20 per cent. To achieve a sufficient number, a major concession had to be made, namely the omission of the deal name and year. Otherwise, the confidentiality issue would have certainly hampered the return rate.

6.1.2. Questionnaire design

As mentioned earlier, the questionnaire for this empirical study deviates from the "standard" type of questionnaires used in similar buyout studies.[700] While standard questionnaires comprise 5-15 pages, the one used here consists of only a single page dedicated to collecting data on transaction characteristics and financial structure plus some additional information included to round off the picture.[701]

To record the financial structure, respondents were asked to indicate the exact share of equity, subordinated and senior debt as a percentage of the total transaction value.[702] Furthermore, they were asked to provide the share of the different instruments used within each class (e.g. mezzanine vs. HYBs).

In contrast, transaction characteristics were recorded by means of numerical scales. While investment managers are likely to be very familiar with the financial structure, they are unlikely to be able to give specific numbers, e.g. earnings volatility, without further calculations. This, too, would have resulted in lower return rates. The problem was overcome by defining categories and

---

[699] Appendix 2 shows the additional notes sheet.
[700] Examples are provided in Kraft, V. (2001), Jakoby, S. (2000), Vest (1995).
[701] Appendix 1 shows the deal record sheet.
[702] For a reconcilement of entreprise value to transaction value, see chapter 2.3.2.2.1.

asking respondents for estimates. This had the benefit of being time-effective without losing the necessary detail. However, as a necessary condition, the balance between clustering and too tight categories had to be achieved.[703]

The scale had to be structured in a way that a balance could be achieved between a sufficient level of detail and the required rate of return. A further constraint was the trade-off between adequate information content (i.e. not too few categories) and the need to reduce dispersion so that all clusters show up indeed.[704] The characteristics were recorded on a scale with 7 categories, since it is seen as the best balance between sufficient information content and an overly complex measurement.[705]

Having decided on the number of categories, the scales had to be calibrated regarding the values and the range of the categories to come up with an adequate taxonomy. As the real distribution of the characteristics was of course unknown, the categories had to be labelled by means of a sample of companies that were likely to exhibit similar characteristics. A set of 100 European companies with revenues between €10m and €2000m was analysed on the basis of publicly available data, particularly annual reports and accounts from the Markus database (Bureau van Dijk). Each determinant was calculated with regard to the average, mean and spread.

In addition to the financial structure and the IBO characteristics, some supplementary information was included, not vital for the empirical study per se but helpful for the overall understanding as this information has also been addressed in other studies.[706] The following areas were covered:

- **Investor activity**: the level of investor activity (hands-on vs. hands-off investors) is expected to have an impact on the capital structure[707]
- **Strategy**: the firm's strategy after the IBO should be of general interest for the overall understanding
- **Motive for buyout**: the motive/source of the IBO is likely to be of general interest of the overall understanding
- **Ownership structure**: the dispersion of ownership can be related to the relevance of agency cost of equity

[703] Bortz, J./ Döring, N. (2002), p. 142.
[704] Beller, S. (2004), pp. 31-33.
[705] Churchill G.A. (1999), pp. 401-402.
[706] For example, a frequently discussed determinant is the ownership structure, see, e.g. Short, H. / Keasey, K./ Duxbury, D. (2002); McConnell, J./ Servaes, H. (1995); Friend, I./ Lang, L. (1988); Leland, H./ Pyle, D. (1977).
[707] See, e.g. Cotter, J.F./ Peck, S.W. (2001).

- **Credit constraint**: in order to give an indication of how difficult it was to obtain the debt financing, two questions addressing this issue were included

The methodology of data collection has to fulfill three conditions in order to ensure the necessary quality of the survey. These are:[708]

- **Objectivity** denotes the independence of the empirical results from the researcher's person
- **Reliability** ensures that the same results would be generated for repeated measurements
- **Validity** describes the overall appropriateness of the measurement for the purpose of the study

However, the conditions do not jointly determine the quality of the constructs. Rather, objectivity represents a necessary condition for reliability, which in turn is a necessary condition for validity. With numerical scales based on real numbers,[709] the methodology allows an objective measurement of the variables. This should ensure that the validity condition is satisfied, which in turn fulfills the other two conditions.

6.2. Univariate data analysis

The data collected on the basis of the questionnaire was analysed by way of several univariate and multivariate methods. As the main univariate analysis, a set of non-parametric tests was performed. At the centre of the multivariate analyses stands the binomial logistic regression (logit) as described in chapter 6.3.

6.2.1. Non-parametric significance tests

A significance test is performed to determine if the observed value of a statistic[710] differs sufficiently from the hypothesized value of a parameter to infer that the hypothesized value of the parameter is not the true value. The hypothesized value of the parameter is called the null hypothesis. Significance tests consist of calculating the probability of obtaining a statistic as different or more different from the null hypothesis (given that the null hypothesis is correct) than the statistic obtained in the sample. If this probability is sufficiently low, then the difference

[708] Mayer, H. (2004), p. 88.
[709] Unlike rating scales that only include an ordinal scaling to record non-metrical variables.
[710] A statistic denotes just a numerical quantity (often, e.g. the mean) calculated in a sample.

between the parameter and the statistic is said to be "statistically significant"[711] To put it another way: a hypothesis is tested whether a difference between a statistic is independent of a certain parameter (in this case whether or not the IBO is structured as an HLT), i.e. whether the difference depends on the envisaged probability of obtaining a difference as large or larger than the sample difference if the parameter had no effect. If the probability is low (below the significance level)[712] then the null hypothesis that the classification of an HLT or Non-HLT makes no difference is rejected in favour of the alternate hypothesis that it does make a difference.

Significance tests can be classified in multiple ways, e.g. tests of independency or homogeneity of parameters, tests based on different scale levels (ordinal vs. metrical), one- or multiple-sample tests and parametric vs. non-parametric tests.[713] The purpose of the following test is to determine whether the statistic of an explanatory variable (e.g. size) is independent of the classification as HLT or Non-HLT, or whether the distribution of the explanatory variable is homogeneous in both samples. Parametric tests require the normal distribution of the variable, which in turn can only be assumed for reasonably large samples, and a continuous distribution of the values.[714] Since the explanatory variables applied in this study are non-continuous (categorical), only non-parametric tests can be applied[715] such as the Mann-Whitney test and Pearson-χ^2 homogeneity test, both of which are frequently used in similar settings.[716]

Mann-Whitney test

The Mann-Whitney test (MW) is one of the most popular two-sample tests and requires at least an ordinal scaling of the variables since it represents a rank-based test. It is equivalent to the Wilcoxon rank sum test for two groups.[717] MW is considered to have a similar power to the equivalent test for continuous variables, the t-test for comparing mean values.[718] A Mann-Whitney test examines whether two sampled populations are equivalent in location, i.e. the distribution of the variable (e.g. size) in both groups.

---

711 Auer, L.v. (2003), pp. 99-106. The threshold probability to observe a value upon or above which the null hypothesis has to be accepted is also known as the *p-value*, see Auer, L.v. (2003), p. 111.

712 The choice of the significance level is somewhat arbitrary. Convention levels of .10 ,.05 and .01 are most commonly used.

713 Bamberg, G./ Baur, F. (2002), pp. 183-185.

714 Brannath, W./ Futschik, A. (2001), p. 154.

715 Bamberg, G./ Baur, F. (2002), p. 185

716 E.g. Ruß, O./ Gebhardt, G. (2002), p. 13.

717 For a detailed discussion of the Mann-Whitney test and the Wilcoxon rank sum test, see, e.g. Sachs, L. (1997), pp. 382-389.

718 MW reaches an asymptotic efficiency of 95 per cent compared to the t-test, i.e. for 100 observations the same power is achieved as a t-test for 95 observations. See Hochstädter, D. (1996), p. 668.

The observations from both groups are combined, ranked and then summed up for each sample (T_1 for sample 1 and T_2 for sample 2). If the distributions are identical in both groups (e.g. HLT and Non-HLT), the sums will be about the same. This implies that if one observation for HLTs and one for Non-HLTs is picked out, then the probability of having, e.g. the size of a deal with $a > b$ is just the same as $b > a$, with a denoting the value of size for the HLT group and b denoting the value for the Non-HLT group. Accordingly, the null and alternate hypotheses are formulated as:

$$H_0: \quad p\{a < b\} = 0.5$$

$$H_a: \quad p\{a < b\} \neq 0.5$$

With N_1 denoting the number of observations in sample 1 and N_2 in sample 2, two metrics can be calculated:

$$U = N_1 N_2 + \frac{N_1(N_2 + 1)}{2} - T_1$$

$$U' = N_1 N_2 - U$$

The Mann-Whitney statistic is the smaller of these two numbers. The Wilcoxon rank sum W statistic, also displayed in SPSS outputs, is the rank sum of the smaller sample. As the value of the MW statistic is normally distributed, it is compared to the critical value of the z-distributed test statistic as for the t-test.[719]

Pearson-χ2 homogeneity test

Similar types of questions albeit with different methodologies can be investigated through a Pearson-χ^2 homogeneity test that examines whether the distribution of variables is homogeneous in two samples, or that the distribution is independent of the classification to one of the samples.[720]

Hence the hypotheses are:

H_0: The distribution of the variable is equal in both groups

H_a: The distribution of the variable is not equal in both groups

---

719 Hartung, J. (2002), p. 517-520.

720 Bleymüller, J./ Gehlert, G./ Gülicher, H. (2004), p. 132. For in-depth discussions of the Pearson-χ^2 homogeneity test, see Hartung, J. (1998), pp. 411-424.

The test statistic χ^2 is based on a contingency table developed from the sample data with relative and absolute frequencies.[721] For a contingency table consisting of *r* categories, *c* different samples and *n* total observations, the χ^2-statistic equals

$$\chi^2 = \sum_{i=1}^{r}\sum_{j=1}^{c}\frac{\left(s_{ij}^0 - \frac{s_i^0 s_j^0}{n}\right)^2}{\frac{s_i^0 s_j^0}{n}}$$

where *i* denotes the category, *j* the sample, s^0_i the number of observations for category *i*, and s^0_j the number of observations in sample *j*. Accordingly, s^0_{ij} describes the frequency (number of observations) in category *i* for sample *j*.[722] The formula can be shortened, using an expected frequency formula for category *i* and sample *j*

$$s_{ij}^e = \frac{s_i^0 \cdot s_j^0}{n}$$

where the expected frequency s^e_{ij} can be retrieved by splitting the total frequency per category *i* across the samples according to the quotient of the samples.[723] This transformation yields the usually reported χ^2-statistic

$$\chi^2 = \sum_{i=1}^{r}\sum_{j=1}^{c}\frac{(s_{ij}^0 - s_{ij}^e)^2}{s_{ij}^e}$$

The resulting statistic has to be compared to the critical value χ_c^2 displayed in the χ^2-table[724] with *v* degrees of freedom given by $v = (r\text{-}1)\ (c\text{-}1)$. If $\chi^2 > \chi_c^2$ the null hypothesis must be rejected.[725] To give a numerical example, a statistic with 6 degrees of freedom yields a χ^2 of 17,863, which equals a significance of 0.7 per cent. Provided there was no relationship between two tested variables, this implies that the probability of achieving a χ^2 of 17,863 would be only 0.7 per cent. Therefore, the confidence to have unequal distributions (rejection of H_0) is very strong.[726]

---

721 In a contingency table all observations are grouped according to the categories (e.g. size categories) for each sample separately. A thorough discussion of contingency tables and relevant definitions can be found in Bamberg, G./ Baur, F. (2002), pp. 31-35.

722 Bleymüller, J./ Gehlert, G./ Gülicher, H. (2004), p. 132.

723 Bleymüller, J./ Gehlert, G./ Gülicher, H. (2004), p. 132.

724 Given the relevance of the χ^2-distribution for the significance tests as well as for the subsequent logit analyses, a brief description of the χ^2-distribution shall be provided in the appendix.

725 Bleymüller, J./ Gehlert, G./ Gülicher, H. (2004), p. 133.

726 Example taken from Brosius, F. (2004), p. 424.

6.2.2. Intercorrelation of explanatory variables (Spearman rank)

Before multivariate methods can be applied, correlation analyses are mandatory to investigate relationships between two parameters. However, for this thesis the correlations are not calculated in order to assess relationships between the explanatory and dependent variables but relationships among the explanatory variables. The significance tests provide reliable indications of dependencies among the groups HLT vs. Non-HLTs and the seven explanatory variables, while the correlation analyses serve to identify problems of multicolliniarity which dilute the power of regressions.[727]

Given the categorical nature of the data used, the most popular coefficient, the Bravais-Pearson correlation, cannot be applied.[728] A more appropriate method is the Spearman rank correlation coefficient, a distribution-free analogue of the correlation analysis.[729] Like a regression, it can be applied to compare two independent random variables, each at several levels (which may be discrete or continuous). Unlike a regression, however, the Spearman rank correlation coefficient works on ranked (relative) data, rather than directly on the data itself. As a distribution-free method, it makes no assumptions about the distribution of the underlying data.[730]

Spearman's method works by assigning a rank to each observation in each group separately.[731] The number of possible ranks *n* (i.e. the number of categories) should not be less than 5 and not exceed 30.[732] Since each explanatory variable may fall into one of 7 categories, the Spearman correlation coefficient can be applied. With R^a_i representing the rank of observation *i* for variable *a* and R^b_i as the equivalent for variable *b*, the following formula calculates the Spearman rank correlation

$$r_s = 1 - \frac{6\sum_{i=1}^{n}(R^a_i - R^b_i)^2}{(n-1)\cdot n(n+1)}$$

---

727 Multicolliniarity arises when substantial correlations among explanatory variables exist (also inter-correlation). The absence of multicolliniarity allows the autonomous variation of explanatory variables by which the changes in the dependent variable can be better attributed to changes in the explanatory variable. For a general introduction in the context of linear regressions, see Auer, L. v. (2003), pp. 461-486. For the specific context of logistic regressions see chapter 6.3.2.

728 See, e.g. Bleymüller, J./ Gehlert, G./ Gülicher, H. (2004), pp. 145-146.

729 See, e.g. Sachs, L. (1997), pp. 510-515 or Hartung, J. (1998), pp. 533-559.

730 Hochstädter, D. (1996), p. 153.

731 Note the difference to the MW test using pooled ranks.

732 Hochstädter, D. (1996), p. 153.

Like the R^2 value produced by a linear regression, Spearman's r_s coefficient indicates a relationship but not necessarily a dependency. A value of r_s near one indicates the presence of a relationship; a value near zero indicates the absence of a relationship between the two variables.[733]

6.3. Binomial logistic regression

In the following section, the use of binomial logistic regression (logit) will be outlined, representing the key statistical instrument applied for the subsequent data analyses. Following an introductory chapter, the three steps in performing logit analyses will be described in detail, the specification of the logit model, its assessment in terms of quality, and the interpretation of the results.

6.3.1. Background

The use of logistic regression modelling has found its way into various fields of research. Originally developed in epidemiological research, logit models are common econometric tools whenever dependencies are explored with a dichotomous (binary) outcome.[734]

As with any regression method, logit analyses aim to explain the impact of exploratory variables (covariates) on one or more dependent variables.[735] In an economic context, problems such as whether or not a borrower is creditworthy or whether or not a product is purchased can be modelled using a logit approach. Similarly, the question of whether or not a firm is highly leveraged can be analysed with logistic regressions that do not directly predict the leverage but the probability that the firm will be highly leveraged, i.e. the likelihood of a certain event $(P(y=1))$.[736]

Since several of the numerous statistical tools would be appropriate to investigate the determinants of capital structure, the question arises why choose logit regressions. First of all, given that the objective of the present thesis is to *confirm* theoretically founded relationships, the technique needs to have a *confirmatory* rather than an *exploratory* character.[737]

---

[733] Bamberg, G./ Baur, F. (2002), pp. 38-39.

[734] Occasionally, "probit" rather than logit models are applied. While the results are very similar for large samples, logit models are more appropriate for smaller samples (<300). Probit models are not "closed form" models because the probability must be expressed as an integral and is therefore analytically less convenient. See Ben-Akiva, M./ Lerman, S. (1985), p. 70. In addition, logit models must be distinguished from "tobit" models which are used for limited outcomes with censored distributions, i.e. if limited knowledge exists regarding the exact distribution of the dependent variable. A comprehensive discussion is provided in Long, J.S. (1997), pp. 187-216.

[735] Hosmer, D.W./ Lemeshow, S. (2000), p. 1.

[736] Backhaus, K. et al. (2003), p. 418.

[737] For a description of both parts of multivariate tools, see Backhaus, K. et al. (2003), pp. 8-9.

Within the segment of confirmatory techniques, the tools must allow incorporation of at least ordinal covariates since the main transaction characteristics are recorded on ordinal scales. The choice between four approaches remains, classical linear regressions, conjoint measurement, variance analysis, and logit analysis.[738] See figure 26 for an overview of the different confirmatory techniques.

Figure 26: Overview of confirmatory multivariate techniques

		Explanatory variables	
		Non-nominal	Nominal
Dependent variable	Non-nominal	• OLS-regression • Linear probability model • Conjoint measurement	• Variance analysis • Linear regression with dummies
	Nominal	• Discriminant analysis • Binary linear regression • Logistic regression (logit)	• Contingency analysis

Source: Author, following Backhaus, K. et. al. (2003), p. 8.

Another group of models which has increasingly attracted the attention of researchers are structural equation models. These prove to be appropriate whenever variables are not directly observable and measurable but are expressed through hypothetical constructs, so-called latent variables, such as motivation or customer satisfaction.[739] However, research questions like those analysed hereafter involve measurable data (e.g. size, profitability, etc.) and do not require structural equation models.

A number of reasons have led the author to choose logistic regression. The main motivation derives from the frequent use by other corporate finance academics, therefore allowing better comparability.[740] In addition, the s-curve relationship intuitively fits reality better than do linear

[738] Having said that the explanatory variables are mainly of non-nominal scaling does not imply that nominal variables cannot be included. Rather, by using dummy variables nominal information can also be handled in the analysis. For the inclusion of nominal variables in logit models, see Tutz, G. (2000), p. 47

[739] For a general review of important structural equation models such as LISREL or PLS, see, e.g. Bollen, K.A. (1989).

[740] See appendix 5.

relationships.[741] Finally, logistic regression does not have to satisfy the same strict assumptions as all other linear regression models (OLS, linear probability model). They include the linearity assumption that requires unrestricted value ranges for the dependent variable and the assumption of homoscedastic error variances.[742] These considerations have justified the use of logit analyses that require the dependent variable to be transformed into a binary nominal variable (HLT vs. Non-HLT). As discussed in chapter 5.1, the use of binary variables is quite common in corporate finance research and is consistent with the objective of the thesis.

Logit models can be classified according to the number of explanatory variables and the number of values that the dependent variable can assume. Models with only one explanatory variable are called univariable binomial models when the dependent variable can take on two values (0/1) and univariable multinomial models when the dependent variable has more than two values. Conversely, when the model includes more than one explanatory variable, it is denoted a binomial and multinomial model. See figure 27 for the classification.

Figure 27: Classification of logit models

Number of possible values of the dependent variable	Number of explanatory variables: One	> One
Two	• Univariable binomial model	• (multivariable) binomial model
> Two	• Univariable multinomial model	• (multivariable) multinomial model

Source: Reisinger, H. (1996), p. 90.

As multivariate technique, the thesis applies (multivariable) binomial models for the final tests. In contrast, univariable binomial models are only used for the model development.[743]

While linear regressions aim to predict the value of the dependent variable directly, logistic regression predicts the likelihood that a dependent variable will take on a certain value (in this case

---

[741] See also chapter 5.1.

[742] Urban, D. (1993), p.23. For a discussion of the assumption of linear models, see Auer, L.v. (2003), pp. 17-44.

[743] See chapter 6.3.2.

that the leverage will be higher than the sample mean). In logistic regressions it is assumed that an unobservable variable z_k exists consisting of a linear combination of covariates x_j plus the respective coefficients.[744] This variable has an aggregated impact on the likelihood of being financed as an HLT and can take on values from $-\infty$ to $+\infty$.[745] For positive values of z_k the IBO k will be financed as a HLT.

$$y_k = \begin{cases} HLT & if\ z_k > 0 \\ Non-HLT\ if & z_k < 0 \end{cases} \quad with\ z_k = \beta_0 + \sum_{j=1}^{J} \beta_j \cdot x_{jk} + u_k$$

However, this relationship must be incorporated into the *logistic function* to achieve a probability relation.[746] This yields

$$p(HLT) = \frac{e^{\beta_0 + \sum_{j=1}^{J} \beta_j \cdot x_{jk} + u_k}}{1 + e^{\beta_0 + \sum_{j=1}^{J} \beta_j \cdot x_{jk} + u_k}} \quad or \quad p(HLT) = \frac{1}{1 + e^{-(\beta_0 + \sum_{j=1}^{J} \beta_j \cdot x_{jk} + u_k)}}$$

where the aggregated influence z_k follows the logistic function and asymptotically reaches 0 at the lower boundary and 1 at the upper boundary. Because the logistic regression assumes a non-linear relationship between the explanatory variables and the likelihood that the IBO is structured as an HLT, the function is also called *linking function*.[747] The parameter β_j determines the rate of increase or decrease on the s-shaped curve, with the sign indicating the direction of influence. The typical shape of a logistic function is displayed in figure 28.

---

744 So far the terms logit analysis and logistic regression have been used synonymously. However, the use of the term logistic regression is limited to models where the explanatory variables are of metrical scale. See Tutz, G. (2000), p. 32. Nevertheless, a differentiation between the two terms does not appear essential for the remainder of the present thesis.

745 Hosmer, D.W./ Lemeshow, S. (2000), p. 5.

746 Backhaus, K. et al. (2003), p. 423. See also the key contributions in Maddala, G. (1983), p. 22, Aldrich, J./ Nelson, F. (1984), p. 22. The approach roots in the works of Berkson, J. (1944) and needs to be distinguished from the conditional logit analysis by McFadden, D. (1974).

747 Cramer, J.S. (1991), p. 7.

Figure 28: Shape of the logistic function

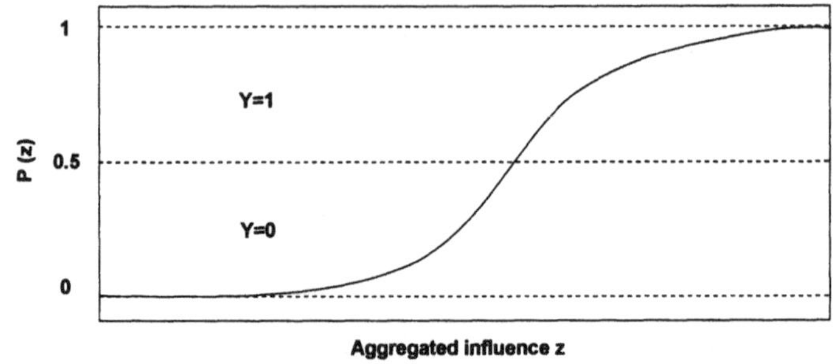

Source: Backhaus, K. et. al. (2003), p. 424.

One may ask why, of all the many different functions that lead to an s-curve, the one above has been chosen. Some considerations, which will be important again in the sections on model quality assessment and interpretation of results, can be helpful to understand the rationale.[748] Assuming a data set where Y_k denotes the result of the observation k in a sample of size N. $P_k(Y_k{=}1)$ describes the probability that a certain event will take place and $(1-P_k(Y_k))$ the counter-probability. When x_k denotes one explanatory variable, a model of the following type would be appropriate for one trial:

$$(y_k|x_k) \sim Bin\ (1, p_k|x_k)$$ [749]

Accordingly, the model can be generalised by $(y_k|n_k,\ x_k) \sim Bin\ (n_k, p_k|x_k)$ for multiple trials n_k for each set of x_k values and the number of events y_k in n_k trials. The logarithmised probability function is referred to as the log-likelihood of the sample.

$$\sum_{k=1}^{N}\left[\log\binom{n_k}{y_k} + y_k \log p_k + (n_k - n_k)\log(1-p_k)\right]$$

Rewriting the likelihood as

$$\sum_{k=1}^{N}\left[y_k \log\left(\frac{p_k}{1-p_k}\right) + n_k \log(1-p_k) + \log\binom{n_k}{y_k}\right]$$

[748] Haberman, S. (1978), pp. 293-295.

[749] For an introduction to binomial distribution as an important discrete distribution, see, e.g. Bamberg, G./ Baur, F. (2002), pp. 99-101.

and considering the form of generalised linear models,[750] of which logit models are sub-groups, with canonical parameter, generates the so-called log-odds (or 'logit').[751] Since a canonical link function for binomial random variable equates the linear predictor the canonical parameter leads to the *logistic linear regression model.*

$$z = \log\left(\frac{p_k}{1-p_k}\right) = \beta_0 + \sum_{j=1}^{J} \beta_j \cdot x_{jk}$$

with the inverse of the logit producing the known form with the desired s-shape.[752]

$$p_k(Y=1) = \frac{e^{\beta_0 + \sum_{j=1}^{J} \beta_j \cdot x_{jk}}}{1 + e^{\beta_0 + \sum_{j=1}^{J} \beta_j \cdot x_{jk}}}$$

6.3.2. Logit model development

Performing logit analyses requires the development of an adequate model, which is a particularly time-consuming task. It constitutes the selection process designed to ensure that all relevant and no irrelevant variables are included in the model. The rationale for restricting the number of variables in the model is that the model becomes more robust with reduced standard errors for the coefficient estimates.[753] Conversely, inclusion of too few covariates leads to underspecification, i.e. the parameter estimates become inconsistent. Rather surprisingly, despite the necessity of selecting the essential variables this procedure is frequently shortened or skipped altogether.[754]

The long list of potential variables must be derived from prior considerations, theories, earlier empirical studies or interviews with practitioners.[755] The process of selecting the right set of explanatory variables varies among model contexts. However, the literature proposes a number of basic steps that may be supplemented by further analyses. The procedure of the subsequent study comprises four steps:

---

750 See, e.g. Simonoff, J.S. (2003), p. 126.

751 $\theta = \log\left(\frac{p}{1-p}\right)$; see also chapter 6.3.5.3.

752 As opposed to the previously mentioned logistic function, the error term u_k has been omitted (and will be omitted for the remainder of the thesis), since, unlike in OLS regressions, the dependent variable does not have to oscillate around a certain expected value in order to achieve a highly qualitative estimate. See Urban. D. (1993), p. 54.

753 Hosmer, D.W./ Lemeshow, S. (2000), p. 92.

754 Gujarati, D. (1995), pp. 456-458.

755 Backhaus, K. et al. (2003), p. 426.

- **Univariate analyses**: The different non-parametric tests already indicate the statistical power of the variables to discriminate between HLT deals and Non-HLT deals. Consequently, they can be used to perform an initial screening. In addition, value distributions for each variable show whether the scale calibrations are adequate and hence able to reflect the actual distribution in the sample.
- **Multicollinearity**: The correlation analyses mentioned above help to identify intercorrelated variables and hence overcome the problem of multicollinearity.[756]
- **Univariable logit analyses**: Based on a set of logistic regressions that only contains one covariate (plus the intercept), the most powerful variables may be selected using the Wald statistic.[757] P-values of 0.25 as a drop-out value are suggested by academics.[758]
- **Interaction effects**: The influence of one explanatory variable on the probability may be conditional on the level of a second explanatory variable.[759] For example, the coefficient for age should be different for males and females when an interaction exists between sex and age.[760] The inclusion of a few highly significant interaction terms (p-value < 0.05) should increase the explanatory power of the model without altering the standard errors.[761]

The upper limit of the number of covariates should be determined by the size of the sample. A general rule of thumb is that there should be a minimum of 10 observations per covariate.[762] Otherwise, the results of the goodness of fit tests will be diluted, as the number of degrees of freedom raises the number of covariates.

6.3.3. Model estimation

The coefficients included in the actual model are then estimated on the basis of the maximum-likelihood method, which aims to determine those coefficient values "which most likely would generate the observed sample observations"[763].

---

756 For an in-depth discussion of multicollinearity, see, e.g. Menard, S.W. (2001), pp. 75-77.
757 See chapter 6.3.5.1.
758 See Hosmer, D.W./ Lemeshow, S. (2000), p. 95 referring to works by Bendel, R.B./ Affiti, A.A. (1977) and Mickey, J./ Greenland, S. (1989).
759 An extensive discussion of the identification and consideration of interaction effects can be found in Jaccard, J. (2001).
760 Hosmer, D.W./ Lemeshow, S. (2000), p. 98.
761 Hosmer, D.W./ Lemeshow, S. (2000), pp. 98-99.
762 See chapter 7.1.1.
763 Pindyck, R.S./ Rubinfeld, D.L. (1991), p. 68.

As previously indicated, the estimation technique roots in the probability theorem for independent events saying that the probability of a simultaneous occurrence of two independent events can be produced through the multiplication of the individual probabilities.[764] Starting with the known relationships

$$p_k(Y) = \begin{cases} \left(\dfrac{1}{1+e^{-(\beta_0+\sum_{j=1}^{J}\beta_j \cdot x_{jk})}}\right) & \text{for} \quad y_k = 1 \\ \left(1-\dfrac{1}{1+e^{-(\beta_0+\sum_{j=1}^{J}\beta_j \cdot x_{jk})}}\right) & \text{for} \quad y_k = 0 \end{cases}$$

they can be transformed into the likelihood function which then has to be maximised.

$$L = \prod_{k=1}^{N} \left(\frac{1}{1+e^{-(\beta_0+\sum_{j=1}^{J}\beta_j \cdot x_{jk})}}\right)^{y_k} \cdot \left(1-\frac{1}{1+e^{-(\beta_0+\sum_{j=1}^{J}\beta_j \cdot x_{jk})}}\right)^{(1-y_k)} \quad \rightarrow \text{max!}$$

For mathematical reasons it is easier to first logarithmise the likelihood, since the maximum of the function remains unchanged but calculation is facilitated.[765]

$$LL = \sum_{k=1}^{N} \left[y_k \cdot \ln\left(\frac{1}{1+e^{-(\beta_0+\sum_{j=1}^{J}\beta_j \cdot x_{jk})}}\right)\right] + \left[(1-y_k)\cdot \ln\left(1-\frac{1}{1+e^{-(\beta_0+\sum_{j=1}^{J}\beta_j \cdot x_{jk})}}\right)\right]$$

In SPSS, the log-likelihood function is maximised, using the so-called *Newton-Raphson algorithm*,[766] an iterative process that calculates for each set of coefficients the log-likelihood several times until no improvement in the value is achieved.[767]

---

764 Backhaus, K. et al. (2003), pp. 428-429.

765 Reisinger, H. (1996), p. 105.

766 Krafft, M. (1997), p. 628.

767 Specifically, following a first-order Taylor row, the coefficient estimates are determined by starting off with standard coefficients of usually β_k=0 until the loglikelihood value does not change by more than 0.1 per cent. See Urban, D. (1993), p. 56. For a formal and graphic discussion of the algorithm, see Ben-Akiva, M./ Lerman, S. (1985), pp. 82-84.

6.3.4. Model assessment

Before interpreting the results, the overall fit of the model needs to be assessed, i.e. its ability to explain the classification of being structured as an HLT or not. The literature on logit modelling controversially debates the appropriateness of different goodness of fit tests.[768] Among the most popular tests are the following four:

- **Pseudo-R^2** measures attempt to directly relate to the familiar coefficient of determination used in linear regression models.[769] They determine how much of the variation can be explained by the set of covariates included
- In contrast, the **likelihood ratio test** determines whether the entire model exhibits statistical significance
- The **Hosmer-Lemeshow test** has become a popular test to assess the model's ability to predict the observed data
- A similar approach is a **classification** of each deal into a 2x2 matrix representing the group membership of predicted and observed values.

6.3.4.1. Pseudo-R^2

Three measures are suggested in the literature, McFaddens-R^2, the Cox & Snell test, and the Nagelkerke test. For this study, the two latter measures will be applied since the McFadden-R^2 has triggered very controversial discussions; it is generally judged to be appropriate only for large samples.[770] Just as the sum of squared errors is the criterion for selecting parameters in the linear regression model, *likelihood* is the criterion in logistic regression models. Pseudo-R^2 measures are derived on the basis of the calculated likelihood. This means that whereas a relevant covariate reduces the sum of squared errors in linear regression, it increases the likelihood in logistic regressions.[771]

[768] See, e.g., Backhaus, K. (2003), pp. 437-450; Hosmer, D.W./ Lemeshow, S. (2000), pp. 144-166; Powers, D.A./ Xie, Y. (2000), pp. 63-71; Krafft, M. (1997), p. 631; Long, J.S. (1997), pp. 104-113; Reisinger, H. (1996); Ryan, T.R. (1997), pp. 266-269; Urban, D. (1993), pp. 57-71.

[769] For general reviews, including less popular measures than those outlined hereafter, see, e.g. Menard, S.W. (2000), Veall, M.R./ Zimmermann, K.F. (1996) and Hagle, T.M./ Mitchell, G.E. (1992).

[770] Powers, D.A./ Xie, Y. (2000), p. 65. The main criticism relates to the lack of consideration of the number of covariates and the sample size. Both the Cox & Snell test and the Nagelkerke measure accommodate the size of the sample and are thus more powerful than the McFadden-R^2. To control for the number of covariates (and hence the degrees of freedom), the literature proposes to use a measure based on the Akaike criterion when the model includes unusually high or low numbers of covariates. See for further discussions Cramer, J.S. (1991), p. 96.

[771] For conceptual reasons, the loglikelihood rather than the likelihood is often multiplied by –2 (for convenience: -*2LL*). Accordingly, the lower the *–2LL* value, the better the prediction. A perfectly fitted model has a *–2LL*=0 and is termed the saturated model. See Pampel, C.F. (2000), p. 46.

Cox & Snell test

The most direct analogue in logistic regression to the linear regression sum of squares is the difference between the *–2LL* of the full model (LL_F), including all covariates and the *–2LL* of the null model (LL_0), the model that just includes the intercept and no covariates.[772] The ratio of the baseline likelihood to the likelihood of the full model raised to the power *2/n* is called the Cox & Snell statistic.[773]

$$C = 1 - \left(\frac{L_0}{L_F}\right)^{\frac{2}{n}}$$

The larger *n* becomes, the smaller will be *C* since $L_o / L_F \leq 1$ and positive. *C* becomes zero when $L_o = L_F$. whereas the model achieves a perfect fit for $L_F = 1$ and $C = 1-(L_o)^{2/n}$.[774] Therefore *C* faces the boundaries

$$0 \leq C \leq 1 - (L_0)^{\frac{2}{n}}$$

In addition to the shortcoming that *C* cannot achieve a value of one even in the case of perfect fit, empirical studies have shown that the Cox & Snell test has a tendency to underestimate the strength of the model.[775]

Nagelkerke test

NAGELKERKE (1991) suggested an adjustment to the Cox & Snell measure to ensure a maximum of one and a counter-balancing of the underestimation.[776] The Nagelkerke statistic is extended to the form

$$N = \frac{1 - \left(\frac{L_0}{L_F}\right)^{\frac{2}{n}}}{1 - (L_0)^{\frac{2}{n}}}$$

---

772 Menard, S.W. (2001), p. 21.
773 Pampel, C.F. (2000), p. 50. See also Cox, D.R./ Snell, E.J. (1989).
774 Reisinger, H. (1996), p. 145.
775 Pampel, C.F. (2000), p. 53.
776 Nagelkerke, N.J.D. (1991), p. 692.

For both measures, the Cox & Snell test and the Nagelkerke test, the literature suggests a value of 0.4 to reflect a good model fit, although in view of the underestimation problem, values in the Cox & Snell-R^2 of 0.3 are considered sufficient.[777]

6.3.4.2. *Likelihood ratio test*

Conceptually close to the *F-test* known from linear regression is the likelihood ratio test designed to test the overall significance of a model. To do so, the null hypothesis is formulated that all coefficients except the intercept equal zero:

$$H_0: \beta_1 = \beta_2 = \ldots = \beta_j = 0$$

The LR test's G statistic is χ^2-distributed with *n* degrees of freedom.[778]

$$G = -2\ln\frac{|L_0|}{|L_F|} = 2(|LL_0| - |LL_F|)$$

The larger the difference between the null and the full model is, the better the model strength. The G statistic is then compared to χ^2-distribution table. The resulting p-value reflects the level with which the null hypothesis must be accepted.[779]

6.3.4.3. *Hosmer-Lemeshow test*

The Hosmer-Lemeshow test extends the idea of the Pearson statistic[780] which tests the null hypothesis if the predicted and observed distributions are equal and thus the model estimate can be regarded as a perfect replication.[781] In this case, a good model fit is indicated by small differences in the observed and predicted classification.

HOSMER / LEMESHOW (1980) proposed that the probability p=[0,1] should be divided into g mutually exclusive groups and a comparison of the observed and predicted frequencies be carried out using a χ^2-statistic. The formula for the Hosmer-Lemeshow test is as follows:

[777] Backhaus, K. et al. (2003), p. 448.
[778] Urban, D. (1993), p. 60.
[779] A measure similar to the LR test is the *deviance*, which calculates the difference between the full model L_F and the perfectly fitted model, the so-called saturated model L_S. See, e.g. Menard, S.W. (2001), pp. 20-21.
[780] See, e.g. Fahrmeir, L./ Hamerle, A./ Tutz, G. (1996), p. 261.
[781] Hosmer, D.W./ Lemeshow, S. (2000), pp.147-149.

$$HL = \sum_{s=1}^{g} \frac{(o_s - n'_s \bar{\pi}_s)^2}{n'_s \bar{\pi}_s (1 - \bar{\pi}_s)}$$

with n'_s denoting the number of observations in group s. With c_s as the number of covariate patterns[782] in the sth decile, o_s, the number of covariate patterns in the sth decile, follows as

$$o_s = \sum_{j=1}^{c_k} y_j$$

The average probability $\bar{\pi}_s$ for the sth group is defined as

$$\bar{\pi}_s = \sum_{j=1}^{c_s} \frac{m_j \pi_j}{n'_k}$$

where m_j denotes the number of observations with the same j^{th} covariate pattern. A good model fit is indicated by a non-significant χ^2-value.[783]

6.3.4.4. *Classification*

Another popular method of assessing the predictive power of a well-fitted model is to make a prediction for each of the observations and contrast the group membership of the predicted value with the actual outcome. This yields a 2x2 table in which a well-fitted model should classify at least 70-80 per cent of the deals correctly.[784]

6.3.5. Model interpretation

Once the full model exhibits an acceptable fit of the data, the estimation coefficients may be interpreted. The subsequent sections discuss three ways of interpreting the results of the model estimation. The component that is most similar to linear regression modelling, the test for significance (Wald statistic), will first be discussed, followed by the interpretation of the coefficient, and finally the logit-typical interpretation of the model odds.

---

[782] Covariate patterns are a distinct set of values for the covariates of the model.
[783] Hosmer, D.W./ Lemeshow, S. (2000), pp.148.
[784] Simonoff, J.S. (2003), p. 370.

6.3.5.1. *Significance of coefficients (Wald statistic)*

Very similar to the *t-test* in linear regression models is the so-called **Wald statistic**, the most popular test for assessing the significance level of an explanatory variable.[785] Following the linear regression methodology, the Wald statistic tests significance with the null hypothesis of a β_j equaling 0:

$$H_0: \beta_j = 0$$

$$H1: \beta_j \neq 0$$

With the parameter's standard error as a measure for the uncertainty of the estimation, the Wald statistic follows as the ratio of the parameter and its standard error.[786]

$$W = \left(\frac{\beta_j}{\sigma(\beta_j)} \right)^2$$

The resulting statistic then has to be compared with the corresponding value in the χ^2-table for 1 degree of freedom.

6.3.5.2. *Interpretation of coefficients*

Although logistic regression is in many respects similar to the linear regression model, the coefficients cannot be interpreted in the same way. Given the non-linear relationship between explanatory and dependent variables, logit regression lacks an analogue interpretation to the coefficients in linear regressions.

Basically, the coefficient β_j determines the influence of x_j on the aggregated influence z, which in turn follows the logistic function. As already outlined, z is also defined as the logged odds, i.e. the logarithm of the ratio of probability and counter-probability.

$$z = \log\left(\frac{p_k}{1 - p_k} \right) = \beta_0 + \sum_{j=1}^{J} \beta_j \cdot x_{jk}$$

---

785 Urban, D. (1993), p. 59.

The coefficients are interpreted in exactly the same way as the coefficients in linear regression, except that the unit of the dependent variable represents the logged odds. For example, a coefficient of β_j=0.8 implies that an increase of the explanatory variable x_j by one unit leads to a decrease of the logged odds by one-fifth. For dummy variables, a change in one unit implicitly compares the indicator group to the reference group.[787]

Since the Newton-Raphson algorithm estimates all logit coefficients simultaneously, the influence of one variable is adjusted for the influence of other variables.[788] It should be noted, however, that coefficients are not comparable among different models since the variances of z changes when new variables are added to the model. The magnitudes of all βs will change even if the added variable is uncorrelated with the original variables.[789]

In addition, the magnitude of the coefficients impacts the shape of the logistic function. Probability values for large βs (β>1) approximate quickly the extremes, while for small coefficients (0<β<1) the dependency on x increases only gradually.[790]

Statements about the influence of variables on changes in logged odds reveal little about the direct relationship and hardly contribute to a general understanding of the results. The baseline interpretation of the coefficient remains the direction of the influence. Despite the general simplicity of the interpretation, logistic regression lacks a meaningful direct metric.

6.3.5.3. Odds-ratio interpretation

While in linear regression marginal effects can be directly retrieved from the regression coefficients, in logit analyses these effects first have to be calculated. Since the coefficients for each parameter in logit regressions are not comparable with each other and their effect varies depending on the position of the s-curve, they have to be transformed in such a way that a standardised interpretation is possible.[791]

---

786 Backhaus, K. et al. (2003), p. 452.
787 Pampel, F.C. (2000), p. 19.
788 Urban, D. (1993), p. 36.
789 Winship, C./ Mare, R.D. (1984), p. 517 and McKelvey, R.D./ Zavoina, W. (1975), pp. 114-116.
790 Backhaus, K. et al. (2003), p. 432.
791 Backhaus, K. et al. (2003), p. 433.

This is achieved by interpreting the odds of the coefficient, the ratio of the probability to the counter-probability. A transformation of the logistic function clearly demonstrates that the odds follow an e-function with the exponential z.[792]

$$p(HLT) = \frac{e^z}{1+e^z} \quad \Leftrightarrow \quad Odds: \frac{p(HLT)}{1-p(HLT)} = e^z$$

Odds extend the value range to [0; +∞] and correspond to those used in horseracing. The actual strength of a coefficient's influence on the probability to be structured as a HLT can be determined on the basis of the change in odds. An increase of x_j+1 improves the odds by a factor $e^{\beta j}$. This factor is called the **odds ratio** or sometimes the **effect coefficient**. The relationship can be illustrated as follows:[793]

$$\begin{aligned} e^{\beta_0+\beta_1\cdot(x+1)} &= e^{\beta_0}\cdot e^{\beta_0\cdot x}\cdot e^{\beta_1} \\ &= e^{\beta_0+\beta_1\cdot x}\cdot e^{\beta_1} \\ &= Odds\cdot e^{\beta_1} \end{aligned}$$

For the exponential coefficients, a coefficient of 1 leaves the odds unchanged, a coefficient greater than 1 increases the odds, and a coefficient smaller than 1 decreases the odds. For example, if p(HLT)=0.5, the respective odds are 1. For an odds ratio of 0.6 an increase of x+1 reduces the odds of being structured as a HLT to 0.6:1 (or 0.38). An odds ratio of 1.2 in turn increases the odds by 20 per cent. Moreover, the more distant the coefficient is from 1 in either direction, the greater will be the effect in changing the odds.[794]

6.4. Summary

The previous section introduced the various analytical techniques used in the empirical study. Of the different univariate analysis techniques non-parametric tests are widely used, because they provide solid indications for the strength of relationships among dependent and explanatory variables, though not the direction of those relationships. As a multivariate technique, the study applies logistic regressions, a powerful tool when the dependent variable has a dichotomous character. Logistic regressions were chosen due to their widespread use in finance research, the

792 Backhaus, K. et al. (2003), p. 435.
793 Backhaus, K. et al. (2003), p. 436.
794 Pampel, F.C. (2000), p. 22.

ability to conform to the saturation aspect in financing, and the robustness of the model given the absence of overly strict assumptions.

Unlike linear regressions, logit analyses model the relationship as the influence of explanatory variables on the probability that a certain event will occur, in this case that an IBO will be structured as an HLT. On the basis of a specific algorithm, an iterative process searches for those coefficients in the regression that simultanenously maximise the likelihood that the IBO will become highly leveraged. Since the coefficients cannot be interpreted in the same way as in linear regressions, logistic regressions provide other metrics that are derived from the coefficients. They are summarised in the following table.

Table 11: Influence of positive and negative coefficients on the likelihood that an event occurs

β	Odds-ratio (effect coefficient)	Logit (z)	Odds [(P(y=1)/P(y=0)]	P(y=1)
$\beta > 0$	$e^{\beta} > 1$	Increases at β	Increases at e^{β}	Increases
$\beta < 0$	$e^{\beta} < 1$	Decreases at β	Decreases at e^{β}	Decreases

Source: Backhaus, K. et. al. (2003), p. 437.

To assess the significance of an explanatory variable, logit regressions include Wald statistics, a two-tailed significance test similar to the t-test used in linear regressions. The fit of the entire model can be assessed using a set of different tests, the easiest to interpret being pseudo-R^2 tests. In addition, the literature favours the likelihood ratio test, the Hosmer-Lemeshow test, and a simple classification. The former two test types reflect the model's power to *explain* the variances in the sample, while the latter three assess the power to *predict* actual outcomes.

7. Empirical results on IBO capital structures

Cross-study comparisons are done with results mostly taken at face value, with maximum possible consideration of differences in measurement, definition and techniques, particularly insofar as these differences are crucial for the understanding and interpretation of the results. Consequently, the thesis followed a stringent structure, from a discussion of the research object through the methodology elaborated in the previous chapter.

The following presentation of empirical results constitutes the core section of the thesis and incorporates mainly three parts presenting the econometric results. First, following the description of the sample (chapter 7.1) and a set of descriptive statistics (7.2), the results of the univariate analyses will be provided (7.3). After that, the core analysis of the study follows: the logistic regression on the classification into HLTs and Non-HLTs (7.4). As add-on analyses, the logistic regressions on the choice of other financial layers will be performed in chapter 7.5. Within this chapter, the logistic regressions on equity (7.5.1) and sub-ordinated debt (7.5.2.) represent complementary regressions to the main analysis on senior debt. In addition to the first-layer instruments, the choice of detailed layers, namely HYB vs. mezzanine (7.5.3.1) and senior A debt vs. senior B/C (7.5.3.2) debt will also be studied. Figure 29 illustrates the different logistic regressions performed in chapters 7.4 and 7.5.

Figure 29: Overview of subsequent logit models

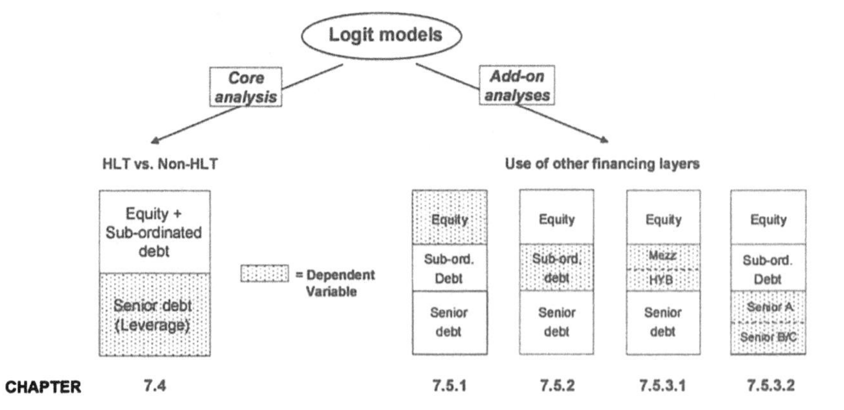

Source: Author.

7.1. Sample description

The sample description comprises two sections, a discussion of the sample in its entirety and a description of the capital structures and characteristics of the reported deals. In an initial step, a review of the sample as such follows, first by presenting the deviation i.e. outlining how the samples evolved, second by illustrating the geographic reach, and finally by testing for potential biases within the sample.

7.1.1. Sample deviation

Out of the 215 contacted PE funds,[795] 26 per cent returned one or more completed deal record sheets. The return rate of 26 per cent appears to be in line with other buyout studies.[796] The 56 responding investors reported 2.25 transactions on average, which results in a total of 126 transactions. However, because answers were seriously incomplete in some cases, 32 transactions had to be substracted from the sample. In the case of only few missing values follow-up calls were done.[797] The resulting sample size of 94 transactions represents a share of 22 per cent based on the total number of 436 IBOs in Europe over the years 1998-2004.[798] Figure 30 depicts the sample deviation.

[795] 215 PE funds out of 454 European PE firms have been identified through database and internet research to have carried out at least one IBO over the last 7 years.

[796] E.g. Jakoby, S. (2000) achieved a rate of 25.3 per cent and Frankfurter, G.M./ Kosedag, A. (1996) a rate of 23 per cent.

[797] Only as far as data on the capital structure or its determinants are concerned. Additional data (e.g. ownership structure) was not followed up.

[798] See figure 1 on page 2.

Figure 30: Sample deviation

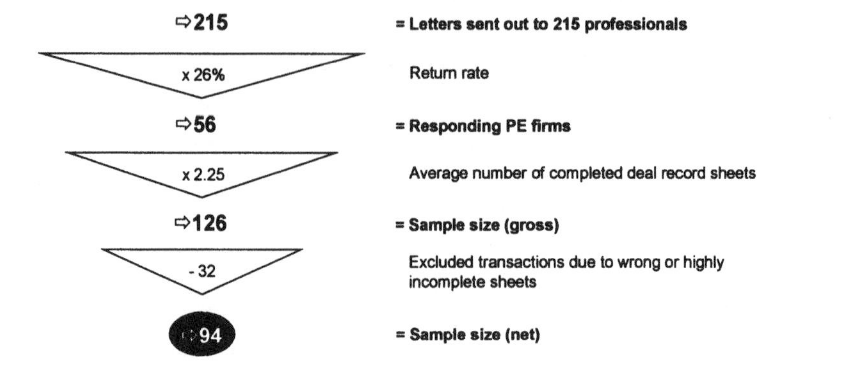

Source: Author.

A number of 94 transactions corresponds to other interview-based buyout studies, while studies that draw the data from public sources (e.g. databases or annual accounts) usually have higher sample sizes than studies based on private sources (e.g. surveys). Compared to the latter studies, this survey ranks at the upper end of the range. Table 12 presents an overview of earlier studies, indicating sample size and the data source in each case.

Table 12: Sample sizes of prior buyout studies

Author(s)	*Year*	*Sample size*	*Data source*
Holthausen / Larcker	1996	90	Public
Roden / Lewellen	1995	107	Public
Kaplan / Stein	1993	124	Public
Long / Ravenscraft	1993	257	Public
Degorge / Zeckhauser	1993	62	Public
Frankfurter / Gunay	1992	110	Public
Liebeskind / Wiersema / Hansen	1992	33	Public
Newbould / Chatfield / Anderson	1992	23	Public
Kaplan / Stein	1990	31	Public
Singh	1990	65	Public
Kaplan	1989	76	Public
Lehn / Poulsen	1988	106	Public
DeAngelo / DeAngelo / Rice	1984	81	Public
Mean		***90***	
Jakoby	2000	67	Private
Frankfurter / Kosedag	1996	131	Private
Vest	1995	29	Private
Gräper	1993	65	Private
Green	1992	35	Private
Forst	1992	38	Private
Bull	1989	25	Private
Warwick Business School	1989	58	Private
Mean		***56***	

To deliver reliable and meaningful results, the sample size must correspond to the number of covariates in the regression. As mentioned earlier, a rule of thumb for logit models suggests a minimum of 10 observations for each parameter.[799] This implies that for a sample of 94 transactions, the number of parameters should not significantly exceed 9. As regards the objective to test buyout financing from a corporate finance perspective, the study by RODEN / LEWELLEN (1995) exhibits most similarities to this study. With a sample size of 107 LBOs, their data set is only slightly larger than the one presented here. Overall, the achieved sample size should be sufficient to generate robust results, since the necessary conditions are fulfilled.

7.1.2. Sample representativeness

In terms of the geographic spread of the sample, a key indicator for its representativeness, the bulk of responses clearly comes from Germany. Therefore, it has to be acknowledged that the study is less representative for Europe than expected. However, the CMBOR (2003) survey shows that for all types of buyouts UK, Germany and France are the top three countries in terms of number and total value of transactions.[800] In addition, since many European IBOs have cross-border dimensions anyway, the European market probably exhibits a higher degree of homogeneity with a supranational relevance of the results.[801] Figure 31 illustrates the geographic dispersion of the sample.

---

[799] Hosmer D.W./ Lemeshow, S. (2000), p. 346.

[800] CMBOR (2003), pp. 79, 89, 171.

[801] In light of the results of earlier international comparisons a better spread might have helped to shed light on nation-specific differences. For example, Rajan, R./ Zingales, L. (1995) found substantial differences within Europe and between European and other countries (p. 1453).

Figure 31: Geographic spread of the sample

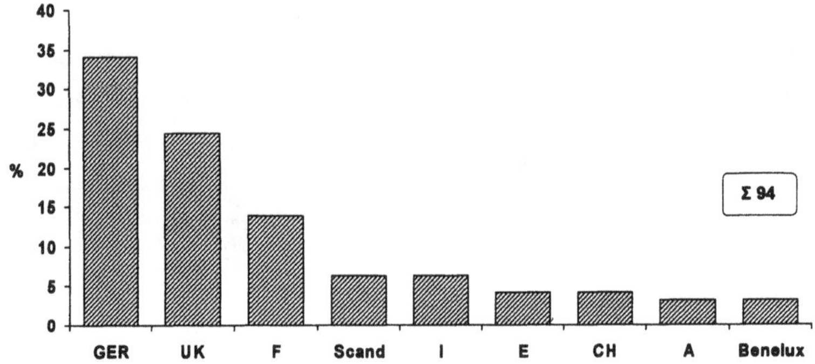

Source: Author.

Two further aspects provide an indication of the overall representativeness of the sample. First of all, the average capital structure across all types of buyouts in Europe exhibits a slightly lower share of debt than that reported for this study. The difference can be attributed to the generally higher share of debt in IBOs than in classical MBOs.[802]

Furthermore, the transaction characteristics of the sample IBOs are consistent with the commonly reported characteristics for buyouts. Particularly the low-risk and low-growth nature of buyouts is reflected in the sample. Overall, the characteristics suggest that the sample is sufficiently representative to ensure the validity of the results.

7.1.3. Sample biases

The problem of a potential non-response bias as well as an informant bias will now be adressed. While the former has to be examined using adequate test methods, the latter can be precluded by structuring the questionnaire in such a way to mitigate the subjectivity of responses.

[802] See Appendix 6.

7.1.3.1. *Test for non-response bias*

Given the return rate of 26 per cent, the quality of the sample had to be tested for a potential non-response bias as discussed in ARMSTRONG / OVERTON (1977).[803] The literature has advanced a number of tests for a potential non-response bias. One intuitive way is to compare sample characteristics with known characteristics from the whole population.[804] However, while data for the financial structure is available for buyouts as a whole, they are not available for IBOs specifically. This holds even more so for characteristics of IBOs such as average profitability or asset structure.

Another method which the literature discusses under the term "extrapolation method" appears feasible. For this, the deal sample has to be divided into two parts, those deals that were reported without follow-up mails/calls and those that were reported only in the second wave. In addition, the sample can be divided according to the time of return, since later respondents are assumed to be similar to non-respondents.[805] For this sample a split according to response waves seems appropriate at first glance. However, a time-dependent classification does not fit the nature of the respondents. Since a PE professional spends a substantial amount of time travelling, the time of awareness of the mailing cannot be assessed and would undermine the validity of the method.[806] In order to pinpoint the respondents who really required some convincing, the sample was split up into those transactions that were reported directly or after a first reminder mail and those that were only reported after a second follow-up mail or subsequent phone calls.

A stringent Kolmogorov-Smirnov two-sample test as well as a χ^2-homogeneity test were performed in order to determine whether systematic differences exist along the transaction characteristics and HLT as key dependent variable.[807] As the tests only display tangibility with a significant difference (at a 5 per cent level) in the Pearson-χ^2 test, the sample appears to be non-response biased. Table 13 summarises the results of both tests.

---

[803] Armstrong, J.S./ Overton, T.S. (1977).

[804] Colombo, R. (2000), p. 86; Armstrong, J.S./ Overton, T.S. (1977), pp. 396-397; Ognibene, P. (1971), p.233.

[805] Armstrong, J.S./ Overton, T.S. (1977), p. 397. Both proceedings have been applied in similar tests as well. See, e.g. Brettel, M. (2002), p. 310.

[806] Armstrong, J.S./ Overton, T.S. (1977), p. 397.

[807] See chapter 6.2.1 for a discussion of the Pearson-χ^2 homogeneity test. The Kolmogorov-Smirnov two-sample test exhibits very similar characteristics to the previously discussed non-parametric tests. For a description see, e.g. Büning, H./ Trenkler, G. (1994), pp. 117-136. The calculations were done with SPSS Version 12.0.

Table 13: Tests for non-response bias

Characteristics	Variable	Pearson-χ2[a]	Kolmogorov-Smirnov[a]
	HLT	1,096	0,523
Risk class	EBITDA_VOL	5,744	0,450
	IND_CYCL	9,281	1,330
Transaction size	TRANS_VALUE	10,126	0,608
	SALES	6,862	0,323
Tangibility	TANG	12,880**	1,158
Growth	EV_EBITDA	4,883	0,666
	CAPEX	9,816	0,793
	CAGR_SALES	6,900	0,704
Profitability	EBITDA_SALES	2,470	0,363
Uniqueness	R_D	0,336	0,283
	MARKET_SH	7,200	0,635
Free cash flow	FCF_SALES	1,174	0,249
	NFL_FCF	7,841	1,029

*, **, *** significant at the 10%-, 5%-, 1%-level

[a] Provided are the test statistics; a high statistic indicates a highly significant value; the same holds for the remaining test statistics of the study

7.1.3.2. *Informant bias and the problem of subjectivity*

A problem often faced by empirical studies is that their surveys are based on self-reported measures to test hypotheses; hence they are informant biased and lead to considerable measurement errors.[808] While that problem appears to be particularly prevalent for sociological and organisational surveys, empirical finance research has to cope with similar concerns as long as the respondents can be referred to as informants who do not express personal attitudes or opinions but statements about patterns of behaviour or actual relations.[809] The data collection methodology has a substantial impact on the degree of informant bias.

As discussed earlier, a key challenge of studying the capital structures of private companies and buyouts in particular is to gather the relevant financial data. Since no sufficiently detailed database exists from which to extract the information, data has to be surveyed through questionnaires. One way to survey characteristics of the firm (e.g. risk class) would be to ask for a positioning on a bipolar rating scale, with poles such as very low risk vs. very high risk. Structuring the scales in this way represents an easy but highly informant-biased way to collect data, as the degree of risk is not related to an objective criterion of which all respondents have an equal understanding. In addition, it

[808] Kumar, N./ Stern, L./ Anderson, J. (1993).
[809] Campbell, D.T. (1955), pp. 339-342.

would imply the unrealistic assumption that all respondents have the same understanding of the distance between two values.[810]

The survey had to be structured in such a way as to overcome the problem of substantial informant bias. The only appropriate way of overcoming this type of subjectivity problem[811] appeared to be the introduction of objective criteria, specifically the introduction of ordinal scales with numerical categories.

7.2. Descriptive statistics

In the following paragraphs, the descriptive statistics of both the different financial layers and the characteristics of the transaction will be presented. They provide a picture of the distribution of capital structure components and indicate what types of buyouts are included in the sample.

7.2.1. Distribution of financing layers

The capital structures of the sampled IBOs prove to be in line with other publications, reporting roughly 40-50 per cent of senior debt and only a minor share for sub-ordinated debt. An average share of 47 per cent of senior notes was reported by CMBOR (2003) for all types of buyouts. Since IBOs are generally assumed to be more highly leveraged, given a smaller equity share in comparison to management buyouts, 53 per cent appears to be a reasonable level.[812]

As regards equity instruments, the capital is split quite evenly between straight common and preferred equity and shareholder loans. Concerning sub-ordinated debt, mezzanine instruments are clearly preferred over high-yield bonds. Within the senior debt segment, yearly amortisable senior A tranches account for the bulk share. See figure 32 for the depiction of the average capital structure in the sample.

[810] Beller, S. (2004), p. 36.
[811] Ernst, H. (2003), p. 2.
[812] See Appendix 6 for buyout capital structures reported by CMBOR.

Figure 32: Average capital structure of sample IBOs

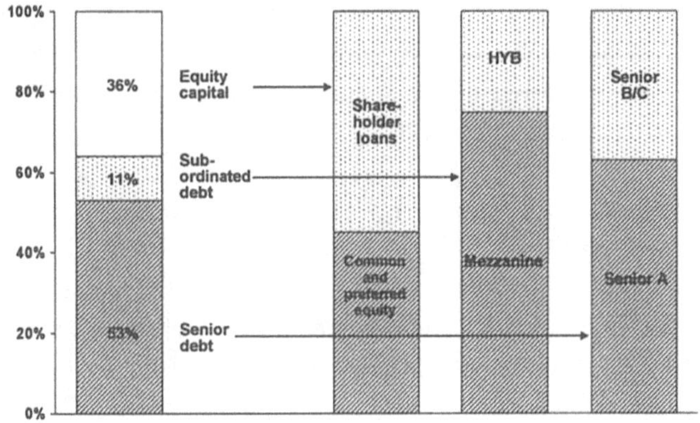

Source: Author.

7.2.1.1. Distribution of senior debt

A more in-depth analysis of the senior debt segment reveals information about systematic patterns. On the left-hand side of figure 33, the frequency of senior debt shares is depicted in 5 per cent groups. As can be seen, with a frequency of 16 deals, a share of 60-65 per cent represents the mode of the distribution, the most common group in the sample. Both very low and very high shares of senior debt are quite rare.

Overall, the distribution is fairly even with a slight right-wing tendency towards higher senior debt shares.[813] Looking at the different tranches, it becomes clear that IBO decision makers prefer either as much senior A as possible or an even mix of both senior A and B/C tranches. This could imply that lower interest rates on senior A tranches are preferred to the deferred-cash nature of senior B/C tranches.[814] Figure 33 depicts the use of senior debt instruments.

[813] The distribution gaps in the categories 45-50 per cent and 55-60 per cent could be due to a respondent's tendency to report rounded numbers (e.g. 50 per cent instead of 48 per cent)

[814] See chapter 4.1.2 for a discussion of the different tranches.

Figure 33: Use of senior debt

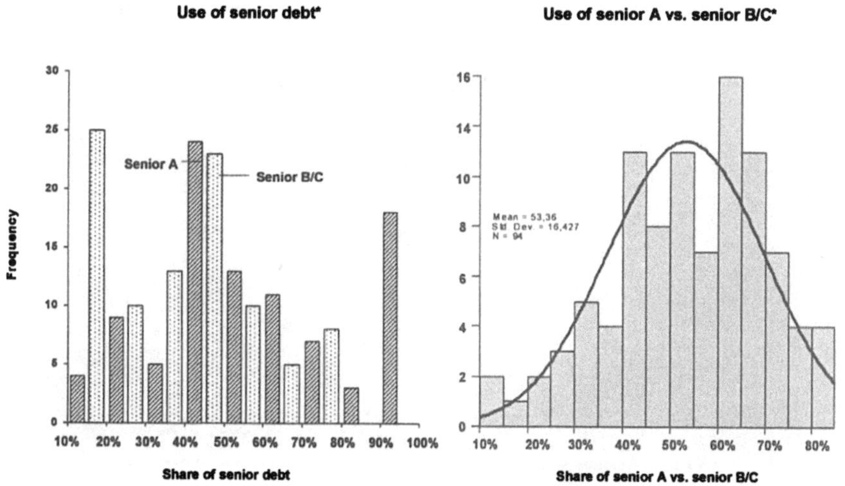

Note: * Each bar represents the number of IBOs that display the share of senior debt (senior A or B/C debt) provided at the bottom of the left (right) graph

Source: Author.

7.2.1.2. Distribution of sub-ordinated debt

As regards the use of sub-ordinated debt, the mean average of 10.5 per cent appears to confirm the commonly reported rare use of sub-ordinated instruments. Only nine transactions carry a substantial share (≥30%) of sub-ordinated debt in the total capitalisation.

In addition, HYBs and mezzanine instruments hardly amount for equal shares in a transaction. Rather, in all but a a few deals, sub-ordinated debt is made up exclusively of either mezzanine or HYBs. Of the 52 IBOs using sub-ordinated debt at all, 37 have 100 per cent in mezzanine and 8 in HYBs. Only 7 employ both instruments jointly. In these deals, the HYB share tends to be larger than the mezzanine share. The usually large portions of HYBs can be explained by the tremendous cost associated with structuring the bond. This makes it necessary to issue large blocks of HYBs at the same time.

Figure 34 depicts the distribution of sub-ordinated debt instruments.

Figure 34: Use of sub-ordinated debt

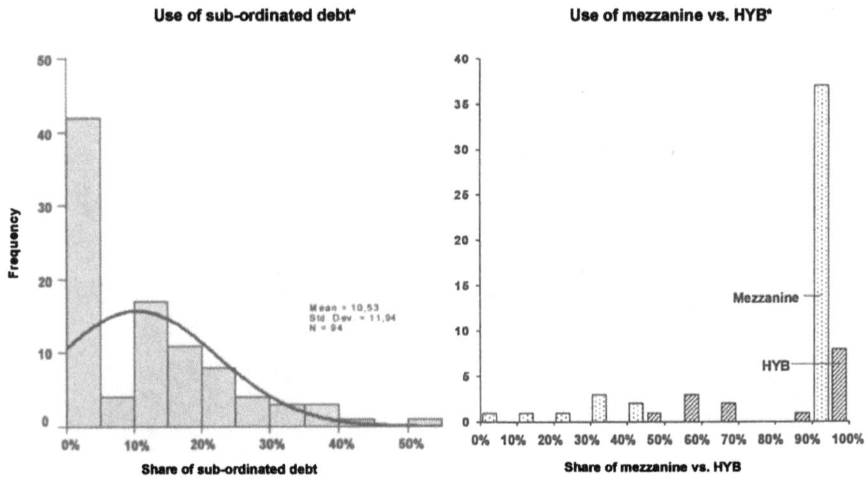

Note: * Each bar represents the number of IBOs that display the share of sub-ordinated debt (mezzanine or HYB) provided at the bottom of the left (right) graph

Source: Author.

7.2.1.3. Distribution of equity

As opposed to senior and sub-ordinated debt, the analysis of equity instruments reveals no clear distribution patterns. The overall shape of the histogramm shows a slight left-wing tendency and reflects the main counterpart to senior debt.

However, there appears to be no systematic pattern in the split between common/preferred equity and shareholder loans. Interviews with PE professionals confirm the varying use of equity instruments among PE funds. Fund-internal reasons as well as legal considerations determine the use of either instrument. Figure 35 shows the distribution of equity capital.

Figure 35: Use of equity capital

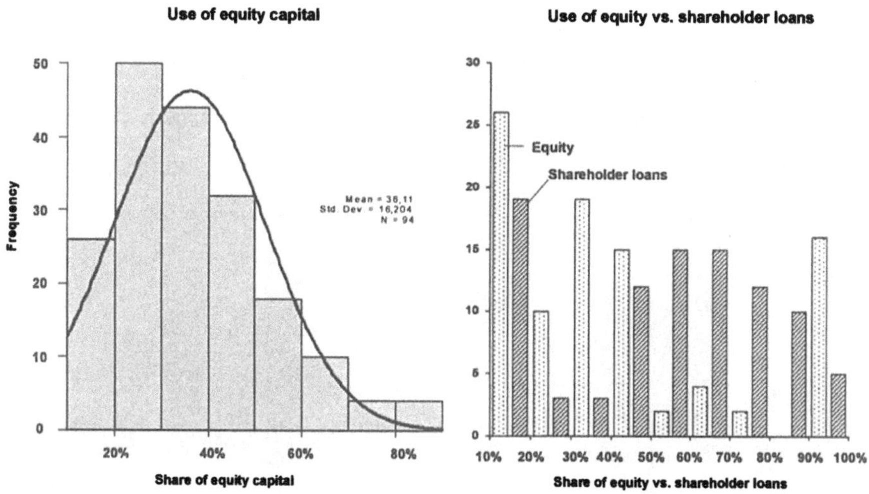

Note: * Each bar represents the number of IBOs that display the share of equity capital (equity or shareholder loans) provided at the bottom of the left (right) graph

Source: Author.

7.2.2. Distribution of characteristics

The descriptive statistics for the various financial instruments aim to pinpoint aggregated financing patterns, irrespective of the underlying characteristics. These are now described with two objectives in mind: first, to obtain an impression of the diversity of the IBO transactions and second, more technically, to ascertain how well the data was recorded. The following paragraphs present the distribution of the variables for each of the seven characteristics.

Risk class was operationalised through EBITDA volatility and the industry's cyclicality. While the scale for EBITDA volatility has numerical categories like all other variables, industry cyclicality is recorded on a simple bipolar scale, given the difficulty of recording an appropriate metric.

As can be seen from figure 36, both variables exhibit low frequencies in the open-end border categories, which suggests an appropriate calibration of the scales to discriminate between high and low-risk deals. Most IBOs cumulate on the lower end of the risk scale, confirming the reputation of buyouts as having less volatile businesses in general. However, only seven deals exhibit very stable EBITDA streams with average standard deviations of 10 per cent around their long-term average. In general, the distribution of industry cyclicality follows the EBITDA volatility with the exception of the third category, which falls short in relevance.

Figure 36: Distribution of characteristics – Risk class

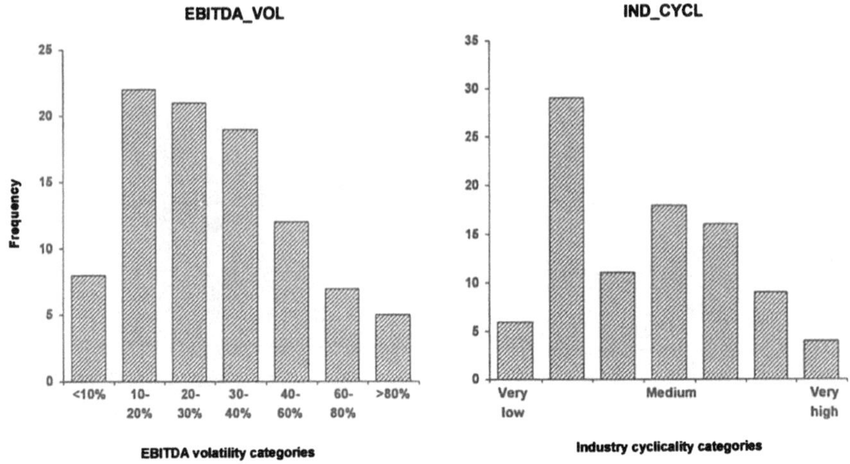

Source: Author.

With regard to **transaction size**, the operationalisation was done by means of the metrics transaction value and sales. Figure 37 shows that concerning transaction value, the category of €150m-300m occurs with the highest frequency. Likewise, the corresponding sales category includes the most IBOs. Clearly, IBOs are in general rather large transactions, while management buyouts tend to be smaller deals. The segment of so-called mega-deals, often public-to-private deals, is represented with 12 deals.

The right-wing skewness conforms to IBOs being generally larger than other types of buyouts. A distribution with high frequencies in the smaller size categories would have been an indication for a severe failure in recording the right transactions. Moreover, the fact that both distributions, sales and transaction value, are fairly similar in shape confirms their equal rights to operationalise a firm's size.

Blatant over- or undervaluations based on sales numbers do not appear to exist, which would have been the case if one proxy was right-skewed and the other left-skewed.

Figure 37: Distribution of characteristics – Transaction size

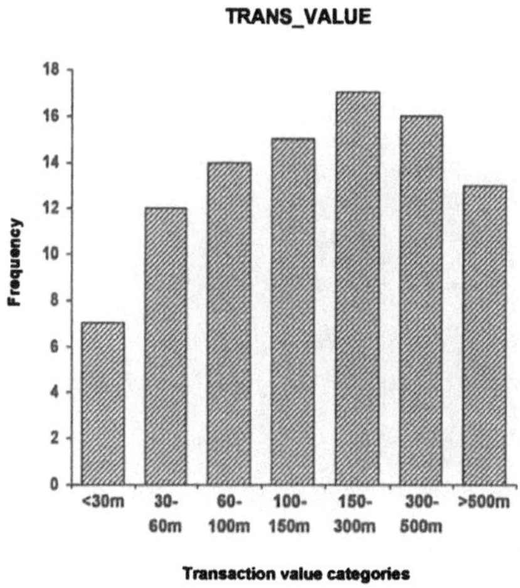

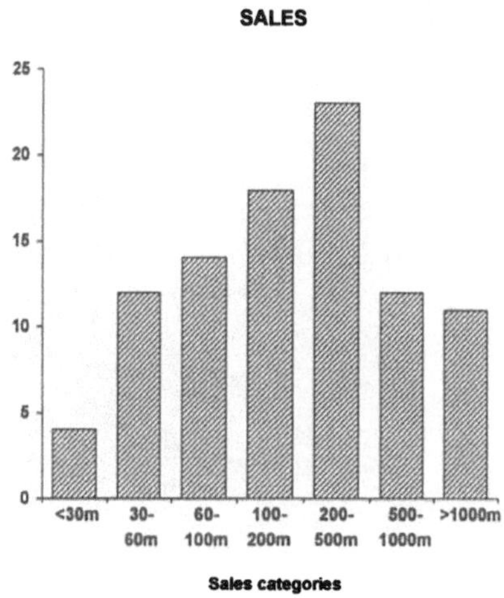

Source: Author.

To consider the **tangibility** of assets, prior studies have made predominant use of a single ratio specifiying tangible assets to total assets. Consequently, this study follows their example and includes only this proxy.

Figure 38 depicts the distribution of the reported deals. Since few deals fall into the border categories, the taxonomy appears to be well-balanced. What can be said is that IBOs are not necessarily characterised by either low or high tangibility ratios. This contradicts the common understanding of buyout targets to be typically industrial goods producers.[815] With the 15-25 per cent category occurring with the highest frequency, the sample appears to comprise more companies with low levels of tangible assets.

815 In fact, some of the best known deals in Germany were companies with highly intangible assets (e.g. BertelsmannSpinger by Candover / Cinven, Scholz & Friends by Electra Partners Europe or Pro7Sat1 by Saban Capital).

Figure 38: Distribution of characteristics – Tangibility

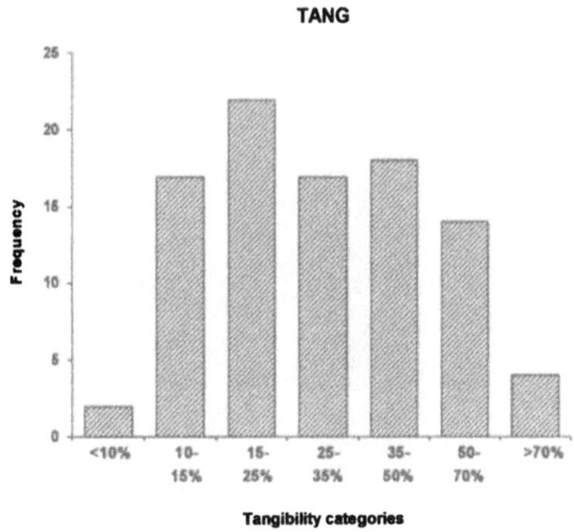

Source: Author.

As with tangibility, the regression includes only one variable to operationalise a firm's **profitability**. As shown in figure 39, the distribution resembles the tangibility distribution insofar as the border categories are clearly underrepresented and the sample does not exhibit an obvious tendency towards low or high profitability firms.

Figure 39: Distribution of characteristics – Profitability

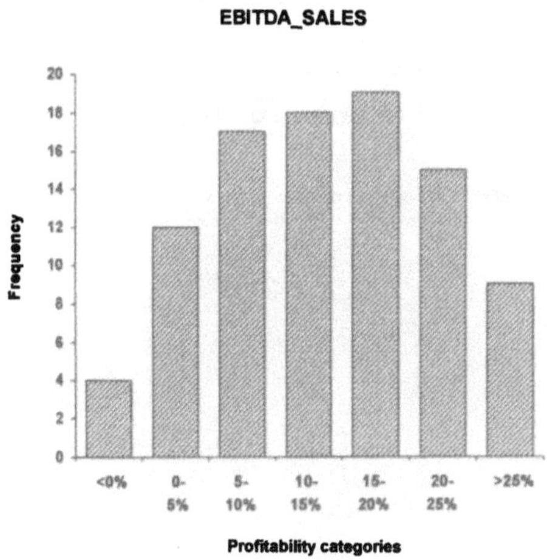

Source: Author.

Moreover, this is an indication that the scale appears to have the right calibration, with no lumping of deals in one of the groups. The fifth category represents the mode category showing that IBOs are usually able to generate solid operating cash flows.

Unlike the previous variables, the decision to operationalise **growth** by way of three metrics was driven by the manifold possibilities to proxy for growth. Accordingly, both forward and backward-oriented metrics were used. Of the three, CAGR_SALES is the only backward-looking metric. As IBOs typically include rather low-growth firms, most deals fall into the groups 0-10 per cent. Only one deal was reported to have experienced significant negative growth rates.

Similarly, the CapEx metric is consistent with the IBO setting since firms are usually not bought out shortly after substantial investments have been made. Both metrics thus show an evident left-wing skewness.

In contrast, EV/EBITDA is similar in nature to Tobin's Q, the most widely applied operationalisation for growth, as the clear future orientation best reflects the agency context. The distribution's right-wing skewness may stem from the fact that in some cases, PE funds acquire firms at premiums associated with reinforced growth efforts.[816] In addition, the high multiples may reflect the buyout as a trigger for extraordinary growth beyond the operating growth potential.

However, all three distributions seem fairly healthy and may serve as a proxy in the regression model. See figure 40 for the distribution of the three variables.

Figure 40: Distribution of characteristics – Growth

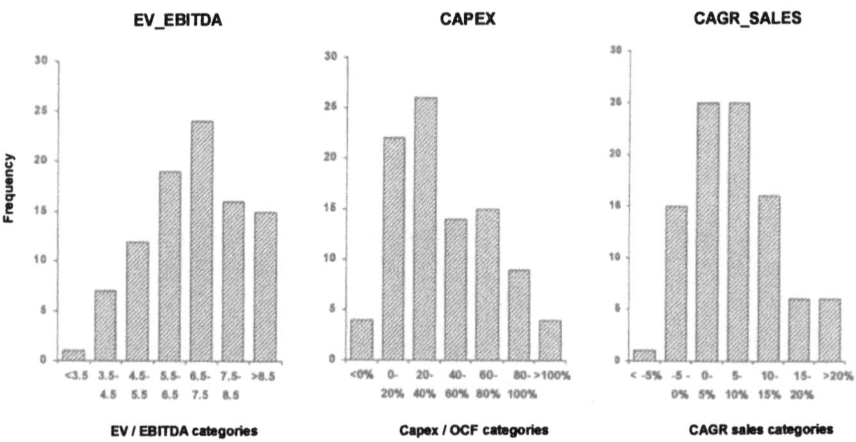

Source: Author.

As regards the adequateness of a metric, incorporating **uniqueness** represents a challenging task, since uniqueness (or asset specificity) has a latent, not measurable character. Since the inverse of an intangibles ratio approximates for tangibility, researchers usually incorporate an R&D figure.

In this case, the numerical taxonomy for R&D/sales unfortunately proved to be entirely inadequate to capture the actual distribution. The underlying distribution of the 100 medium-sized firms that were analyzed to calibrate the scales dramatically overestimated the R&D intensity of the IBOs. In light of the cumulation in the left border category, R&D/sales cannot serve as an adequate proxy in the regression model.

[816] Butler, P.A. (2001), pp. 143-144.

Instead, the well-balanced market share record shall be applied, although its appropriateness may be questioned.[817] Almost one-quarter of the deals fall into the middle category, showing that IBO firms rarely dominate the market as in a monopolistic environment but still hold substantial market shares. This underlines the typical IBO profile of being one of the market leaders in an oligopolistic market. This is illustrated in figure 41.

Figure 41: Distribution of characteristics – Uniqueness

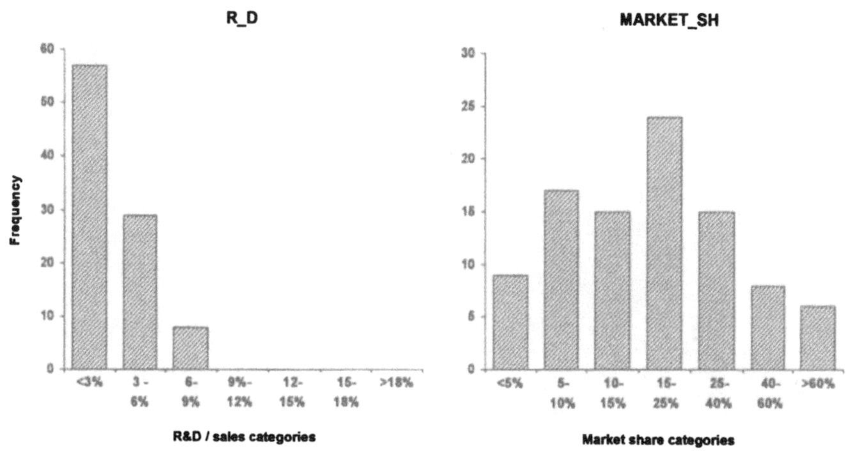

Source: Author.

The distribution of **free cash flow** metrics reflects that the calibration of FCF/sales is less problematic than the calibration of the NFL/FCF figure. Retrieving the net financial liabilities from the medium-sized company reports was a time-consuming task with imprecise results given the different levels of detail in the annual accounts.

The variable FCF/sales, however, has a solid normal distribution-like shape with low border category frequencies. Nevertheless, despite the satisfactory shape itself, the distribution somewhat contradicts the typical IBO characteristic of having strong free cash flow levels. One would have expected the distribution to show a clear right-wing skewness. However, interviews suggested that not only the level but also the stability of the free cash flows characterises an IBO candidate.

[817] One may argue that market share could also be correlated with other characteristics such as profitability, as c.p. a higher market share should lead to a better fixed cost degression. However, as will be shown in table 18, market share only exhibits a correlation of about 0.2 with the profitability metric EBITDA_SALES.

Moreover, the analysis of the 14 IBOs with negative free cash flows reveals that they are primarily turnaround deals subject to financial restructurings. Much of their cash flows are absorbed by existing credit facilities.

Overall, the free cash flow variable should be the more adequate proxy in the regression model. See depiction 42 for a comparison of the two variables.

Figure 42: Distribution of characteristics – Free cash flow

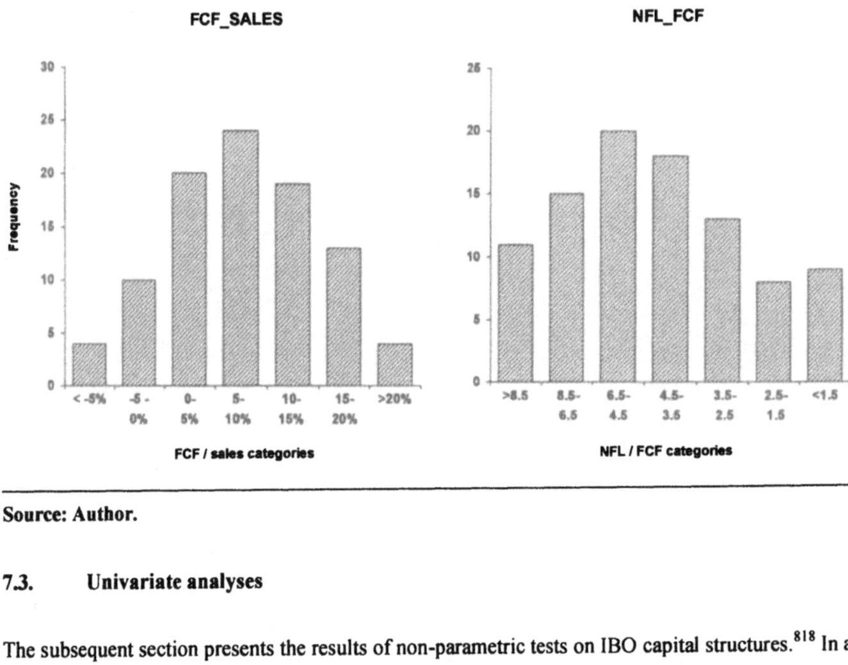

Source: Author.

7.3. Univariate analyses

The subsequent section presents the results of non-parametric tests on IBO capital structures.[818] In a first step, the differences between HLT and Non-HLT groups are studied by way of box-plot illustrations in addition to the two-sample tests. The tests are then applied to determine the use of other financial instruments, e.g. by examining the classification in groups that use sub-ordinated debt and groups that do not. However, compared to the discussion of the HLT/Non-HLT classification, this section will be short since the focus clearly lies on the former analysis.

[818] The tests were performed by means of SPSS Version 12.0.

In addition to the two-sample tests, a Spearman rank correlation analysis of the explanatory variables will be performed in order to detect potential multicolliniarity problems.

7.3.1. Non-parametric tests of the choice between debt and equity

The tests consist of two parts, one being the statistical analyses (Pearson-χ^2, Mann-Whitney)[819] and the other a graphical comparison of the characteristic distribution within each group of HLTs and Non-HLTs.

The graphical comparison is done by means of so-called box plots,[820] which split up the sample into two groups and apply percentile comparisons to illustrate the mean and the dispersion of the IBOs. Figure 43 depicts the structure of box plots as used subsequently.

Figure 43: Box-plots

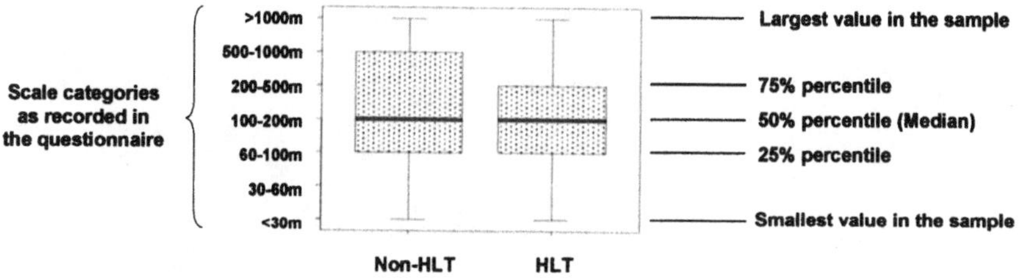

Source: Author.

As a supplement to the two-sample tests that do not provide an indication of the direction of relationships, the box plots give a first idea of a potentially positive or negative relationship.

7.3.1.1. Risk class

Having performed both a Pearson-χ^2 and Mann-Whitney test, variable EBITDA_VOL showed up as significant in the latter. The MW test confirms a significant difference between highly leveraged and non-highly leveraged IBOs at the 5 per cent level as regards the risk class measured by the volatility in EBITDA. The box plot confirms an expected inverse relation between risk and

[819] See chapter 6.2.1.
[820] For a discussion of box plots and their fields of application, see, e.g. Schlittgen, R. (2000).

leverage, with the median of volatility being one category lower in the HLT than in the Non-HLT group.

Conversely, the variable IND_CYCL does not appear to exhibit a substantial dependency on the leverage. The box-plot comparison confirms the non-parametric test given the very similar distribution in both groups. Not only is the median located in the same category, the spread measured by the 25% to the 75% percentile is also of equal magnitude.

Consequently, going forward the regression models should include EBITDA_VOL instead of IND_CYCL, since the former metric has more power to discriminate between HLTs and Non-HLTs. See figure 44 for a comparison of both variables.

Figure 44: Univariate analyses – Risk class

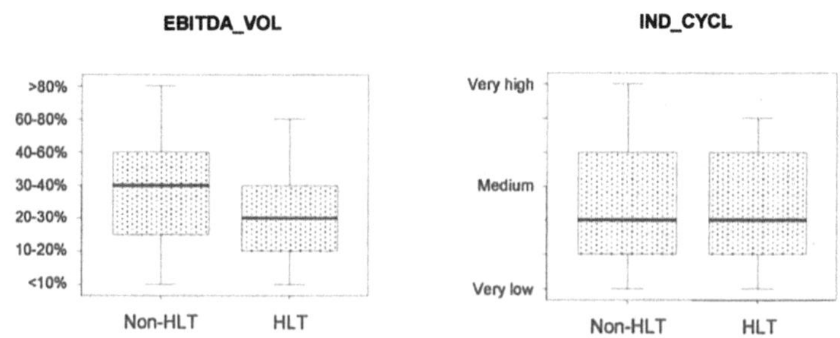

Tests	Mann-Whitney	Pearson-χ2
EBITDA_VOL	810,0**	9,731

Tests	Mann-Whitney	Pearson-χ2
IND_CYCL	970,0	7,252

*, **, *** significant at the 10%-, 5%-, 1%-level

Source: Author.

7.3.1.2. Transaction size

A similar picture arises when comparing the two proxies for transaction size, TRANS_VALUE and SALES. On the basis of the MW test, TRANS_VALUE reveals a difference among HLTs and Non-HLTs, while SALES does not. Though only at the 10 per cent level, a relationship between size and leverage appears to exist.

However, the direction reported by practitioners is not what one would commonly expect, namely that in general larger deals carry more debt. Instead, as figure 45 clearly shows, there is an inverse relationship between transaction value and leverage class.

Figure 45: Univariate analyses – Transaction size

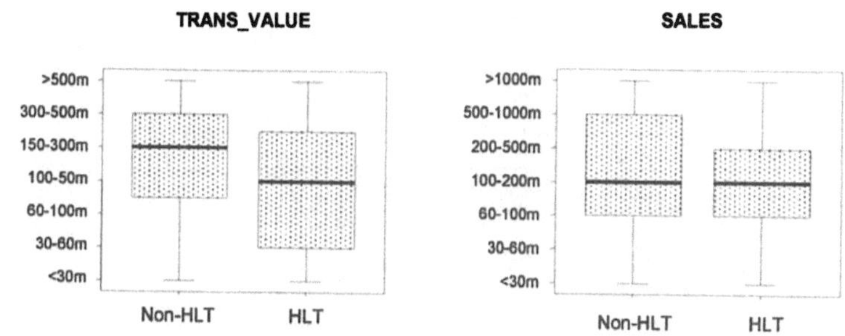

Tests	Mann-Whitney	Pearson-χ2
TRANS_VALUE	852,5*	4,4

Tests	Mann-Whitney	Pearson-χ2
SALES	992,5	4,461

*, **, *** significant at the 10%-, 5%-, 1%-level

Source: Author.

The sales metric, however, does not graphically discriminate between the two groups. They have equal median categories, whereas the spread is higher in the Non-HLT group. Though at first glance the transaction value appears to be a more adequate proxy for the logit regression, the unexpected relationship has to be interpreted on the basis of other analyses.

7.3.1.3. Tangibility

As regards the tangibility variable TANG, again the MW test confirms a significant difference, while the Pearson-χ^2 test fails to identify the relationship. The HLT classification depends on tangibility at the 5 per cent level.

However, the inverse relation as illustrated in figure 46 is surprising and does not conform to the general view of tangible assets being more suited to debt financing. However, given the significant dicriminatory power of TANG, the variable should be a proper metric for the logit model.

Figure 46: Univariate analyses – Tangibility

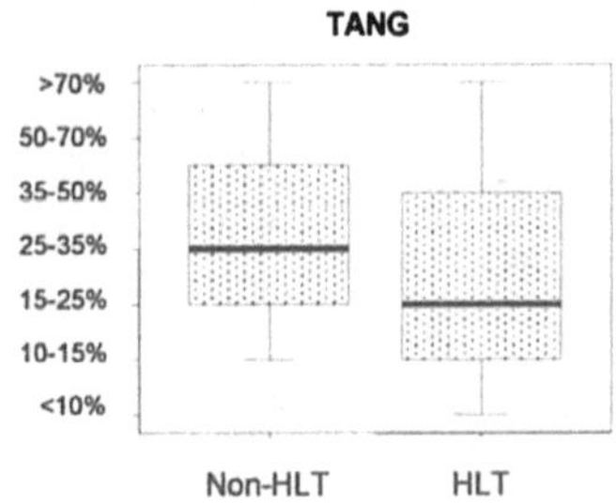

Tests	Mann-Whitney	Pearson-χ2
TANG	794,5**	6,743

*, **, *** significant at the 10%-, 5%-, 1%-level

Source: Author.

7.3.1.4. Growth

A non-parametric test of all three growth metrics generates quite homogenous results as illustrated in figure 47. Yet, while CAPEX and CAGR_SALES are only significant at the 10 per cent level in the MW test, EV/EBITDA shows significance at the 1 per cent level even in the more restrictive Pearson-χ^2 test. The median value differs by one category and the value ranges hardly overlap.

The clear discrimination of HLTs and Non-HLTs reflects the consideration that growth shall be rather financed with equity. Virtually no low-leveraged transactions fall into the lower half of the EV/EBITDA scale.

The box plot for CAGR_SALES does not, despite the significance, appear capable of classifying both groups, since the median categories are equal and the ranges overlap substantially. This might be an indication for the reduced relevance of backward-looking measures.

Figure 47: Univariate analyses – Growth

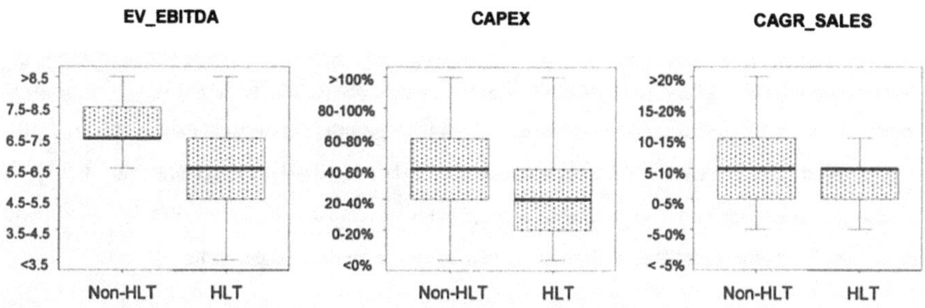

Tests	Mann-Whitney	Pearson-χ2
EV_EBITDA	632,5***	17,834***

Tests	Mann-Whitney	Pearson-χ2
CAPEX	868,5*	8,191

Tests	Mann-Whitney	Pearson-χ2
CAGR_SALES	868,5*	8,191

*, **, *** significant at the 10%-, 5%-, 1%-level

Source: Author.

7.3.1.5. Profitability

EBITDA_SALES as the operationalisation for profitability clearly has a strong influence on the classification as HLT or Non-HLT. Significant at the 1 per cent level in both tests, profitability exhibits a clear positive relationship with debt levels. Figure 48 depicts the box plots and test results of EBITDA_SALES.

Figure 48: Univariate analyses – Profitability

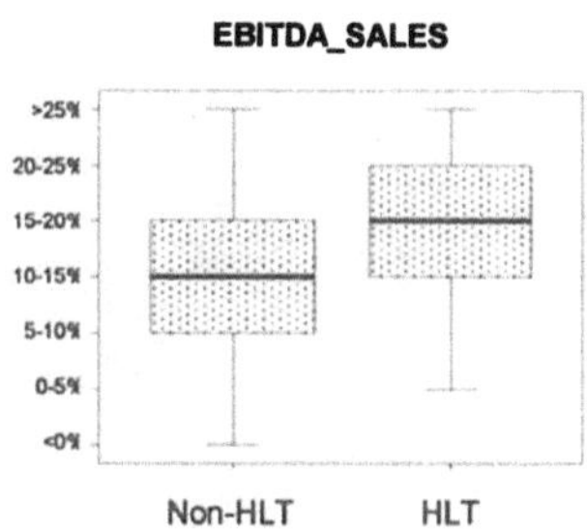

Tests	Mann-Whitney	Pearson-χ2
EBITDA_SALES	638,5***	19,757***

*, **, *** significant at the 10%-, 5%-, 1%-level

Source: Author.

7.3.1.6. *Uniqueness*

The variables approximating a firm's uniqueness, R_D and MARKET_SH, show test results in accordance with the discussions about the variable distributions. The tests and box plots on R_D reflect the inappropriate calibration of the scales. In both groups, the location parameters are equal, showing that R_D is unable to discriminate between HLTs and Non-HLTs. Consequently, both tests exhibit the least significant values, with test statistics of almost zero for the Pearson-χ^2 test and more than 1.000 for the MW test. Both result in p-values exceeding 90 per cent.

In contrast, the variable MARKET_SH shows a high significance level of 1 per cent in both tests. The Pearson-χ^2 test even exhibits the highest value among all variables. The inverse relation conforms to the common understanding that specific assets are rather inappropriate for debt financing. The univariate analysis confirms prior results that instead of R_D, the MARKET_SH should be used in the regression model. See figure 49 for a comparison of both variables.

Figure 49: Univariate analyses – Uniqueness

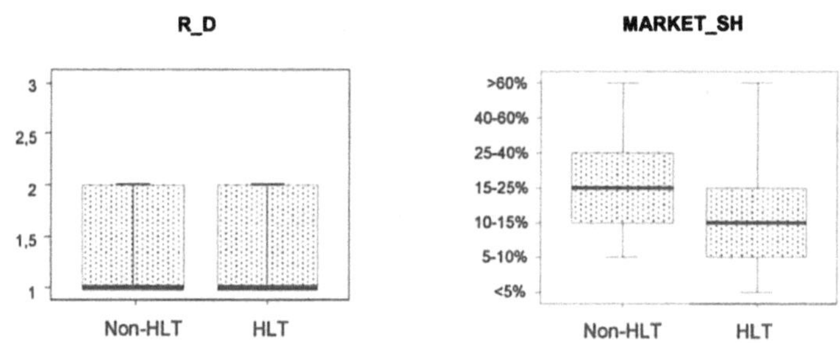

Tests	Mann-Whitney	Pearson-χ2
R_D	1064,5	0,552

Tests	Mann-Whitney	Pearson-χ2
MARKET_SH	683,0***	22,031***

*, **, *** significant at the 10%-, 5%-, 1%-level

Source: Author.

7.3.1.7. Free Cash Flow

For the free cash flow characteristic too, one variable (FCF) proves to be significant in the non-parametric tests. Though only significant at the 10 per cent level in the Pearson-χ^2 test, FCF is highly significant at the 1 per cent level in the MW test.

However, the box plots do not confirm the strong relationship, since both groups share the same median category. In addition, the distribution in the HLT group is right-skewed with many deals cumulating at the upper end of the value range. NFL_FCF conversely, does not appear to have a significant bearing on a firm's leverage. Both tests show unfavourable test statistics, particularly the MW test with a statistic of 1.101. This confirms the earlier notion that FCF appears to be the more powerful operationalisation for an empirical study.

Figure 50: Univariate analyses – Free cash flow

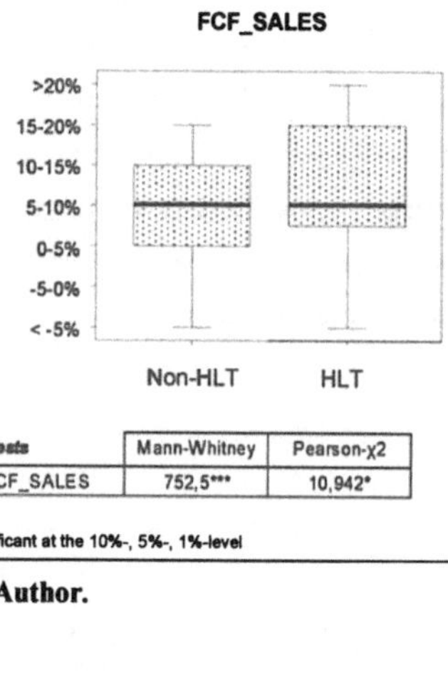

Tests	Mann-Whitney	Pearson-χ2
FCF_SALES	752,5***	10,942*

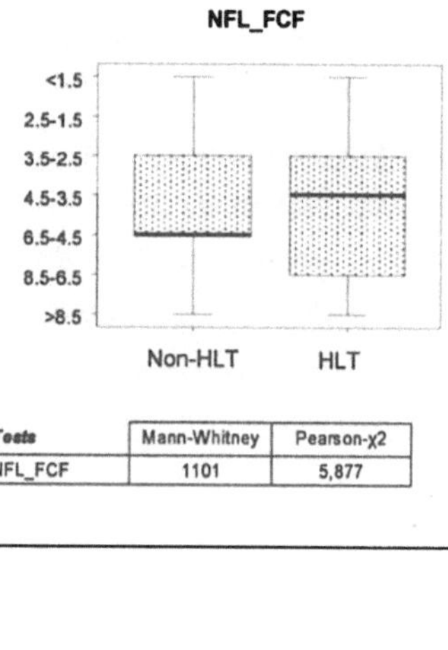

Tests	Mann-Whitney	Pearson-χ2
NFL_FCF	1101	5,877

*, **, *** significant at the 10%-, 5%-, 1%-level

Source: Author.

7.3.2. Non-parametric tests of the use of other financial instruments

Though the study of IBO capital structures focuses on the classification in HLTs and Non-HLTs, the analysis of other financing layers appears necessary to complement the understanding of capital structure decisions. As for the debt/equity choice, the two non-parametric tests shall be applied here, too.[821] Given the minor relevance compared to the HLT classification, the box plots shall be omitted. The following choices are analysed subsequently.[822]

- Equity vs. senior and sub-ordinated debt
- Sub-ordinated debt vs. senior debt and equity
- HYB vs. mezzanine
- Senior A vs. senior B/C

7.3.2.1. Equity capital

In comparison to the HLT/Non-HLT classification, the use of equity can be similarly explained, based on the univariate structure of the characteristics. Since equity represents the counterpart together with sub-ordinated debt, both instruments jointly should exhibit quite the same relationship.[823] As can be seen from table 14, the use of equity shows significance in most variables where senior debt is significant, too. Particularly EBITDA_SALES, MARKET_SH and FCF_SALES are highly significant at the 1 per cent level in the MW test, though the latter shows no significance in the Pearson-χ^2 test. Also, the significance of TANG corresponds to the results for senior debt. However, risk class (EBITDA_VOL and IND_CYCL) reveals adverse results. Moreover, the non-significant relationship between equity share and EV_EBITDA appears surprising since the literature typically proposes a significant positive relation. However, as will be seen in the next chapter, the role of absorbing growth appears to accrue largely to sub-ordinated debt. When measured as CAPEX growth exhibits a significant relation at the 5 per cent level in the MW test and at the 10 per cent level in the Pearson-χ^2 test.

---

821 See chapter 5.3.2.2 for a description of the dummy coding for the four analyses.

822 The use of common/preferred equity vs. shareholder loans is forgone given the results of the descriptive statistics and interviews indicating a split exclusively based on fund-internal considerations.

823 Deviations arise from different underlying definitions of the dummy coding.

Table 14: Two-sample tests - Use of equity

	EQUITY (0/1)	
Variable	Mann-Whitney	Pearson-χ2
EBITDA_VOL	935,0	3,340
IND_CYCL	880,0*	11,323*
TRANS_VALUE	983,5	6,034
SALES	970,5	10,143*
TANG	797,0**	8,580
EV_EBITDA	973,0	5,438
CAPEX	814,0**	11,722*
CAGR_SALES	1030,0	3,179
EBITDA_SALES	523,5***	22,415***
R_D	1075,0	0,158
MARKET_SH	721,0***	12,695**
FCF_SALES	762,0***	9,352
NFL_FCF	920.5	9,647

*, **, *** significant at the 10%-, 5%-, 1%-level

7.3.2.2. Sub-ordinated debt

With only four fairly significant variables, the univariate use of sub-ordinated debt can only be marginally explained by transaction characteristics.

The significance of EV_EBITDA (5 per cent level in the MW test) points to the relevance of sub-ordinated debt in financing growth companies as proposed by VC researchers.[824] Moreover, this aspect is also reflected in the significance of TRANS_VALUE due to the previously mentioned correspondence between TRANS_VALUE and a firm's future growth potential. SALES comes up significantly in both tests, which can be explained by the frequent use of HYBs in predominantly large deals.

Beyond these variables, the two-sample tests do not provide answers to the question of what determines the use of sub-ordinated instruments in general. Only growth and size appear to positively influence the use of sub-ordinated debt in IBOs. See table 15 for the results of the tests.

[824] E.g. Cornelli, F./ Yosha, O. (2003); Gompers, P. (1998); Billingsley, R./ Smith, D. (1996).

Table 15: Two-sample tests - Use of sub-ordinated debt

	SUB (0/1)	
Variable	Mann-Whitney	Pearson-χ2
EBITDA_VOL	978,0	3,346
IND_CYCL	947,5	6,251
TRANS_VALUE	820,5**	7,697
SALES	868,5*	11,370*
TANG	1010,0	7,863
EV_EBITDA	794,5**	8,562
CAPEX	1086,5	13,706**
CAGR_SALES	995,5	2,093
EBITDA_SALES	956,5	5,514
R_D	1058,0	2,698
MARKET_SH	1065,5	5,109
FCF_SALES	1075,5	6,722
NFL_FCF	1063,5	8,458

*, **, *** significant at the 10%-, 5%-, 1%-level

7.3.2.3. HYB vs. mezzanine

The results for the use of HYBs compared to mezzanine as shown in table 16 unambiguously show the dependency on the size of the transaction. Both variables, TRANS_VALUE and SIZE, are highly significant in the tests indicating the imperative need to scale down the enormous issuing cost for publicly traded high-yield bonds. From a univariate perspective, other transaction characteristics do not play a substantial role in determining the use of HYBs.

Table 16: Two-sample tests - Use of HYBs

	HYB (0/1)	
Variable	Mann-Whitney	Pearson-χ2
EBITDA_VOL	555,5	2,849
IND_CYCL	426,0*	5,761
TRANS_VALUE	304,5***	12,594**
SALES	223,0***	19,232***
TANG	574,5	12,094*
EV_EBITDA	452,0	3,890
CAPEX	516,0	3,479
CAGR_SALES	572,5	2,757
EBITDA_SALES	519,0	4,534
R_D	556,5	3,451
MARKET_SH	436,0*	9,824
FCF_SALES	480,5	3,905
NFL_FCF	508,0	2,559

*, **, *** significant at the 10%-, 5%-, 1%-level

7.3.2.4. Senior A vs. senior B/C

So far, all financial instruments have been associated with one or more comprehensible determinants. In contrast, as regards the use of senior A tranches compared to senior B/C tranches, the two tests reveal only minor significance. Besides the significant CAPEX variable in the MW test, only the firm's risk class imposes some noteworthy influence on the choice of instruments.

This might be explainable in light of the cash flow effect of each tranche. While A tranches are redeemable annually, senior B/C debt usually follows a bullet-payment pattern, hence only repayable at maturity.[825] Therefore, in volatile businesses, the positive effect of lower ongoing cash flow payments might compensate for higher interest coupons. Though the direction is not provided in a non-parametric test, the cash flow effect could also explain the significance in CAPEX, since firms requiring high levels of capital expenditures[826] may run short of cash and hence carry more senior B and C tranches. See table 17 for the results of the tests.

Table 17: Two-sample tests - Use of senior A

	SENIOR A (0/1)	
Variable	Mann-Whitney	Pearson-χ2
EBITDA_VOL	971,0	11,363*
IND_CYCL	803,0**	11,278*
TRANS_VALUE	1103,0	9,110
SALES	863,5*	10,609*
TANG	883,5*	5,069
EV_EBITDA	1101,0	3,285
CAPEX	794,0**	6,263
CAGR_SALES	902,0	7,144
EBITDA_SALES	1025,5	3,771
R_D	1064,0	0,150
MARKET_SH	1000,5	3,099
FCF_SALES	1069,0	7,694
NFL_FCF	1086,0	6,233

*, **, *** significant at the 10%-, 5%-, 1%-level

825 See chapter 4.1.2 for a delineation of the types of senior debt.

826 However, the explanation may only hold for firms where past CapEx proxies for equal levels in the future.

7.3.3. Correlation analyses

Having analysed the univariate structure of the explanatory variables, the subsequent section is dedicated to testing the correlation among them. As in all types of regression models, multicolliniarity interferes with the coefficient estimates. An absense of multicolliniarity would require partial correlation coefficients of less than 0,3-0,4 for all coefficient pairs. Otherwise, appropriate counter-measures have to be taken, such as the omission of one of the intercorrelated variables.[827]

As previously discussed, the structure of the data set, ordinal scales and non-normal distributed variables, requires a distribution-free correlation analysis. Of the different potential tools the rank correlation after Spearman is by far the most popular.

Table 18 summarises the pair-wise rank correlation coefficients for all variables.

[827] See Urban, D. (1982), pp. 182-192 for a detailed discussion of multicolliniarity issues and the various methods to overcome them.

Table 18: Intercorrelation of the explanatory variables

	EBITDA_VOL	IND_CYCL	TRANS_VALUE	SALES	TANG	EV_EBITDA	CAPEX	CAGR_SALES	EBITDA_SALES	MARKET_SH	FCF_SALES	NFL_FCF
EBITDA_VOL	1,000	0,096	-0,146	-0,157	0,213**	0,000	-0,096	0,036	-0,227**	0,021	-0,144	-0,028
IND_CYCL		1,000	-0,022	-0,030	0,151	-0,022	0,138	-0,025	-0,222**	-0,148	-0,075	0,126
TRANS_VALUE			1,000	0,399***	-0,130	0,270***	0,088	-0,116	0,048	0,067	0,019	-0,211**
SALES				1,000	0,020	0,176	0,132	-0,093	-0,041	0,184	-0,188	-0,156
TANG					1,000	0,042	0,122	-0,003	-0,241**	-0,003	-0,069	-0,105
EV_EBITDA						1,000	0,046	0,183	0,156	0,001	-0,093	-0,126
CAPEX							1,000	0,093	0,328***	-0,059	-0,196	-0,091
CAGR_SALES								1,000	-0,049	-0,128	0,038	0,219**
EBITDA_SALES									1,000	0,199*	0,196*	0,082
MARKET_SH										1,000	-0,111	-0,082
FCF_SALES											1,000	0,107
NFL_FCF												1,000

*, **, *** significant at the 10%-, 5%, 1%-level

In the correlation analysis, the variable R_D has been omitted due to the miscalibration. All other variables do not exhibit overly strong correlations. None of the pairs exceeds a coefficient of more than 0,5, which would be considered to be a critical correlation.[828] With a coefficient of 0,399, the pair SALES and TRANS_VALUE exhibits the strongest relationship which, however, is not surprising given that they are both proxies for the size of the transaction. Besides SALES, TRANS_VALUE is also significantly intercorrelated with NFL_FCF and EV_EBITDA. While the correlation with NFL_FCF cannot be coherently explained, the correlation with EV_EBITDA reflects the previous discussions. The aspect also explains the surprising univariate result of an inverse relation between TRANS_VALUE and leverage, as growth is associated with lower debt levels. To avoid muddied results, TRANS_VALUE will be omitted in further analyses.

Similarly, CAPEX and CAGR_SALES shall also be excluded from the multivariate regressions, in particular CAGR_SALES given the correlation with EBITDA_SALES. In turn, this variable exhibits further significant (at the 10 per cent level) correlations with EBITDA_VOL, IND_CYCL, and TANG. However, given that EBITDA_SALES represents the only operationalisation for profitability, it needs to remain in the analysis. Moreover, since the risk proxy EBITDA_VOL will be applied, IND_CYLC will drop out of the model. Therefore, only three significant correlations remain, though all pairs only have coefficients slightly above 0.2, which is not likely to trigger any substantial interference.

7.3.4. Summary

The univariate analyses represented a first step in the analysis of IBO capital structures. Of the four sections, the first one constitutes the sample description. Providing a general understanding of the characteristics of the recorded IBOs, it also tested the adequacy of the sample composition for the purpose of the thesis. The results are summarised as follows:

- The unbiased sample size of 94 transactions is in line with previous buyout studies. Given the diversity of the selected IBOs, the sample provides a solid foundation for robust and meaningful results.
- The average capital structure in the sample consists of 53% senior debt, 36% equity capital, and 11% sub-ordinated debt; within the sub-ordinated debt segment mezzanine is clearly preferred by PE professionals
- Except for R_D, all variables have been appropriately recorded in a way that border categories clearly exhibit the lowest frequencies

[828] Urban, D. (1982), p. 187.

- Typical IBO characteristics such as low volatility, low historical growth and rather large transactions are confirmed in the data

Following the descriptive statistics, two non-parametric tests were applied to the influence of a characteristic on the classification as a HLT or Non-HLT. Supported by box-plot illustrations, the results provided an indication for the direction of influence imposed by the various characteristics.

- For all characteristics at least one variable has a significant relationship with the classification as HLT or Non-HLT. Particularly those characteristics for which only one variable was specified (tangibility and profitability) showed significance at the 1 per cent level
- Four variables are significant at least at the 10 per cent level in both tests: EV_EBITDA (growth), EBITDA_SALES (profitability), MARKET_SH (uniqueness), and FCF_SALES (free cash flow)
- Positive associations are exhibited by EBITDA_SALES and FCF_SALES, while EV_EBITDA and MARKET_SH have a negative association
- TRANS_VALUE (size) has an unexpected inverse relation with leverage due to the positive correlation with EV_EBITDA as growth metric
- Four variables are not related to the leverage: IND_CYCL (risk), SALES (size), R_D (uniqueness), and NFL_FCF (free cash flow)
- In addition to senior debt, the use of other financial instruments was also examined. The first two analyses are dedicated to equity and sub-ordinated debt as complementary positions to senior debt. Following these, the detailed layers of HYBs, mezzanine, senior A and senior B/C were examined.
- The analyses display equity to be the main counter-position, while sub-ordinated debt only represents a source of capital to fill the gap between senior debt and equity
- An exception to the use of sub-ordinated debt appears to be the significance of the growth proxies, particularly EV_EBITDA, which confirms the common view of sub-ordinate debt being an adequate instrument for high-growth firms.
- The use of HYBs compared to mezzanine seems to be exclusively associated with the size of the transaction due to the tremendous cost of issuing HYBs. Beyond this, no significant patterns were identified.
- The firm's risk class was identified as the only characteristic having a notable influence on the use of senior A debt vs. senior B/C debt. The different cash flow

profiles probably determine the split between the tranches, depending on the volatility of the business.

Finally, in anticipation of the discussion of multicolliniar variables, the Spearman rank correlation was performed. Besides the positive correlation of SALES and TRANS_VALUE, no critical relationships were identified.

7.4. Binomial logistic regression of the choice debt vs. equity

The nature of univariate analyses does not fully allow challenging the theoretical hypotheses on the financing of IBOs, since the effect of one characteristic is not adjusted for the effects of other characteristics. Instead, a simultaneous estimation of the influences needs to be made by means of a multivariate method. The binomial logistic regression satisfies this condition and shall allow us to test the hypotheses developed in chapter 5. The subsequent chapters elucidate the four-step process of performing logit analyses:

- Model development (1)
- Model estimation (2) and assessment (3)
- Model interpretation (4)

7.4.1. Model development

The development of the main binomial logit model for the classification into HLTs/Non-HLTs must be conditioned on the thesis' objective and preceding analyses. Starting with a long list that comprises all main variables for the seven characteristics and the additional variables recorded in the deal record sheet, the filtering process includes the four steps discussed in chapter 6.3.2.[829] A pre-selection is based on the results of the univariate analyses and multicolliniarity tests followed by the univariable logit analysis that constitutes the last selection stage. Finally, the model specification will be concluded by the introduction of interaction effects.

7.4.1.1. Univariate analyses

Given the importance of selecting the most influential variables for the IBO characteristics, the univariate structure of the tests does not suffice to make final selections on each variable.

---

[829] The additional variables such as ownership structure are only selected on the basis of a Mann-Whitney and Pearson χ^2 test and the subsequent univariable logit analysis.

However, the two-sample non-parametric tests may serve as a filter for the selection of the *additional variables*, as long as clear patterns permit a delineation of influential and non-influential parameters. Hence, in a similar fashion to chapter 7.3.1, the set of variables was screened by means of the Mann-Whitney and Pearson-χ^2 test.

Table 19 summarises the results for both tests, including the p-values to extract the significant variables. As can be seen, only three variables, ASSET_SALES, MGMT_EQUITY[830], and BULK_SHARE exhibit a significant influence (<10 per cent in the MW test) on the classification in HLTs or Non-HLTs. In the more restrictive Pearson-χ^2 test only ASSET_SALES reaches a significant value.

The next most significant variable is the definition as future IPO candidate with a p-value of 0,268 in the MW test and only 0,600 in the Pearson-χ^2 test. As it represents quite a substantial gap vis-à-vis the three mentioned variables, the non-parametric test allows us to discriminate between relevant and irrelevant covariates. Therefore, only these three variables shall be considered going forward. As an additional test of the robustness of the selection, the three variables will be tested by means of a univariable logit analysis.

Table 19: Two-sample tests - Additional variables

	Mann-Whitney-Test (HLT/Non-HLT)		Pearson-χ2 (HLT/Non-HLT)	
Variable	MW-Wert	p-value	χ2-Wert	p-value
SUPERVISORY	1081,000	0,319	0,103	0,748
MGMT_BOARD	1034,000	0,338	0,927	0,336
GROWTH_OPTION	1057,500	0,681	0,170	0,680
BUY_BUILD	1051,000	0,667	0,172	0,678
ASSET_SALES	634,500***	0,000	18,952***	0,003
IPO	989,000	0,268	0,275	0,600
TRADE_SALE	1023,500	0,397	0,327	0,542
SUCCESSION	1098,000	0,709	0,547	0,460
TURNAROUND	991,500	0,356	0,881	0,365
GOING_PRIVATE	1081,000	0,642	0,121	0,721
DIVESTMENT	1010,500	0,392	0,707	0,401
PRIVATISATION	1124,000	0,891	0,382	0,536
MGMT_EQUITY	934,500*	0,094	N/A[a]	N/A
BULK_SHARE	843,500**	0,042	7,255	0,298
INCUMB_MGMT	1034,000	0,401	0,714	0,398
EXT_MGMT	1081,000	0,821	0,052	0,820

*, **, *** significant at the 10%-, 5%, 1%-level

[a] Not applicable due to metrical scale

830 MGMT_EQUITY could not be tested for the Pearson-χ^2 statistic given the metrical scale.

7.4.1.2. Multicolliniarity

As discussed in chapter 7.3.3, a number of variables can be reasonably excluded based on the results of the rank correlation (table 18). Though the correlation coefficients are fairly low, TRANS_VALUE, CAPEX and CAGR_SALES shall be omitted in further analyses. Through this step only four noteworthy correlations remain, of which three are associated with the profitability measure EBITDA_SALES, which, however, needs to remain in the model. In the logit regression, the transaction size has to be proxied by SALES instead of TRANS_VALUE due to the significant correlation with EV_EBITDA.

7.4.1.3. Univariable logit-analysis

Within the selection process, the univariable logit analyis represents the most restrictive filter when based on Wald statistics.[831] The significance of a covariate can be determined on the basis of the improvement in the likelihood of a logit model that includes one covariate as opposed to a model with just the constant. Since the algorithm is equal to the multivariable logit models, the results should best reflect the essential variables. Table 20 summarises the results.[832]

Table 20: Univariable logit analysis

	Univariable logit analysis (HLT/Non-HLT)			
Variable	b_j	s.e. b_j	Wald	p-value
EBITDA_VOL	-0,350**	0,147	5,642	0,018
IND_CYCL	**-0,151**	**0,131**	**1,330**	**0,249**
SALES	-0,115	0,125	0,851	0,356
TANG	-0,346**	0,145	5,691	0,017
EV_EBITDA	-0,562***	0,163	11,931	0,001
EBITDA_SALES	0,496***	0,146	11,465	0,001
MARKET_SH	-0,413***	0,141	8,609	0,003
FCF_SALES	0,436***	0,157	7,696	0,006
NFL_FCF	**0,007**	**0,116**	**0,003**	**0,954**
ASSET_SALES	2,135***	0,526	16,453	0,000
MGMT_EQUITY	**-0,015**	**0,013**	**1,329**	**0,249**
BULK_SHARE	0,305*	0,163	3,496	0,062

*, **, *** significant at the 10%-, 5%-, 1%-level

The table includes all main variables not excluded so far, plus the three selected additional variables. Most of the variables exhibit a clear influence on the classification as a HLT or Non-HLT and therefore confirm the univariate results. However, the variables in *bold* lack sufficient influence

[831] See chapter 6.3.5.1.
[832] Univariable and multivariable binomial logit analyses performed with SPSS Logistic Regression Version 12.0.

and will be omitted in the multivariable regression model. At the same time, the omission of IND_CYCL further reduces the number of interrelated pairs, so that going forward no multicolliniarity problems should exist. Excluding NFL_FCF and MGMT_EQUITY[833] leaves only highly significant variables in the model. The only insignificant variable remaining in the regression is SALES as a proxy for the size of the transaction.

7.4.1.4. Interaction effects

As a last step in the selection process, some relevant interaction effects need to be considered to generate the final model. This is done with a univariable analysis including the arithmetic products of the variable pairs, i.e. the reported ranks for each of the two variables are multiplied. The literature proposes the inclusion of only those interaction effects that are really essential, limiting the total number to 2-3. Otherwise, as a result of higher degrees of freedom, the increased standard errors would overcompensate the improvement in the power of the model.[834] Therefore, only those interactions with significance levels of at least 5 per cent shall be included. Appendix 8 summarises the logits for each of the interaction terms. Two terms are selected that exceed the threshold significance. SALES*EBITDA_VOL is rather surprising since SALES alone does not contribute significantly to the likelihood of the model. However, the influence of the firm's risk conditioned on the firm's size is a good example of the need for simultaneous multivariate regressions. The second term, EV_EBITDA*EBITDA_SALES, reflects the need to distinguish between profitable and unprofitable growth firms.

Table 21 summarises the selection process from the long list to the full model of the binomial logit analysis.

[833] Unlike in the MW test, MGMT_EQUITY shows up insignificantly in the logit analysis, a deviation that roots in the different underlying test methodologies.
[834] Hosmer, D.W./ Lemeshow, S. (2000), p. 98.

Table 21: Logit model development

Selection step	(1) Long list	(2) Univariate analyses	(3) Multicolliniarity	(4) Univariable logit analysis	(5) Interaction effects	Full model logit analysis
Risk class	EBITDA_VOL	X	X	X	X	EBITDA_VOL
	IND_CYCL	X	X			
Transaction size	TRANS_VALUE	X				
	SALES	X	X	X	X	SALES
Tangibility	TANG	X	X	X	X	TANG
Growth	EV_EBITDA	X	X	X	X	EV_EBITDA
	CAPEX	X				
	CAGR_SALES	X				
Profitability	EBITDA_SALES	X	X	X	X	EBITDA_SALES
Uniqueness	R_D					
	MARKET_SH	X	X	X	X	MARKET_SH
Free cash flow	FCF_SALES	X	X	X	X	FCF_SALES
	NFL_FCF	X	X			
Additional variables	SUPERVISORY					
	MGMT_BOARD					
	GROWTH_OPTION					
	BUY_BUILD					
	ASSET_SALES	X	X	X	X	ASSET_SALES
	IPO					
	TRADE_SALE					
	SUCCESSION					
	TURNAROUND					
	GOING_PRIVATE					
	DIVESTMENT					
	PRIVATISATION					
	MGMT_EQUITY	X	X			
	BULK_SHARE	X	X	X	X	BULK_SHARE
	INCUMB_MGMT					
	EXT_MGMT-					
Interaction effects	SALES * EBITDA_VOL				X[a]	SALES * EBITDA_VOL
	EV_EBITDA * EBITDA_SALES				X[a]	EV_EBITDA * EBITDA_SALES

[a] selected upon wald statistics (<5%) in a univariable logit analysis

7.4.2. Model estimation and assessment

The resulting model contains all essential variables and can be subjected to the estimation by means of the Newton-Raphson algorithm. The results are presented in table 22.

Besides the full model, a reduced model was developed which incorporates the six most significant variables.

Table 22: Binomial logit estimation and assessment

		Full logit model (HLT vs. Non-HLT)					Reduced logit model (HLT vs. Non-HLT)				
Characteristics	Variables	b_j	s.e. b_j	Wald	p-value	OR e^b	b_j	s.e. b_j	Wald	p-value	OR e^b
Risk class	EBITDA_VOL	-0,946*	0,521	3,302	0,069	0,388	-0,811**	0,428	3,594	0,042	0,444
Transaction size	SALES	0,104	0,229	0,207	0,649	1,110					
Tangibility	TANG	-0,400*	0,217	3,397	0,065	0,670	-0,466**	0,194	5,769	0,016	0,628
Growth	EV_EBITDA	-1,450*	0,793	3,342	0,068	0,235	-0,564***	0,212	7,055	0,008	0,569
Profitability	EBITDA_SALES	-0,607	0,886	0,469	0,494	0,545					
Uniqueness	MARKET_SH	-0,407**	0,205	3,968	0,046	0,665	-0,415**	0,174	5,661	0,017	0,660
Free cash flow	FCF_SALES	0,750**	0,309	5,889	0,015	2,117	0,546**	0,231	5,557	0,018	1,726
Additional variables	ASSET_SALES	2,189***	0,765	8,198	0,004	8,930	2,077***	0,698	8,843	0,003	7,977
	BULK_SHARE	0,397	0,265	2,247	0,134	1,488					
Interaction effects	SALES * EBITDA_VOL	-0,063	0,400	2,468	0,116	0,939					
	EV_EBITDA * EBITDA_SALES	0,165	0,168	0,972	0,324	1,180					
Constant		6,453	4,867	1,758	0,185		4,608	2,060	5,003	0,025	
	Test	Value	p-value				Value	p-value			
Model significance	LR-Ratio test	63,429***	0,000				53,089***	0,000			
Goodness-of-fit	Cox & Snell-R^2	49,10%	n/a				43,20%	n/a			
	Nagelkerke-R^2	65,40%	n/a				57,50%	n/a			
Predictive power	Hosmer / Lemeshow test	5,905	0,658				10,606	0,225			
	Classification	81,90%	n/a				78,70%	n/a			
-2 Log likelihood		66,882	n/a				77,223	n/a			

*, **, *** significant at the 10%-, 5%, 1%-level

The table reports the results of the binomial logit analysis both for the full and the reduced model. Each estimation contains the regression coefficient b_j, the associated standard error, the resulting Wald statistic, the p-value, and, finally, the odds ratio. In addition, the bottom lines comprise the various tests to assess the quality of the model.

At the 1 per cent level, the likelihood-ratio test confirms the high significance of both the full and the reduced model. Also the two pseudo-R^2 tests included to assess the model's goodness-of-fit achieve high values. At some 50 per cent, even the restrictive Cox & Snell test exhibits an R^2 that clearly exceeds the threshold of 30-40 per cent, as mentioned in the literature.[835] Being closest to the R^2 as known from linear regressions, the Nagelkerke-R^2 reaches 65 per cent, i.e. about two-thirds of the variations in the data can be explained through the logistic regression. The reduced model exhibits lower values, indicating that although the omitted values were insignificant relative to the other covariates, their omission leads to a reduction in the model fit.

As regards the tests on the predictive power of the model, the Hosmer-Lemeshow test and the classification, both results are in line with the goodness-of-fit tests. With a statistic of 5,905 and a p-value of 65.8 per cent, the Hosmer-Lemeshow test is very distant to a significant χ^2-value reflecting a good predictive power. Similarly, the classification shows that for 81.9 per cent of the IBOs, the capital structure would have been predicted correctly as regards allocation to the groups HLT and Non-HLT. The reduced model exhibits a substantially lower predictive power when subjected to the Hosmer / Lemeshow test given the higher χ^2-value (p-value 22.5 per cent). However, in terms of classification, the reduced model would also be a good basis for predicting allocation to the HLT and Non-HLT categories.

The lower loglikelihood multiplied by –2 in the full model also indicates the better predictive power of the full model. However, since the reduced model has fewer degrees of freedom, the standard errors of each coefficient are substantially mitigated, leading to lower p-values. Overall, the tests confirm that the model is of a high quality and that results for the individual convariates are robust.

7.4.3. Model interpretation and discussion of IBO financing hypotheses

Having estimated a robust logistic regression, the subsequent section is devoted to the interpretation and discussion of the model results. Confirming the general picture of the univariate analyses, the binomial logit analyses of the IBO capital structures generate a number of interesting findings. The trade-off theory appears to best explain the capital structures of IBOs, whereas agency considerations fail in part to describe the financial policy. The outcome is surprising to the extent that a number of academics have refused to support the trade-off theory in the past.[836]

[835] See chapter 6.3.4.1.
[836] See chapter 3.1.4.2.

Table 23 summarises the hypotheses and the evidence from this empirical study. Contrasted with results from prior corporate finance studies, the table depicts whether a hypothesis is accepted or rejected.

Table 23: Hypotheses and empirical evidence on IBO financing

	Prior empirical evidence	*Results of this study*	Trade-off theory	Agency context
Risk class	-	-	- (H1a) ✓	- (H1b) ✓
Transaction size	+	o	+ (H2a) ✗	+ (H2b) ✗
Tangibility	+	-	- (H3a) ✓	+ (H3b) ✗
Growth	-	-	- (H4a) ✓	- (H4b) ✓
Profitability	-	o	+ (H5a) ✗	+ (H5b) ✗
Uniqueness	-	-	- (H6a) ✓	o (H6b) ✗
Free Cash Flow	o	+	+ (H7a) ✓	+ (H7b) ✓

Note: + = significantly positive relationship; - = significantly negative relationship; o = not significant or indeterministic relationship

The empirical study confirms 8 of the overall 14 hypotheses. The trade-off theory accounts for 5 correct predictions. Except for transaction size and profitability, the directions of all variables were predicted correctly.

Agency considerations only conform to the influence of risk class, free cash flow and growth, the other hypotheses are rejected. However, the observed influences must also be discussed in light of the different sources of agency cost, since the hypotheses were inconclusive in the case of uniqueness. The influence of uniqueness can be explained by the threat of underinvestment. Overall, the results underpin agency cost of debt to be slightly more prevalant. That means, leverage rather serves to mitigate the agency cost of debt than the cost of equity. At first glance, the weak impact of the agency cost of equity might generally be explained by the management equity share.

The subsequent section contains an in-depth discussion of the model results. Specifically, the observed influences are discussed in light of the hypotheses developed in chapter 5.2. and respective prior empirical results.

7.4.3.1. *Risk class*

EBITDA_VOL as proxy for risk class exhibits a significant (at 10 per cent level) negative relation to the HLT group membership, which conforms to the results of the majority of prior empirical studies. Since hypothesis 1a stated the inverse relation, the trade-off theory can be confirmed in the case of risky firms. The results also confirm hypothesis 1b suggesting the relevance of both agency cost of debt and equity for risky businesses.

To further interpret the effect, the absolute stength of the influence should be studied by way of the odds ratio given in the last column of the model. An odds ratio of 0,388 implies that an increase by one in the risk class reduces the odds of being structured as an HLT by more than 60 per cent. Given this substantial influence, it underpins the relevance of the financial distress cost.

7.4.3.2. *Transaction size*

The transaction size operationalised through the SALES of the firm exhibits an insignificant positive relation, a surprising result given that both hypotheses, 2a for the trade-off theory and 2b for the agency context, predict a significant positive relation. Therefore, with regard to the deal size, both theories must be rejected for IBOs.

The lack of a size-dependent effect also contradicts the majority of prior corporate finance studies that obeserved a significantly positive influence. Many of them also applied sales as a proxy for firm size.[837] Moreover, the odds ratio of 1,11 confirms the minor relevance of the firm's size for determining classification as a highly leveraged deal. In interviews, most practitioners have acknowledged a market dichotomy with regard to financing large and small deals in that it is easier to obtain senior debt for large than for small and medium-sized transactions. In light of the anecdotal evidence, the results appear even more surprising. In order to further investigate the results, the questions at the end of the deal record sheet are analysed in more detail, addressing a potential credit constraint.

Figure 51 reports the results for two analyses based on these questions. One question addressed the difficulty of obtaining senior debt, allowing answers of "*easy*", "*as usual*", and "*difficult*". To enable a non-parametric Pearson-χ^2 test of the answers, the sales results have to be allocated to

[837] See chapter 5.3.1.2.

large deals (≥ category 4 on the scale equalling ≥ €100m sales[838]) and small deals (categories 1-3). This allows a cross-tabulation of the results and a subsequent test of the two samples. The left-hand side in the figure depicts the results that prove a significant relationship at the 10 per cent level. A brief glance at the distribution in the table already shows that large deals obtained senior debt more easily than small deals. Therefore, the results confirm the general claim of practitioners.

However, the obvious contradiction to the insignificant coefficient in the logit model requires a direct comparison of the credit constraint classification and the HLT/Non-HLT group membership. The result of the respective Pearson-χ^2 test is reported on the right-hand side of figure 51. With a two-tailed significance level of 81,6 per cent, a relationship between credit constraint and leverage must be rejected.

Considering that the answer to the second question in the deal record sheet "*Have you received the amount of senior debt you asked for?*" was "*yes*" for 82 per cent of the transactions, one can only assume an additional equity or sub-ordinated debt buffer in large transactions. Raising this point in follow-up interviews, some of the interviewees confirmed that despite more available senior debt they had decided to stick to a conservative senior debt level. In their view a more aggressive capital structure would have jeopardised the opportunity of realising the future value appreciation of their investment. In addition they feared the reputation loss for the next fund raising. In other words, beyond the known cost of financial distress,[839] the expected opportunity cost prompt PE professionals to use less senior debt than they could well have obtained. For PE funds the indirect cost are obviously of greatest relevance and impose substantial pressure to pursue a defensive financing strategy. Consequently, going forward theoretical discussions on the relevance of direct and indirect distress cost need to consider the specific background of the borrower ideally from a dynamic perspective.[840]

838 Applying €100m as the cut-off value is somewhat arbitrary but conforms to the threshold mentioned by practitioners.

839 In fact, the study of Cays, S.E. (2001) identified a positive relationship between size and indirect cost of financial distress as defined today (p. 11).

840 For example, the previously mentionned empirical study by Warner, J. (1976) might have revealed a different outcome if he had incorporated indirect cost.

Figure 51: Credit constraint and leverage

Crosstable: difficulty of obtaining senior debt and firm size

Sales_binär * difficulty Crosstabulation

Count

		difficulty			
		easy	as usual	difficult	Total
Sales_binär	<4*	6	12	12	30
	>= 4	19	33	12	64
Total		25	45	24	94

Chi-Square Tests

	Value	df	Asymp. Sig. (2-sided)
Pearson Chi-Square	4,904ᵃ	2	,086
Likelihood Ratio	4,713	2	,095
Linear-by-Linear Association	3,711	1	,054
N of Valid Cases	94		

a. 0 cells (,0%) have expected count less than 5. The minimum expected count is 7,66.

* < 4 equals a sales value of < €100m

Crosstable: difficulty of obtaining senior debt and HLT/Non-HLT classification

HLT * difficulty Crosstabulation

Count

		difficulty			
		easy	as usual	difficult	Total
HLT	Non-HLT	13	21	13	47
	HLT	12	24	11	47
Total		25	45	24	94

Chi-Square Tests

	Value	df	Asymp. Sig. (2-sided)
Pearson Chi-Square	,407ᵃ	2	,816
Likelihood Ratio	,407	2	,816
Linear-by-Linear Association	,020	1	,887
N of Valid Cases	94		

a. 0 cells (,0%) have expected count less than 5. The minimum expected count is 12,00.

Note: The black arrows indicate the relevant chi-aquare statistics

Source: Author.

7.4.3.3. Tangibility

With a negative coefficient, the tangibility covariate represents another surprising influence that contradicts prior empirical research. Significant at the 10 per cent level, TANG exhibits an odds ratio of 0,670 that indicates a substantial absolute strength of the influence. As stated in chapter 5.2.3, the common belief that collateralisable tangible assets are more apt for debt financing cannot be assumed for IBOs, given that senior debt is mainly granted on a future cash flow basis. The cognition of a negative influence complies with hypothesis 3a predicting an inverse relation based on the existence of non-debt tax shields which are higher for depreciation-intense firms. Depreciation of tangible assets reduces the taxable income and thus mitigates the benefits from interest deduction. This result contradicts earlier studies that question the relevance of non-debt tax shields.[841] Hypothesis 3b of a positive relation based on agency considerations must however be rejected.

The increased earnings volatility as a result of a higher operating leverage underpins the relevance of the trade-off theory for the explanation of the negative influence. Tangible asset-intensive industries often have higher shares of fixed cost (e.g. maintenance) resulting in a higher sensitivity to sales fluctuations.

The intercorrelation in table 18 confirms a significant, albeit minor, correlation between the variables EBITDA_VOL and TANG. Therefore, as far as cash-flow lending transactions are concerned (e.g. classical project financing), the influence of a firm's tangibility must be related to the increased cash-flow volatility rather than to the potential to collateralise assets.

7.4.3.4. Growth

From the perspective of both the trade-off theory and agency considerations, growth was seen to impose higher cost of leverage leading to lower senior debt levels. Measured by EV_EBITDA, the binomial logit analysis confirms a significantly stronger inverse relation than previously identified both in the non-parametric tests and in prior corporate finance studies.

EV_EBITDA particularly exhibits a very low odds ratio of 0,235 reflecting the strong influence of growth on a firm's capital structure. Therefore, both hypotheses 4a and 4b can be accepted at the 10 per cent level.

Interestingly, EV_EBITDA has a substantially higher odds ratio in the reduced logit model with an increase from 0,235 to 0,569. A general reduction in the odds ratios for variables with very low or very high ratios can be explained by a lower goodness-of-fit of the reduced model. However, the significant increase is due to the omission of the interaction effect that incorporates the variable.

7.4.3.5. Profitability

Pure economic reasoning would suggest a positive relation between profitability and leverage. However, corporate finance studies have predominantly found an inverse relation explained by the pecking-order theory which has been excluded from he theoretical framework for explaining IBO capital structures.

Hypothesis 5a relates to the economic reasoning given that the expected cost of financial distress is lower for profitable firms for a specific business risk. Conversely, hypothesis 5b also predicts a positive relation. However, here the reason relates to an increased level of agency cost of equity since a higher profitability implies c.p. higher free cash flow levels.

Neither of these two hypotheses can be accepted, though the observed negative influence is not significant. With a low Wald statistic and high p-value of 0,494 respectively, the influence of

[841] See chapter 3.3.3.

profitability represents a surprising result. And as the existence of a pecking order cannot be assumed, it appears difficult to explain. However, one cause may be found in the relevance of EBITDA. Interviewees have acknowledged EBITDA only in conjunction with capital expenditures and the effective tax rate for determining the debt capacity. According to interview results, free cash flow (i.e. EBITDA minus CapEx and change in working capital) is the appropriate measure for determining the maximum amount of senior debt for the deal. Therefore, the insignificant coefficient could just reflect a limited relevance of EBITDA as a stand-alone indicator.

7.4.3.6. Uniqueness

The proxy for uniqueness, the firm's market share, confirms the results from the univariate analysis. Significant at the 5 per cent level, MARKET_SH exhibits a negative influence on the likelihood of being structured as a HLT. The result confirms hypothesis 6a that relates the negative influence to the higher level of liquidation cost, since specific assets are less marketable given that there are fewer available buyers.

In an agency context, highly specific assets impose a substantial degree of outcome uncertainty, i.e. the agent's actions are more difficult to assess in light of a certain outcome. However, since the uncertainty applies to debtholders and shareholders alike, both types of agency cost tend to rise resulting in an indeterminate net influence. Therefore, given the univariate and multivariate results, hypothesis 6b of an indeterminate relation must be rejected.

The impact of a firm's uniqueness appears to be best described by the predictions of the trade-off theory, specifically the argumentation based on the expected cost of financial distress. However, from an agency perspective the negative influence supports the argumentation by WALD (1999) that firms are more likely to be underinvested if they exhibit specific assets.

7.4.3.7. Free cash flow

As already mentioned in the section on profitability, free cash flow is considered by practitioners to be one of the main determinants of IBO capital structures. Similar to the prediction of profitability, free cash flow is considered to reduce the expected cost of financial distress and increase the existence of agency cost of equity. Consequently, both hypotheses 7a and 7b express a positive relation.

In fact, the practitioner's view and theoretical predictions can be confirmed by the logit model. Being significant at the 5 per cent level, FCF_SALES has the highest odds ratio among the 7 characteristics, with a value of 2,117. This implies a doubling of an IBO's odds of being highly leveraged for an increase by one category in the FCF_SALES variable.

7.4.4. Discussion of additional explanatory variables

In addition to the main characteristics, the final logit model includes asset sales and the number of bulk shareholders. Both have been selected from a larger set of variables based on the results in the two-sample tests and univariable logit analyes.

7.4.4.1. Asset sales

Whether a firm plans to sell off parts of its asset base has a tremendous influence on the likelihood of becoming an HLT. At a significance level of 1 per cent, the null hypothesis of an independency of asset sales can be clearly rejected. Even more striking appears the odds ratio of 8,930. However, it has to be remembered that the questionnaire records planned asset sales only as a binary variable with yes/no answers, whereas the main firm characteristics have a 7-category scale. Therefore, an increase by one for asset sales implies a far stronger shift in the explanatory variable than would the same increase for the rest. An odds ratio of 8,9 implies that the odds of being structured as an HLT are 9 times higher if the firm plans to sell off assets.

The straightforward reason for the significant influence lies in the increased debt capacity beyond the level of the yearly free cash flow. IBO managers attempt to match the amortisation schedule of the senior debt with the one-off cash-in from asset sales.

7.4.4.2. *Bulk shareholding*

The number of bulk shareholders is the second additional variable. The relevance of ownership dispersion has been frequently discussed in the context of agency cost.[842] However, its significance in the univariate analysis was not confirmed in the multivariate model. Although the influence is not significant, the positive relation becomes manifest in a high odds ratio of 1.488, i.e. one additional bulk shareholder increases the odds by almost 50 per cent. Nonetheless, the result does not conform to earlier empirical evidence that the involvement of bulk shareholders reduces the level of agency cost of equity and hence should lead to lower debt levels.[843]

7.5. Logit analyses of other financing layers

The analysis of the use of equity capital represents the first analysis of a set of logistic regressions on other financing layers. So far, the dependent variable consisted of senior debt to classify a deal as HLT or Non-HLT. Going forward, the discussions of equity capital and sub-ordinated debt constitute the complementary analyses and round off the picture on the top-level capital structure choice. These two analyses will be followed by a discussion of second-layer instruments, notably the choice between mezzanine and HYB and senior A versus senior B/C debt tranches. In general, the subsequent sections follow the same procedure as the previous logit analysis except for the model development. Drawing on the selection of variables, the analysis of the other financial instruments focuses solely on the 7 main characteristics, as they stand in the center of the theoretical discussions and allow comparisons with the HLT/Non-HLT model.

7.5.1. Binomial logistic regression of the use of equity

As a first step in understanding the financial policy with regard to instruments other than senior debt, the choice of equity versus senior and sub-ordinated debt will be examined. As discussed in chapter 5.3.2.2, the dummy variables for high and low shares of equity derived from the sample median, therefore assuming a classification methodology analogous to the HLT/Non-HLT classification.

---

[842] E.g. Lins, K.V. (2003); LaPorta, R./ Lopez-de-Silanes, F./ Shleifer, A. (1999); Inderst, R./ Müller, H.M. (1999); Shleifer, A./ Vishny, R.W. (1997); McConnell, J.J./ Servaes, H. (1995).

[843] Lins, K.V. (2003), p. 181.

7.5.1.1. *Model estimation and assessment*

Below are the results from the binomial logit estimation of the use of equity capital. For each characteristic the coefficient, Wald statistic and odds ratio are reported. Overall, the model passes all quality tests quite satisfactorily. With significance below 1 per cent, the covariates contribute substantially to the understanding of the use of equity. The two goodness-of-fit statistics confirm the quality of the model with 43 per cent and 45 per cent respectively.

In addition, the classification tests underpin the significance of the model. Interestingly, however, the classification of some 82 per cent matches the previous logistic regression exactly despite worse results in all other tests. This reflects the fact that the classification achieves better results if the model contains few highly significant variables (p-value < 1 per cent) with the others being insignificant than if all variables had minor levels of significance (p-value 5-10 per cent). Conversely, goodness-of-fit statistics reflect the reverse constellation, where few insignificant variables decrease the value of the statistic. In other words, a mixture of variables with very high and very low p-values achieves the best classification outcome.[844]

Table 24: Binomial logit analysis - Use of equity

			EQUITY (0/1)	
Characteristics	Variable	b_j	Wald	Odds-ratio e^b
Risk class	EBITDA_VOL	-0,069	0,156	0,934
Transaction size	SALES	-0,482**	5,541	0,652
Tangibility	TANG	0,308*	2,964	1,361
Growth	EV_EBITDA	0,124	0,461	1,132
Profitability	EBITDA_SALES	-0,578***	10,733	0,561
Uniqueness	MARKET_SH	0,462***	7,051	1,587
Free cash flow	FCF_SALES	-0,432**	5,972	0,649
Constant		2,620	1,556	
	Test	Value	p-value	
Model significance	LR-Ratio test	39,232***	0,000	
Goodness-of-fit	Cox & Snell-R^2	43,10%	n/a	
	Nagelkerke-R^2	45,50%	n/a	
Predictive power	Hosmer / Lemeshow-test	6,792	0,559	
	Classification	81,90%	n/a	
-2 Log likelihood		90,909	n/a	

*, **, *** significant at the 10%-, 5%, 1%-level

[844] Pampel, F.C. (2000), p. 25.

7.5.1.2. Model interpretation

Focussing on the individual covariates, what clearly comes out of the regression is the complementarity to the senior debt coefficients. With the exception of risk class and profitability, all variables show the reverse direction to the previous regression. This had not been anticipated since the influence of sub-ordinated debt could have interfered with the coefficients of equity. For example, as will be seen in the next chapter, the interference becomes transparent for the risk class and growth variable. While both are significant for sub-ordinated debt, they are not relevant for equity, a fact that comes as a surprise because equity is considered to be particularly essential for high-growth and high-risk firms. Below are the interpretations for each variable:

- The use of equity shows an insignificant negative relationship with **risk class**. Given the odds-ratio close to 1, this model does not suggest that risk is an important determinant of the equity volume injected by the PE fund.
- In contrast, **transaction size** exhibits a highly significant (5 per cent) negative relation with the use of equity and a low odds ratio. As opposed to the senior debt regression, this could be a result of fund-internal considerations. In order to avoid bulk risks through investment in only few deals, they limit the equity injections for large deals. Otherwise, just a small number of deals would absorb substantial shares of a fund. Therefore, with growing deal sizes, the equity injections tend to be lower, which would explain the inverse relation.
- **Tangibility** as a determinant shows some significant influence. Also, the odds ratio of 1,361 does indicate a certain impact on the use of equity. However, apart from complementarity, there is no conclusive explanation for the influence.
- The influence of **growth** is not significant, i.e. the hypothesis of a non-existent influence cannot be rejected. The odds ratio of 1,132 underlines the absence of a substantial impact.
- With a Wald statistic of 10.7, **profitability** exhibits the most significant negative influence on the choice of equity. Moreover, an odds ratio of 0,561 reflects a substantial absolute impact of this characteristic. Unlike the HLT/Non-HLT regression, the use of equity better reflects the theoretical predictions in the way that according to both trade-off and agency considerations more profitable firms should carry more senior debt and less equity.

- With an odds ratio of 1,587, a firm's **uniqueness** has the strongest positive influence in absolute terms. With a significance of <1 per cent, unique firms are clearly financed with more equity than non-unique firms. This could be an indication that increases in agency cost due to the higher outcome uncertainty are lower for shareholders than debtholders.
- The significant negative influence of **free cash flow** confirms the senior debt regression in the way that shareholders face higher agency cost in the presence of strong free cash flow levels. The odds ratio of 0,649 indicates that the use of equity capital is quite sensitive to free cash flow.

7.5.2. Binomial logistic regression of the use of sub-ordinated debt

Beyond the debt/equity choice, probably the most interesting and theoretically relevant analysis is the question which firm characteristics determine the use of sub-ordinated debt.

7.5.2.1. Model estimation and assessment

Examining the use of sub-ordinated debt, the respective logit model shows results clearly inferior to the two previous ones. A *–2LL* of 115,210 indicates a low model quality. Accordingly, the likelihood ratio test confirms only a significance at the 10 per cent level. Even less satisfactory results are indicated by the R^2-tests with goodness-of-fit statistics of 13,9 per cent and 18,6 per cent respectively. This reflects the lack of significant covariates in the model. Conversely, the two predictive power tests indicate an average quality. As previously mentioned, however, this result roots in the different structure of the tests.

The results for the individual covariates as well as the model tests are somewhat muddied given the rather low number of 52 IBOs that employ sub-ordinated debt instruments. Although with as few as 7 explanatory variables the logit specification should be sufficiently robust, the standard error of the estimation is higher than for the previous regressions, leading to generally lower significance levels. This means that the relation between the characteristics and the use of sub-ordinated debt may be underestimated by the model. However, the general outcome of the estimation should not alter substantially for larger sample sizes. Table 25 summarises the results of the use of sub-ordinated debt.

Table 25: Binomial logit analysis - Use of sub-ordinated debt

		SUB (0/1)		
Characteristics	Variable	b_i	Wald	Odds-ratio e^b
Risk class	EBITDA_VOL	0,283*	3,082	1,328
Transaction size	SALES	0,280*	3,534	1,323
Tangibility	TANG	-0,690	0,204	0,933
Growth	EV_EBITDA	0,356**	4,771	1,428
Profitability	EBITDA_SALES	0,238	2,298	1,269
Uniqueness	MARKET_SH	-0,032	0,049	0,969
Free cash flow	FCF_SALES	0,103	0,398	1,109
Constant		-4,678	5,621	
	Test	Value	p-value	
Model significance	LR-Ratio test	14,036*	0,051	
Goodness-of-fit	Cox & Snell-R^2	13,90%	n/a	
	Nagelkerke-R^2	18,60%	n/a	
Predictive power	Hosmer / Lemeshow-test	8,154	0,398	
	Classification	68,10%	n/a	
-2 Log likelihood		115,210	n/a	

*, **, *** significant at the 10%-, 5%, 1%-level

7.5.2.2. Model interpretation

With only three significant covariates, the use of sub-ordinated debt does not appear to be highly determined by characteristics of the transaction. This may lead one to the conclusion that sub-ordinated debt serves to fill a potential gap between equity and senior debt, particularly given that only 52 out of 94 IBOs use sub-ordinated instruments at all. PE funds seem mainly to fall back on sub-ordinated instruments when other sources of bank capital are scarce. Exceptions appear to be situations with severe agency problems.

- With a significance level of 10 per cent, **risk class** has a positive influence on the use of sub-ordinated debt. Given the insignificant impact on equity, a high level of risk seems to be absorbed by above-average amounts of sub-ordinated debt.
- **Transaction size** exhibits an almost identical result to risk class. The reason for the slightly positive influence may be twofold. First of all, the gap-filling function appears to hold again, given the significant inverse relation between size and equity together with an insignificant influence on senior debt. Moreover, as will be shown in the next chapter and was mentioned in the section on the two-sample tests[845], size

[845] See chapter 7.3.2.2.

has a highly significant influence on the use of high-yield bonds. The strong influence may also reflect the frequent use of HYBs in large deals.

- Both the significance level and the odds ratio indicate that a firm's **tangibility** does not have a substantial influence on the use of sub-ordinated debt.
- In contrast, **growth** exhibits a highly significant influence on the use of sub-ordinated debt, and this is also expressed by the odds ratio of 1,428. Confirming the univariate result, sub-ordinated debt appears to be well suited to finance growth options. The flexibility of sub-ordinated instruments mitigates the relevance of agency cost faced by debtholders in growing firms.
- The result for **profitability** does not reflect a distinct impact on the use of sub-ordinated debt.
- **Uniqueness**, as expressed by the firm's market share, has the lowest impact both in terms of significance and odds ratio. With the latter achieving merely 0,969 the use of sub-ordinated debt will remain quite the same, no matter how unique the firm may be.
- Finally, **free cash flow** also exhibits only insignificant results. The complementary use of senior debt and equity appears to be the only determinant of sub-ordinated debt.

7.5.3. Binomial logistic regression of second-layer instruments

All three generic types of capital, senior debt, equity and sub-ordinated debt, have been analysed in depth, and the results provide a comprehensive picture of their use in IBOs. However, the discussion of IBO capital structures should include an analysis of second-layer instruments, as substantial differences can be expected given the diverse characteristics which instruments may incorporate.

The structure follows the approach of the univariate analyses by studying first the use of high-yield bonds versus mezzanine instruments and second, the use of senior A versus senior B/C debt.

7.5.3.1. Sub-ordinated debt: High-yield bonds vs. Mezzanine

As the descriptive statistics have suggested, PE professionals prefer either to use only HYBs or mezzanine. A mixture of both was only identified in 9 transactions. By sharply differentiating between HYB-based deals and mezzanine-based deals, it should be possible to identify the factors of influence.

7.5.3.1.1. Model estimation and assessment

At first glance, the analysis of the use of HYBs reveals contradictory results with regard to the quality of the model. While the R^2-statistics reflect a rather poor model quality, particularly in the Cox & Snell test, all other tests show quite strong results. Especially the classification suggests a powerful regression.

However, as mentioned earlier, the presence of a single highly significant covariate in conjuction with all other variables being neglegible leads to the strong classification result, which proves to be even stronger than in the HLT regression. Though clearly less significant than in the HLT and equity regression, the likelihood-ratio test shows that the model achieves high significance levels of 1 per cent. Obviously, the results are based exclusively on the influence of the characteristic transaction size. Without the other 6 covariates, quite similar results could have been expected.

The outcome of both R^2-statistics and the Cox & Snell test have a strong tendency to underestimate the power of regression models, given that all other statistics including the –2 loglikelihood generated robust results.

Table 26 depicts the regression estimates on the use of HYBs.

Table 26: Binomial logit analysis - Use of HYBs

		HYB (0/1)		
Characteristics	Variable	b_j	Wald	Odds-ratio e^b
Risk class	EBITDA_VOL	0,019	0,008	1,019
Transaction size	SALES	0,804***	8,708	2,234
Tangibility	TANG	0,009	0,001	1,009
Growth	EV_EBITDA	0,219	0,881	1,244
Profitability	EBITDA_SALES	0,222	1,047	1,249
Uniqueness	MARKET_SH	0,250	1,428	1,284
Free cash flow	FCF_SALES	0,028	0,013	1,029
Constant		-8,954	9,303	
	Test	Value	p-value	
Model significance	LR-Ratio test	20,464***	0,005	
Goodness-of-fit	Cox & Snell-R^2	19,60%	n/a	
	Nagelkerke-R^2	33,50%	n/a	
Predictive power	Hosmer / Lemeshow-test	7,343	0,5	
	Classification	87,20%	n/a	
-2 Log likelihood		62,061	n/a	

*, **, *** significant at the 10%-, 5%, 1%-level

7.5.3.1.2. Model interpretation

In light of the estimated coefficients, the interpretation is straightforward, and the variables do not need to be discussed separately. Transaction size measured by SALES is found to have the most distinct influence on the use of HYB. As raised in the univariate analysis,[846] issuing HYB requires substantial resources, e.g. for the rating process and the development of an adequate bondholder reporting. The cost associated with the entire process can only be scaled down in large transactions. With a high odds ratio of 2,234 an increase in the sales category more than doubles the chances of HYB financing. Conversely, all other characteristics have no systematic influence on the use of HYBs. Since the covariates only achieve minor Wald statistics and odds ratios, there is no base for further interpreting the surprising result.

7.5.3.2. Senior debt: Senior A vs. Senior B/C

The amortisation schedule and the interest level distinguish mainly A and B/C tranches of senior debt. The factors that determine the use of the different types will be studied in the final regression.

[846] See chapter 7.3.2.3.

7.5.3.2.1. Model estimation and assessment

Except for the classification, all model assessment tests reflect a very low quality of the logit model for the choice of senior A debt. Low values for the R^2-tests in conjunction with a poor LR-statistic prove that the choice of senior A tranches are hardly influenced by transaction characteristics. However, as in the previous regressions, the good result in the classification can be explained by the single significant variable transaction size.

Table 27: Binomial logit analysis - Use of senior A

		SENIOR A (0/1)		
Characteristics	Variable	b_j	Wald	Odds-ratio e^b
Risk class	EBITDA_VOL	-0,175	1,357	0,839
Transaction size	SALES	-0,340**	5,187	0,712
Tangibility	TANG	0,268	3,135	1,307
Growth	EV_EBITDA	0,071	0,219	1,073
Profitability	EBITDA_SALES	-0,025	0,031	0,975
Uniqueness	MARKET_SH	0,150	1,179	1,162
Free cash flow	FCF_SALES	-0,005	0,001	0,975
Constant		-0,043	0,142	
	Value	Wert	p-value	
Model significance	LR-Ratio test	10,106	0,183	
Goodness-of-fit	Cox & Snell-R^2	10,20%	n/a	
	Nagelkerke-R^2	13,60%	n/a	
Predictive power	Hosmer / Lemeshow-test	10,343	0,242	
	Classification	78,70%	n/a	
-2 Log likelihood		120,163	n/a	

*, **, *** significant at the 10%-, 5%, 1%-level

7.5.3.2.2. Model interpretation

Only transaction size is seen to have a significant influence on the use of senior A debt. However, tangibility also has some considerable impact.

Transaction size exhibits a substantial inverse relation between the use of senior A and senior B/C tranches. With a significance level of 5 per cent, the use of senior A tranches is relatively less frequent in large deals. This result might be attributable to the fact that for large volumes banks split senior debt into several tranches, some of which are provided in the form of B/C tranches.

With a Wald statistic of 3,135 and an odds ratio of 1,307, tangibility also has a fairly significant influence. As mentioned earlier, senior A levels are sometimes referred to as secured senior debt.

Although the collateralisation aspect does not play a vital role in IBOs, higher shares of tangible assets may nevertheless give rise to more senior A debt. Therefore, as soon as assets are collateralised for the sake of securing debt positions, these are usually denoted as senior A tranches.

The residual 5 characteristics were not found to influence the use of the different senior debt tranches. To a large extent, the use may be explained by non transaction-specific factors such as the individual contract design or debt syndication aspects.

7.5.4. Summary of the results on other financing layers

Four analyses have been performed to gain an understanding of IBO capital structures beyond the use of senior debt. To complement the first layer, logistic regressions on the use of equity and sub-ordinated debt have been carried out. In addition, the use of HYBs (vs. mezzanine) and senior A debt (vs. senior B/C debt) have been studied to fathom financial policies beyond the generic types of capital. The results can be summarised as follows:

- With strong model assessment results, **equity capital** represents the main counter-position to senior debt.
- Exhibiting mostly inverse relations to the senior debt regression coefficients, the use of equity follows the theoretical predictions as regards growth, profitability, uniqueness, and free cash flow.
- With regard to the size of the transaction, fund-internal considerations appear to interfere with the results in that PE funds tend to reduce their equity injection with increasing firm size in order to avoid bulk risks.
- As regards **sub-ordinated debt**, its use cannot be satisfactorily explained by the different transaction characteristics. Rather, sub-ordinated debt predominantly fills the gap left by equity and senior debt
- An exception is the influence of growth. As predicted by theoretical contributions, sub-ordinated debt appears to suit situations where agency cost are particularly high.
- With good results in the model assessment tests, the logit model on the use of **HYBs** vs. mezzanine instruments identified transaction size to be the single most important characteristic. All other characteristics fail to explain the use of HYBs.
- The use of **senior A** tranches compared to B/C tranches can be only traced back to the transaction size. Banks provide large amounts of debt in several tranches, some

of which are B or C notes, in order to achieve a more diversified spectrum of cash flow and interest profiles.

7.6. Discussion of the empirical results

The structure of the thesis and the empirical study was designed to provide answers to the three research questions which were formulated at the beginning. However, before carrying on to discuss the results a number of general points shall be recapitulated:

- With 94 reported IBOs, the sample size comprises a sufficiently large number of deals to produce robust results, given the limited number of covariates in the logistic regressions.
- Descriptive statistics have provided preliminary indications of certain patterns in capital structure decisions, although to explore relationships univariate and multivariate analyses are mandatory.
- The scales in the record sheet proved to be sufficiently well calibrated with the exception of R_D.
- Univariate non-parametric tests indicated potential relationships between an IBO's capital structure and its characteristics. Overall, the results from the logistic regressions do not contradict the univariate tests, which indicates the absence of significant multicolliniarity and interaction effects.
- In general, the focus of the logit regression was on the 7 characteristics included in most empirical finance studies in the past. Complementing the core study of why IBOs are structured as HLT or Non-HLT, two additional characteristics were considered.
- Developing a logit model on the basis of several analyses represents a necessary but intricate step in logistic regressions. Since the regression of HLT vs. Non-HLT deals is at the center of interest, only this model will be developed extensively. However, the remaining regressions capitalise on the result in that the same main variables are included. This in turn allows the model outcomes to be cross-interpreted.

Having considered these general comments on the study, the discussion of the three research questions follows as:

1.) Which established corporate finance theories best predict the financing of IBOs?

- Two theoretical approaches were followed in developing hypotheses on IBO capital structure decisions. The results of the logit model on HLT vs. Non-HLT favour the trade-off theory which correctly predicted the influence of 5 out of 7 characteristics. In contrast, only 3 hypotheses were confirmed for the agency context.
- The agency perspective partly fails to explain the study observations. It appears that particularly the agency cost of equity can be efficiently mitigated through management equity participation. The efficient mechanism was not anticipated since management shares are usually only between 5-10 per cent. However, the substantial private assets locked-in the transaction might explain the outcome. This view is supported by the fact that equity held by management does not significantly correlate with the leverage found in the transactions.
- The observed leverage adjustments reflect rather the relevance of the associated cost of debt as a result of potential underinvestment (uniqueness) or both the threat of asset substitution and underinvestment (risk class and growth).
- Within the trade-off theory context, the various analyses addressing the lack of empirical support for the influence of transaction size generated interesting results. First, the potential credit constraint of small deals as claimed by practitioners was confirmed by the results. However, this did not lead to higher senior debt levels for large transactions, which could serve as evidence for less aggressive financing than expected.
- The discount on senior debt volumes appears to be due to direct and indirect cost (e.g. lost opportunities, reputation losses) that are particularly emphasised for buyouts. As opposed to most early works this study revealed these types of distress cost to be highly relevant for the decision.

2.) *What particular influence do the various transaction-specific characteristics have on the capital structure decisions?*

- The evidence provided by the study partly confirms the identified influences of previous empirical corporate finance studies. Only tangibility and profitability were found to exhibit the opposite influence. Both characteristics reflect the specific nature of IBOs and might be representative of cash-flow lending transactions in general.
- Most of the characteristics have a negative influence on the likelihood that a deal will be structured as an HLT or Non-HLT. Risk, tangibility, growth and uniqueness exhibit a significant inverse relation with senior debt. The picture of buyouts as typically low-risk and low-growth firms with substantial amounts of senior debt can thus be confirmed by the study.
- Conversely, free cash flow and asset sales both have a positive impact on senior debt, the latter being the single most influential determinant. The probability of IBOs with planned asset sales being highly leveraged is about 9 times higher than IBOs without planned asset sales.
- Surprisingly, as discussed above, size does not impose a substantial impact on the senior debt level. A set of non-parametric tests investigating the results point to the existence of further cost affecting the use of senior debt.
- Another surprising result is the negative influence of tangibility, which can be explained by two factors. First, the IBOs are cash flow-based transactions in which debt positions are less closely linked to the existence of collateralisable assets. Second, tangible asset-intensive firms exhibit slightly higher cash flow volatilities, which reduces the debt capacity.
- Finally, the result for profitability confirmed neither prior studies nor the theoretical prediction. While prior studies identified a negative relation due to the pecking order, this argumentation does not hold for IBOs. Also, the clear positive prediction from the viewpoint of both the trade-off theory and agency cost, however, was not confirmed either.

3.) Which factors determine the use of financial instruments beyond the debt/equity choice?

- Results on the financial instruments beyond senior debt reflect the complementarity of equity and sub-ordinated debt.
- Equity represents the main counter-position to senior debt The negative relation with transaction size could be due to fund-internal considerations.
- Apart from growth, sub-ordinated debt appears to exclusively serve to fill the gap between equity and senior debt.
- As regards high-growth firms, the benefits of sub-ordinated debt, namely the mitigation of agency cost, seem effective given the significant positive relation.
- The size of the transaction is the predominant determinant of the use of HYBs. Not surprisingly, the substantial issuing cost require a large deal.
- Senior A cannot be well explained by transaction-specific characteristics. Only the size of the transaction has a negative effect on the share of senior A debt.

In sum, the empirical results show that basic capital structure decisions can be satisfactorily explained by traditional capital structure theories, though only in the light of the IBO context. In essence, the results hold for the senior debt level in the transaction with equity as the main counter-position. Sub-ordinated debt, however, lacks support for theoretical considerations except for its use in growth-intensive firms. As concerns the second-layer instruments, it appears that fund-specific reasons prevail.

8. Conclusion

The present thesis examines the determinants of capital structure decisions in institutional buyouts. Based on prior empirical studies, 7 characteristics plus a number of additional variables have been selected as the explanatory variables in a set of binomial logistic regressions. These regressions were sub-divided into two sections:

- Influence on the classification into HLTs and Non-HLTs
- Influence on the use of other financial instruments

While the objective of the first section was to test the validity of the static trade-off model vis-à-vis popular agency models for IBO capital structures, the second section supplemented both the theoretical and the practical view.

The results of the survey on the classification as HLTs and Non-HLTs are both reassuring and puzzling. Previous empirical evidence for the influence of individual determinants was confirmed in part, although the IBO-specific characteristics are clearly reflected in the results. In particular, the cash-flow lending nature distinguishes IBO financing from "usual" corporate financing. The results pave the way for further empirical studies which might shed additional light on certain aspects of the theories.

As regards the two theories, the results of the study demonstrate that the trade-off theory best describes the capital structure decisions in IBOs. With 5 correct predictions on the influence of the 7 characteristics, the trade-off theory explains the financial structure accurately, while only 3 hypotheses were confirmed as regards agency considerations. However, the first-glance impression on the explanatory power of agency models has to be decomposed in the different elements, as the results suggest that the agency cost of debt have a slightly greater impact on IBO capital structures than the agency cost of equity.

The evidence on taxes and the cost of financial distress confirms the theoretical reasoning and conversely rejects results of earlier empirical studies on the trade-off theory. A reason for the failure of earlier studies could be the misspecification of financial distress cost and how they may affect a borrower's decision. The capital structure's independence of size suggests that the borrower – here the buyout responsible – faces certain counter-balancing cost forcing him to pursue a defensive financing strategy. Given that promoters of large deals are in a better position to obtain senior debt, it comes as a surprise that they do not in fact borrow more than for small deals. Having controlled for other effects, the reason appears to be the PE fund's fear of losing the opportunity to realise the upside in the deal and the loss in reputation as regards future fund raising. In other words empirical results on the existence of distress costs vary by borrower and his long-term perspective. The present thesis emphasises indirect cost to be the main driver in the trade-off model. Future work should contribute to a better understanding of these cost. In particular, the considerations must be extended towards a dynamic perspective.

As regards the agency context, the lack of evidence in the data suggests that either the respective cost are less pronounced than expected or they can be mitigated without substantial efforts by instruments other than leverage. Concerning the agency cost of equity, these appear to be efficiently reduced through management's equity participation. However, the minor management shares raise some doubts about the direct proportionality of the agency problems and equity share as claimed by theorists.[847] Instead, it could be that the considerable private fortune locked in the IBO firm plays a more substantial role in explaining the incentive alignment than the mere equity share in the firm.[848] This could be a starting point for future empirical studies, which may help to better understand the influence of the personal situation of the management on the capital structure decision. Given that the LBO association is considered to be a future model of corporate governance,[849] the results could be of interest for both organisation and management incentivation topics.

The evidence on the agency cost of debt suggests two conclusions. First, the observed influence on the leverage indicates a higher relevance compared to the agency cost of equity. Second, however, the result that the friction show up less explicitly than the neo-classic effects might be evidence for the effectiveness of other instruments. Two aspects in particular could play a role in mitigating the agency problems, which should both be further examined in the future. First, PE firms are repeat borrowers with long-standing relationships to the banking industry. They have an incentive to safeguard the interests of their debtholders, which in turn allows the banks to reduce efforts spent on monitoring and bonding the target through contractual covenants.[850] Second, if the contracts include a wide range of covenants, the cost of surveilling them might be less costly than presumed. Given that buyout targets usually exhibit healthy business models, banks might have managed to keep the monitoring processes lean.

847 See chapter 3.3.2.1.
848 See also chapter 2.1.3.4.
849 E.g. Kester, C.W./ Luehrmann, T.A. (1995).
850 DeAngelo, H./ DeAngelo, L. (1986), p. 43.

The econometric results concerning the choice of other financial instruments and the underlying determinants of this choice indicate that the use of more elaborate and flexible financial instruments, such as sub-ordinated instruments, are not significantly related to the severity of agency cost, as confirmed by other studies, with the exception of growth firms. While growth firms apply sub-ordinated debt more frequently than other firms, other characteristics do not have a systematic influence on its use. It appears that sub-ordinated debt still serves primarily to fill the existing capital structure gap. Probably, either the benefits of hybrid instruments can be achieved more cost-efficiently by other means, or practitioners have not yet fully grasped how to make use of the flexibility these instruments offer. Also the use of cash flow-reduced senior tranches should become more popular in small and mid-cap deals, since they allow the debt capacity to be increased, while preserving the value-enhancing tax shield.

Overall, the thesis has made some suggestions for future studies on corporate finance as a number of questions are still not fully answered, owing to the complexity of capital structure decisions. However, it appears that understanding financial policies approximates a consensus on some of the most important determinants. Already with risk class, growth and the level of free cash flow a deal can be reasonably classified as a highly- or non highly-leveraged transaction. Therefore, the recent statement by FRANK / GOYAL (2003) can be confirmed in that financial structure variations "can be explained using a fairly small set of factors"[851]. Yet, the study also shows that specific circumstances such as the setting (e.g. cash flow lending) or the type of borrower (e.g. IBO firms as repeat borrowers) matter a lot as regards the impact these factors may exert. With more available buyout data and possibly insights into financing contracts, the remaining questions should be addressed in the future as buyouts prove to be excellent settings for studying capital structure decisions.

[851] Frank, M./ Goyal, V. (2003), p. 28.

Appendix

Financial Structure

Equity ☐ %		Subordinated Debt ☐ %		Senior Debt (incl. WC facility) ☐ %	
Equity	Shareholder Loan	Mezzanine	High Yield Bond	A	B/C
%	%	%	%	%	%

Share PIK	
of total Mezzanine	of total Senior Debt
%	%

Transaction Characteristics

Comments

CHARACTERISTIC	*SPECIFICATION*	*UNIT*							
SIZE	Transaction value *	m€	<30	30-60	60-100	100-150	150-300	300-500	>500
	Sales	m€	<30	30-60	60-100	100-200	200-500	500-1000	>1000
RISK CLASS	EBITDA volatility *	%	0-10	10-20	20-30	30-40	40-60	60-80	>80
	Industry cyclicality *	%	None			Medium			Very high
ASSET STRUCTURE	Fixed tangibles / Total assets	%	0-10	10-15	15-25	25-35	35-50	50-70	>70
FREE CASH FLOW	FCF / Sales *	%	<-5	-5-0	0-5	5-10	10-15	15-20	>20
	Net financial liabilities / FCF *	#	>8.5	8.5-6.5	6.5-4.5	4.5-3.5	3.5-2.5	2.5-1.5	<1.5
GROWTH	EV / EBITDA	#	<3.5	3.5-4.5	4.5-5.5	5.5-6.5	6.5-7.5	7.5-8.5	>8.5
	Capex / Operating cash flow *	%	<0	0-20	20-40	40-60	60-80	80-100	>100
	CAGR Sales growth *	%	<-5	-5-0	0-5	5-10	10-15	15-20	>20
PROFITABILITY	EBITDA / Sales	%	<0	0-5	5-10	10-15	15-20	20-25	>25
UNIQUENESS	R&D / Sales	%	0-3	3-6	6-9	9-12	12-15	15-18	>18
	Market share	%	0-5	5-10	10-15	15-25	25-40	40-60	>60

ADDITIONAL INFORMATION

INVESTOR ACTIVITY	Supervisory board seats	☐ Yes ☐ No
	Direct mgmt board seats	☐ Yes ☐ No
STRATEGY	Growth option	☐ A=Acquistion / O=Organicly
	Buy-and-build	☐ Yes ☐ No
	Major asset sales planned	☐ Yes ☐ No
	Envisaged exit channel	☐ I=IPO / T=Trade-Sale S=Secondary
MOTIVE FOR BUYOUT	Succession	☐
	Turnaround	☐
	Going private	☐
	Divestment	☐
	Privatisation	☐
OWNERSHIP STRUCTURE	% Management Equity	☐
	# of Equity bulk shareholders	☐
	Limited Partner shareholdings	☐ Yes ☐ No
	Incumbent Management	☐
	External Management	☐
CREDIT CONSTRAINT	How difficult was it to receive senior debt?	☐ Easy ☐ As usual ☐ Difficult
	Have you received the amount of senior debt you asked for?	☐ Yes ☐ No ☐ Yes, but at inferior conditions

* Further explanations provided on note sheet

Appendix 2: Additional notes sheet

General Information

- The deal record sheet is the only way of collecting information which is sufficiently detailed (as opposed to public databases and bank loan letters) to test the validity of capital structure theories.
- We would be grateful if you would complete three deal record sheets, one for each transaction. Of course, we would also be happy to receive less, should you not yet have been involved in three deals.
- Please do not disclose the name of the transaction.
- Some of the figures might be irrelevant from a practitioner's view, but they are necessary for theoretical purposes.
- If you do not have the relevant deal data at hand, please try to guess or give an estimate. For (purposes of) the econometric analysis, we primarily need to have an idea whether a deal ranks below or above an average deal with regard to its characteristics.
- Please subsume working capital facilities under the senior debt position and replace bridge loans by the eventual financing.
- Any data will be processed anonymously and published on an aggregated level across all deals. Only the author of the Ph.D thesis will have access to individual information. In no case will the reader of the thesis or any other person be able to trace back data to individual deals or funds.
- With your help we shall be able to develop the largest study on financial structures of investor-driven buyouts in the European buyout industry. Of course, we will be happy to provide you with agreggated results of the study.
- **Thank you very much for your help.**

Explanations: Deal Record Sheet

• Transaction value	=> Entreprise value plus any additional cost (e.g. fees)
• EBITDA volatility	=> The average percentage (stdev.) the company's EBITDA oscillates around a 7-year average. Try to capture the average amplitude of a full business cycle which the target firm undergoes
• Industry cyclicality	=> Refers to the medium to long-term cyclicality of the target industry
• Fixed tangibles	=> Property, plant and equipment
• FCF / Sales	=> Unlevered free cash flow (after investments and before financing activities) divided by total sales
• Net financial liabilities / FCF	=> Total (long and short-term) financial liabilities less cash & cash equivalents divided by the unlevered free cash flow (after investments and before financing activities. Please exclude negative ratios
• CapEx / Operating cash flow	=> Capital expenditure without acquisitions/divestments as percentage of the operating cash flow
• CAGR sales growth	=> Compound annual growth rate of total sales over the last 5 years
• % management equity	=> Refers to the combined percentage share of all managers involved in the deal
• Equity bulk shareholders	=> How many bulk shareholdings are involved (usually two, one management and one PE investor)?
• LP shareholding	=> Are limited partners given the opportunity to invest directly in the deal?
• Incumbent/External mgmt.	=> Please indicate whether incumbent and/or external managers are involved in the transaction

Appendix 3: Description and coding of the additional variables

Variable	Specification	Coding	Description
Investor activity	SUPERVISORY	No=0 / Yes=1	PE investor holding a seat on the supervisory board
	MGMT_BOARD	No=0 / Yes=1	PE investor holding a seat on the management board
Strategy	GROWTH_OPTION	A=Acquisition O=Organicly	Firm growth by aquisition or organically
	BUY_BUILD	No=0 / Yes=1	Planned buy-and-build strategy
	ASSET_SALES	No=0 / Yes=1	Any major asset sales planned?
	EXIT_ROUTE	I=IPO / T=Trade sales S=Secondary	Preferred exit route
Motive for buyout	SUCCESSION	No=0 / Yes=1	Buyout resulting from a succession problem
	TURNAROUND	No=0 / Yes=1	Buyout resulting from a turnaround situation
	GOING_PRIVATE	No=0 / Yes=1	Quoted company taken private by a PE investor
	DIVESTMENT	No=0 / Yes=1	Buyout resulting from a divestment of a larger company or group
	PRIVATISATION	No=0 / Yes=1	State-owned company privatised by way of a buyout
Ownership structure	MGMT_EQUITY	In %	Equity share held by management as % of total equity
	BULK_SHARE	Number	Number of bulk shareholders in the buyout
	LTD_SHARE	No=0 / Yes=1	Presence of limited partner (fund investors) shareholders
	INCUMB_MGMT	No=0 / Yes=1	Involvement of incumbent senior managers in the buyout
	EXT_MGMT	No=0 / Yes=1	Involvement of external senior managers in the buyout
Credit constraint	DIFFICULTY	0=Easy / 1=As usual 2=Difficult	How difficult was it to receive senior debt?
	AMOUNT	No=0 / Yes=1	Have you obtained the amount of senior debt you asked for?

Appendix 4: The χ2-distribution

The χ^2-distribution represents a continuous probability distribution over the entirety of positive real numbers. Usually, when talking about the χ^2-distribution, authors refer to the central χ^2-distribution. Unlike the standard normal distribution, which can be fully characterised by variance and expected value, the only parameter necessary for describing a χ^2-distribution is the number of degrees of freedom ν that denotes the number of independent random variables. The χ^2-distribution equals a stochastic model: For ν different normally distributed random variables (Z_1, Z_2, ..., Z_ν), all characterised by an expected value of 1 with variance 0, the squared sum $X^2 = Z_1^2 + Z_2^2 + ... + Z_\nu^2$ follows a χ^2-distribution. The density function of the χ^2-distribution equals χ^2 for ≥ 0

$$f(\chi^2/\nu) = (\chi^2)^{(\frac{\nu}{2}-1)} \cdot \frac{1}{2^{(\frac{\nu}{2})} \cdot \Gamma(\frac{\nu}{2})} \cdot e^{(\frac{\chi^2}{2})}$$

Accordingly, the distribution function results as

$$F(\chi^2/\nu) = \frac{1}{2^{(\frac{\nu}{2})} \cdot \Gamma(\frac{\nu}{2})} \int_0^{\chi^2} e^{-\frac{\nu}{2}} \nu^{(\frac{\nu}{2}-1)} \, d\nu$$

The subsequent figure shows some density functions for different degrees of freedom:

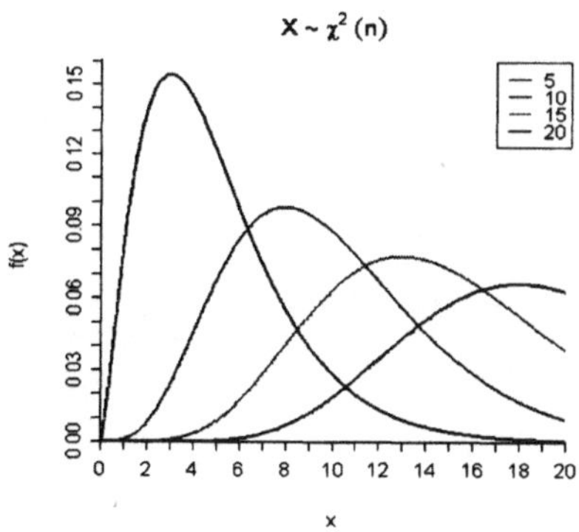

Source: Bleymüller, J./ Gehlert, G./ Gülicher, H. (2004), p. 132

Appendix 5: Overview of corporate finance studies

Author(s)	*Year*	*Methodology*
Frank / Goyal	2003	OLS
Brailsford / Oliver / Pua	2002	OLS
MacKay / Phillips	2002	OLS
Schwenhold I	2001	Logit
Schwenhold II	2001	Logit
Ozkan	2001	OLS
Hovakimian / Opler / Titman	2001	Logit
Wald	1999	Tobit
De Jong / Veld	1998	Logit
Jung / Kim / Schulz	1996	Logit
Opler / Titman	1996	Logit
Rajan / Zingales	1995	OLS
Bayless / Chaplinsky	1991	Logit
MacKie / Mason	1990	Logit
Lehn / Poulsen	1989	Logit
Billingsley / Lamy / Thompson	1988	Logit
Titman / Wessels	1988	Lisrel
Kim / Sorenson	1986	ANOVA
Bradley / Jarrell / Kim	1984	OLS
Marsh	1982	Logit / Probit
Ferri / Jones	1979	Discriminant A.
Taub	1975	Probit
Martin / Scott	1974	Discriminant A.
Mean		

Appendix 6: Development of capital structures as recorded by CMBOR (1999-2003)

Type of Finance (Average %)	1998	1999	2000	2001	2002
Equity	53.5	40.0	47.2	44.1	38.1
Mezzanine	0.3	3.8	7.5	9.5	8.0
Senior Debt	42.5	54.2	40.3	43.1	42.9
Loan Note	0.0	0.5	0.3	1.0	4.4
Other Finance	3.9	1.5	4.6	2.4	6.7

Appendix 7: Development of global long-term interest rates

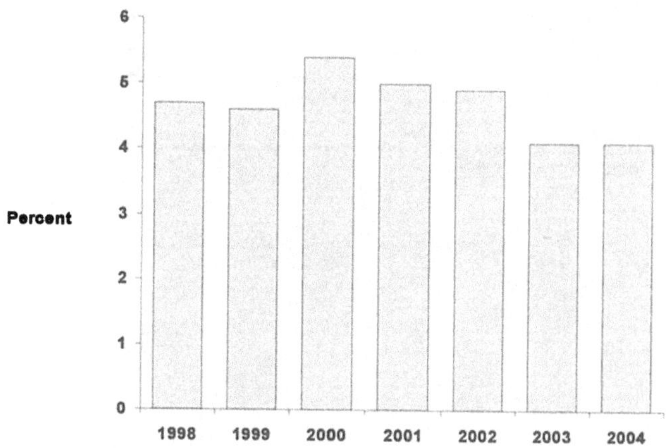

Source: OECD 2004.

Appendix 8: Univariable logit results of the interaction terms

	HLT vs. Non-HLT		
Interaction terms	b_j	Wald	Odds-ratio e^b
Sales * EBITDA vol	**-0,749****	**6,038**	**0,014**
Sales * Tangibles	-0,468	2,208	0,137
Sales * FCF_Sales	0,021	0,004	0,950
Sales * EV_EBITDA	0,427	2,152	0,142
Sales * EBITDA_Sales	0,277	1,891	0,169
Sales * Market share	0,15	0,605	0,437
EBITDA vol * tangibles	-0,398*	2,745	0,098
EBITDA vol * FCF_sales	-0,559*	2,948	0,084
EBITDA vol * EV_EBITDA	0,405	2,568	0,109
EBITDA vol * EBITDA_sales	0,244	0,984	0,321
EBITDA vol * market share	0,285	1,173	0,279
Tangibles * FCF_Sales	0,033	0,014	0,906
Tangibles * EV_EBITDA	0,223	0,874	0,350
Tangibles * EBITDA_Sales	-0,025	0,02	0,888
Tangibles * Market share	0,202	0,62	0,431
FCF_sales * EV_EBITDA	0,021	0,007	0,932
FCF_sales * EBITDA_sales	0,499*	3,114	0,078
FCF_sales * market share	0,101	0,123	0,725
EV_EBITDA * EBITDA_sales	**0,637****	**4,066**	**0,044**
EV_EBITDA * market share	-0,511*	3,085	0,079
EBITDA_sales * market share	-0,058*	0,071	0,79

*, **, *** significant at the 10%-, 5%-, 1%-level

Bibliography

ACHLEITNER, A.-K./ WAHL, S. (2004): Private Debt als alternative Finanzierungsform für mittelständische Unternehmen, in: Achleitner, A.-K./ Einem, C.v./ Schröder, B.v. (Ed.) (2004): Private Debt – alternative Finanzierung für den Mittelstand, Schäffer-Poeschel, Stuttgart 2004, pp. 41-80.

AGHION, P./ BOLTON, P. (1992): An incomplete contracts approach to financial contracting, in: Review of Economic Studies, Vol. 59, pp. 473-494.

AKERLOF, G.A. (1970): The market for lemons: Quality uncertainty and the market mechanism, in: Quarterly Journal of Economics, Vol. 84, pp. 488-500.

ALBACH, H. (2001): Finanzierungsregeln und Kapitalstrukturen der Unternehmung, in: Breuer, R.-E. (Ed.) (2001): Handbuch Finanzierung, Gabler-Verlag, Wiesbaden 2001.

ALDERSON, M.J./ BETKER, B.L. (1995): Liquidation cost and capital structure, in: Journal of Financial Economics, Vol. 39, pp. 45-69.

ALDRICH, J./ NELSON, F. (1984): Linear probability, logit, and probit models, Newbury Park, London 1984.

ALLEN, D.E./ MIZUNO, H. (1989): The determinants of corporate capital structure: Japanese evidence, in: Applied Economics, Vol. 21, pp. 569-585.

ALLEN, J.R. (1999): LBOs – The evolution of financial structures and strategies, in: Chew, D.H. (Ed.) (1999): The New corporate finance: Where theory meets practice, Mc-Graw-Hill, New York 1999, pp. 708-719.

ALTMAN, E. (1984): A further investigation of the bankruptcy cost question, in: Journal of Finance, Vol. 39, pp. 1067-1089.

AMIHUD, Y. (1989): Leveraged management buyouts and shareholder wealth, in: Amihud, Y. (Ed.) (1989): Leveraged management buyouts, Homewood IL, Dow Jones-Irwin, pp. 3-34.

AMIHUD, Y./ LEV, B. (1981): Risk reduction as a managerial motive for conglomerate mergers, in: Bell Journal of Economics, Vol. 12, pp. 605-617.

AMIR, E./ LEV, B. (1996): Value-relevance of non-financial information: The wireless communication industry, in: Journal of Accounting and Economics, Vol. 22, Nr. 1-3, p. 3-30.

ANDERS, G. (1992): The barbarians in the boardroom, in: Harvard Business Review, July/August, pp. 79-87.

ANDRADE, G./ KAPLAN, S. (1998): How costly is financial (not economic) distress? Evidence from highly leveraged transactions that became distressed, in: Journal of Finance, Vol. 53, No. 5, pp. 1443-1493.

ANG, J.S. (1991): Small business uniqueness and the theory of financial management, in: Journal of Small Business Finance, Vol. 1, pp. 1-13.

ARBEITSKREIS FINANZIERUNG DER SCHMALENBACH-GESELLSCHAFT DEUTSCHE GESELLSCHAFT FÜR BETRIEBSWIRTSCHAFT E.V. (1990): Analyse der für die Entwicklung eines Buyout-Marktes notwendigen Bedingungen in der Bundesrepublik Deutschland unter besonderer Berücksichtigung von MBOs, in: Zeitschrift für betriebswirtschaftliche Forschung 1990, pp. 830-850.

ARMSTRONG, J.S./ OVERTON, T.S. (1977): Estimating nonresponse bias in mail surveys, in: Journal of Marketing Research, Vol. 14, pp. 396-402.

ARROW, K. (1985): The economics of agency, in: Pratt, J.W./ Zeckhauser, R.J. (Eds.) (1985): Principals and agents – Structure of business, Boston 1985, pp. 37-51.

ARZAC, E.R. (1992): On the capital structure of leveraged buyouts, in: Financial Management, Spring (1992), pp. 16-26.

ARZAC, E.R. (1996): Valuation of highly leveraged firms, in: Financial Analysts Journal, July/August, pp. 42-50.

ASQUITH, P./ GERTNER, R./ SCHARFSTEIN, D. (1994): Anatomy of financial distress: An examination of junk bond issuers, in: Quarterly Journal of Economics, Vol. 109, pp. 625-658.

ATTESLANDER, P. (1995): Methoden der empirischen Sozialforschung, Springer-Verlag, Berlin / Heidelberg 1995.

AUER, L. v. (2003): Ökonometrie, Springer-Verlag, Berlin / Heidelberg 2003.

BADER, H.P. (1996): Private Equity als Anlagekategorie, Verlag Peter Haupt, Bern 1996.

BACKHAUS, K./ ERICHSON, B./ PLINKE, W./ WEIBER, R. (2003): Multivariate Analysemethoden – Eine anwendungsorientierte Einführung, Springer-Verlag, Berlin / Heidelberg 2003.

BACKHAUS, K./ WERTHSCHULTE, H. (2003): Projektfinanzierung – wirtschaftliche und rechtliche Aspekte einer Finanzierungsmethode für Großprojekte, Schäffer-Poeschel, Stuttgart 2003.

BAKER, G.P. (1992): Beatrice: A study in the creation and destruction of value, in: Journal of Finance, vol. 47, no. 3 (July), pp. 1081-1119.

BAKER, G.P./ MONTGOMERY, C. (1994): Conglomerates and LBO association: a comparison of organisational forms, Working Paper, Harvard Business School 1994.

BAKER, G.P./ SMITH, G.D. (1998): Private Equity comes of age, in: The New Financial Capitalists: Kohlberg Kravis Roberts and the Creation of Corporate Value, Cambridge University Press, Cambridge 1998.

BAKER, S.H. (1973): Risk, leverage, and profitability: An industry analysis, in: Review of Economics and Statistics, Vol. 55, No. 4, pp. 503-507.

BALLWIESER, W. (1985): Informationsökonomie, Rechnungslegungstheorie und Bilanzricht-linien-Gesetz, in: zfbf, Vol. 37, pp. 47-66.

BALLWIESER, W. (1987): Kapitalmarkt und Informationsversorgung mit Jahresabschlüssen, in: Claussen, C.P./ Hübl, L./ Schneider, H.P. (Ed.) (1987): Zweihundert Jahre Geld und Brief – Herausforderungen an die Kapitalmärkte, Frankfurt a. M., p. 163-178.

BAMBERG, G./ BAUR, F. (2002): Statistik, Oldenbourg Verlag, München / Wien 2002.

BARCLAY, M./ MORELLEC, E./ SMITH, C.W. (2001): On the debt capacity of growth options, Working Paper No. FR 01-07, The Bradley Policy Research Center, University of Rochester, downloaded from SSRN.

BARCLAY, M.J./ SMITH, C.W. (1995a): The maturity structure of corporate debt, in: Journal of Finance, Vol. 50, No. 2, pp. 609-631.

BARCLAY, M.J./ SMITH, C.W. (1995b): The priority structure of corporate liabilities, in: Journal of Finance, Vol. 50, No. 3, pp. 899-917.

BARNEA, A./ HAUGEN, R./ SENBET, L. (1981): An equilibrium analysis of debt financing under costly tax arbitrage and agency problems, Vol. 36, No. 3, pp. 569-581.

BARTHOLD, B. (2000): Mezzanine-Finanzierung von Unternehmensübernahmen und Jungunternehmen, in: Schweizerische Zeitschrift für Wirtschaftsrecht, 5/2000, pp. 224-237.

BARTON, S.L./ GORDON, P.J. (1987): Corporate strategy: Useful perspective for the study of capital structure, in: Academy of Management Review, Vol. 12, pp. 67-75.

BARTON, S.L./ HILL, N./ SUNDARAM, S. (1989): An empirical test of stakeholder theory predictions of capital structure, in: Financial Management, Vol. 18, pp. 36-44.

BASCHA, A./ WALZ, U. (2001): Financing practices in the German venture capital industry: an empirical assessment, Working paper downloaded from SSRN, 2001.

BAYLESS, M./ CHAPLINSKY, S. (1991): Expectations of security type and the information content of debt and equity offers, in: Journal of Financial Intermediation, Vol. 1, pp. 195-214.

BAXTER, N./ CRAGG, J. (1970): Corporate choice among long-term financing instruments, in: Review of Economics and Statistics, Vol. 52, pp. 225-235.

BEAVER, G. (2001): Management Buy-Outs: Who Dares Wins?, in: Strategic Change, Vol.10, No.6, pp.307-309.

BECKER, W. (2003): Buy-outs machen dem Mezzanine-Markt Beine, in: Börsen-Zeitung v. 09. Oktober 2003, pp. 52-54.

BEHR, G./ WIRTH, O. (1999): Einsatz von Mezzanine-Kapital bei der Wachstums-finanzierung – High-Yield Anleihen, Wandelobligationen und Going Public Optionsanleihen im Vergleich, in: Der Schweizer Treuhänder, 3/99, pp. 161-170.

BEN-AKIVA, M./ LERMAN, S. (1985): Discrete choice analysis - Theory and application to travel demand, The MIT Press, Cambridge 1985.

BENDEL, R.B./ AFFITI, A.A. (1977): Comparison of stopping rules in forward regression, in: Journal of the American Statistical Association, Vol. 72, pp. 46-53.

BEISEL, W./ KLUMPP, H.H. (1996): Der Unternehmenskauf – Gesamtdarstellung der zivil- und steuerrechtlichen Vorgänge einschließlich gesellschafts-, arbeits- und kartellrechtlicher Fragen bei der Übertragung eines Unternehmens, München 1996.

BELLER, S. (2004): Empirisch forschen lernen – Konzepte, Methoden, Fallbeispiele, Tipps, Verlag Hans Huber, Freiburg i.B. 2004.

BERENS, J.L./ CUNY, C.J. (1995): The capital structure puzzle revisited, in: Review of Financial Studies, Vol. 8, No. 4, pp. 1184-1205.

BERENS, W./ SCHMITTING, W./ STRAUCH, J. (2002): Funktionen, Terminierung und rechtliche Einordnung der Due Diligence, in: Berens, W./ Brauner, H./ Strauch, J. (Eds.) (2002): Due Diligence bei Unternehmensakquisitionen, Schäffer-Poeschel, Stuttgart 2002, pp. 77-120.

BERG, A./ GOTTSCHALG, O. (2003): Understanding value generation in buyouts, in: INSEAD Working Paper Series 2003/42/SM.

BERGER, A.N./ KLAPPER, L./ UDELL, G.F. (2001): The ability of banks to lend to infor-mationally opaque small businesses, in: Journal of Banking and Finance, Vol. 21, pp. 2127-2167.

BERGER, A.N./ UDELL, G.F. (1998): The economics of small business finance: The roles of private equity and debt markets in the financial growth cycles, in: Journal of Banking and Finance, Vol. 22, pp. 613-673.

BERGER, M. (1993): Management Buy-Out und Mitarbeiterbeteiligung – Finanzwirtschaft-liche Analyse von Konzepten zur Übernahme von Unternehmen durch Management und Belegschaft, Köln 1993.

BERGER, P./ OFEK, E./ YERMACK, D.L. (1997): Managerial entrenchment and capital structure decisions, in: Journal of Finance, Vol. 52, pp. 1411-1438.

BERKSON, J. (1944): Application of the logistic function to bio-assay, in: Journal of the American Statistics Association, Vol. 39, pp. 357-365.

BERLE, A./ MEANS, G. (1932): The modern corporation and private property, MacMillan, New York 1932.

BERNET, B./ DENK, C.L. (2000): Finanzierungsmodelle für KMU, Geiger, H. et al. (Eds.), Verlag Paul Haupt, Bern 2000.

BETSCH, O./ GROH, A./ LOHMANN, L. (2000): Corporate Finance – Unternehmens-bewertung, M&A und innovative Kapitalmarktfinanzierung, Verlag Franz Vahlen, München 2000.

BIELER, S. (1996): Die Unternehmernachfolge als finanzwirtschaftliches Problem, Diss., Gabler-Verlag, Wiesbaden 1996.

BILLINGSLEY, R.S./ SMITH, D.M. (1996): Why do firms issue convertible debt?, in: Financial Management, Vol. 25, No. 2, pp. 93-99.

BILLINGSLEY, R.S./ LAMY, R./ THOMPSON, G. (1988): The choice among debt, equity, and convertible bonds, in: Journal of Financial Research, Vol. 11, No. 1, pp. 43-55.

BINDER, P./ LANZ, R. (1993): ‚Due Diligence': Systematisches und professionelles Instrument für erfolgreiche Firmen-Akquisitionen, in: INDEX 4-5/93, pp. 15-19.

BING, G. (1996): Due diligence: techniques and analysis, London 1996.

BITZ, M. (2001): Theorie der Kapitalstruktur, in: Gerke, W./ Steiner, M. (Eds.) (2001): Handwörterbuch des Bank- und Finanzwesens, Stuttgart.

BLACK, F./ SCHOLES, M. (1973): The pricing of options and corporate liabilities, Journal of Political Economy, Vol. 81, No. 3, pp. 637-654.

BLEX, W./ MARCHAL, G. (1990): Risiken im Akquisitionsprozeß – ein Überblick, in: Betriebswirtschaftliche Forschung und Praxis, Vol. 42, pp. 85-103.

BLEYMÜLLER, J./ GEHLERT, G./ GÜLICHER, H. (2004): Statistik für Wirtschaftswissen-schaftler, Verlag Vahlen, München 2004.

BOLLEN, K.A. (1989): Structural equation models with latent variables, Wiley & Sons, New York 1989.

BOLTON, P./ SCHARFSTEIN, D. (1990): A theory of predation based on agency problems in financial contracting, in: American Economic Review, 80, pp. 94-106.

BORIO, C. (1990): Banks' involvement in highly leveraged transactions, BIS Economic Papers, No. 28, October 1990.

BORTZ, J./ DÖRING, N. (2002): Forschungsmethoden und Evaluation für Human- und Sozialwissenschaftler, Springer-Verlag, Heidelberg / Berlin 2002.

BOWMAN, J. (1980): The importance of a market value measurement of debt in assessing leverage, in: Journal of Accounting Research, Vol. 18, pp. 242-254.

BOYLE, G.W./ ECKHOLD, K.R. (1997): Capital structure choice and financial market liberalisation: Evidence from New Zealand, in: Applied Financial Economics, Vol. 7, pp. 427-437.

BOXBERG, F. v. (1991): Das Management Buyout-Konzept, Hamburg 1991.

BRADLEY, M./ JARRELL, G./ KIM, E.H. (1984): On the existence of an optimal capital structure: Theory and evidence, in: Journal of Finance, Vol. 39, pp. 857-878.

BRAILSFORD, T./ OLIVER, B./ PUA, S. (2002): On the relation between ownership structure and capital structure, in: Accounting and Finance, Vol. 42, pp. 1-26.

BRANDER, J.A./ LEWIS, T.R. (1986): Oligopoly and Financial Structure: The limited liability effect, in: American Economic Review, Vol. 76, pp. 956-970.

BRANNATH, W./ FUTSCHIK, A. (2003): Statistik für Wirtschaftwissenschaftler, WuV-Universitätsverlag, Wien 2001.

BREALEY, R.A./ MYERS, S.C. (2000): Principles of Corporate Finance, McGraw-Hill, New York 2000.

BRENNAN, M./ SCHWARTZ, E. (1988): The case for convertibles, in: Journal of Applied Corporate Finance, Summer, 1 (2), pp. 55-64.

BRETTEL, M. (2002): Entscheidungskriterien von Venture Capitalists, in: DBW, Vol. 62, No. 3, pp. 305-325.

BREUER, W. (1995): Optimale Kapitalstrukturentscheidungen von Unternehmen bei groben Informationsstrukturen, in: ZfB, Vol. 65, No. 6, pp. 609-631.

BREUER, W. (1998): Finanzierungstheorie – Eine systematische Einführung, Gabler-Verlag, Wiesbaden 1998.

BREUER, W. (2000): Die Finanzierung eines Leveraged Buy-out über Anleihen mit Reset-Klausel, in: WISU, Vol. 29, No. 6, pp. 827-828.

BREUER, W. (2001): Kapitel 4 – Finanzierung, in: Jost, P.J. (Ed.) (2001): Die Spieltheorie in der Betriebswirtschaftslehre, Schäffer-Poeschel, Stuttgart 2001, pp. 135-174.

BREUER, W./ HARTMANN, N./ KLEEFISCH, A. (2003): Finanzinnovationen der Beteiligungsfinanzierung – Überblick und Würdigung, in: Österreichisches Bank-Archiv, 5/2003, pp. 325-335.

BREWIS, J. (1998): High-Yield market widens its reach, Euromoney, August 1998, p. 21.

BRIDS, C. (2002): Basel II und die Folgen für den M&A-Markt, in: ConVent GmbH (Ed.): M&A-Jahrbuch 2003, pp. 111-114.

BRINGHAM, E. (1966): An analysis on convertible debentures: Theory and some empirical evidence, in: Journal of Finance, Vol. 21.

BROMAN, K.L. (1963): The use of convertible subordinate debentures by industrial firms 1949-59, in: Quarterly Review of Economics and Business, No. 3, pp. 65-75.

BROSIUS, F. (2004): SPSS 12, mitp-Verlag, Bonn 2004.

BÜNING, H./ TRENKLER, G. (1994): Nichtparametrische statistische Methoden, De Gruyter, Berlin / New York 1994.

BUREAU VAN DIJK (2004): Zephyr database, in: www.zephyr.bvdep.com, 14.07.2004.

BULL, I. (1988): Management performance in leveraged buyouts: An empirical analysis, Presented at the conference on management buyouts, NY University Graduate School of Business Administration, May 20, 1988.

BULL, I. (1989): Financial performance of leveraged buyouts: An empirical analysis, in: Journal of Business Venturing, 4. (1989), pp. 263-289.

BUSSE V. COLBE, W. (1993): Die Entwicklung des Jahresabschlusses als Informations-instrument, in: zfbf Sonderheft, Vol. 32, pp. 11-29.

BUTLER, P.A. (2001): The alchemy of LBOs, in: McKinsey Quarterly, no. 2, p. 140-151.

CAMPBELL, D.T. (1955): The informant in quantitative research, in: American Journal of Sociology, Vol. 60, pp. 339-342.

CASTANIAS, R. (1983): Bankruptcy risk and optimal capital structure, in: Journal of Finance, Vol. 38, pp. 1617-1635.

CAYS, S.E. (2001): A study on the measurement and prediction of the indirect costs of bankruptcy, Working Paper, Stern School of Business at New York University, April 2001.

CHAPLINSKY, S./ NIEHAUS, G. (1993): Do inside ownership and leverage share common determinants, in: Quaterly Journal of Business and Economics, Vol. 32, No. 4, pp. 51-65.

CHEVALIER, J.S. (1995a): Do LBO supermarkets charge more? An empirical analysis of the effects of LBOs on supermarket pricing, in: Journal of Finance, Vol. 50, 4. (1995), pp. 1095-1112.

CHEVALIER, J.S. (1995b): Capital structure and product market competition: Empirical evidence from the supermarket industry, in: American Economic Review, Vol. 85, No. 3, 415-435.

CHOWDHURY, D./ MILES, G. (1989): Modelling companies' debt and dividend decisions with company accounts data, in: Applied Economics, Vol. 21, pp. 1483-1507.

CHUNG, K.H. (1993): Asset characteristics and corporate debt policy: An empirical test, in: Journal of Business Finance and Accounting, Vol. 20, No. 1, pp. 83-98.

CHURCHILL G.A. (1999): Marketing research: Methodological foundations, The Dryden Press Dillman, New York 1999.

CMBOR (2003): European Management Buy-out Review, University of Nottingham, April 2003

COASE, R. (1937): The nature of the firm, in: Economica, Vol. 4, pp. 386-405.

COENENBERG, A.G. (2003): Jahresabschluss und Jahresabschlussanalyse: Betriebs-wirtschaftliche, handelsrechtliche, steuerrechtliche und internationale Grundsätze – HGB, IAS, US-GAAP, Landsberg a. L. 2003.

COENENBERG, A.G./ JAKOBY, S./ MAAS, G. (1996): Nachfolgeregelung durch MBO? – Ergebnisse einer Befragung mittelständischer Unternehmen in Deutschland, in: M&A Review, pp. 529-535.

COLE, J.E./ SOKOL, A.L. (1998): Structuring venture capital investments, in: Bokser, D. (Ed.) Pratt's guide to venture capital sources, 1998 Edition, New York: Securities Data Publishing, 1998, pp. 31-39.

COLLIN-DUFRESNE, P./ GOLDSTEIN, R.S./ SPENCER, M. (2001): The determinants of credit spread changes, in: Journal of Finance, Vol. 56, No. 5, pp. 2177-2207.

COLOMBO, R. (2000): A model for diagnosing and reducing nonresponse bias, in: Journal of Advertising Research, January/April 2000, pp. 85-93.

CORNELLI, F./ PORTES, R./ SCHAFFER, M.E. (1996): The capital structure of firms in Central and Eastern Europe, in: CEPR Discussion Paper No. 1392, Centre of Economic Policy Research (London).

CORNELLI, F./ YOSHA, O. (2003): Stage financing and the role of convertible securities, in: Review of Economic Studies, Vol. 70, pp. 1-32.

COTTER, J.F./ PECK, S.W. (2001): The structure of debt and active equity investors: The case of the buyout specialist, in: Journal of Financial Economics, Vol. 59, 2001, 101-147.

COX, D.R./ SNELL, E.J. (1989): The analysis of binary data, Chapmann and Hall, London 1989.

CRAMER, J.S. (1991): The logit model – An introduction for economists, Edward Arnold, New York 1991.

CRUTCHLEY, C.E./ HANSEN, R.S. (1989): A test of the agency theory of managerial ownership, corporate leverage and corporate dividends, in: Financial Management, Vol. 18, pp. 33-46.

CULLOM, P./ STEIN, C. (2001): MBO/ MBI – Private Equity als Chance für den Start ins Unternehmerleben, in: Stadler, W. (Ed.) (2001): Venture Capital und Private Equity – Erfolgreich wachsen mit Beteiligungskapital, Dt. Wirtschaftsdienst, Köln 2001, pp. 123-140.

CULP, C.L. (2002): The art of risk management: alternative risk transfer, capital structure, and convergence between insurance and capital markets, John Wiley & Sons, New York 2002.

CUMMING, D.J. (2002): The convertible preferred equity puzzle in Canadian venture capital finance, Working Paper, University of Alberta School of Business, downloaded from SSRN.

DAMMON, R./ SENBET, L. (1988): The effect of taxes and depreciation on corporate investment and financial leverage, in: Journal of Finance, Vol. 43, pp. 357-373.

DEANGELO, H./ DEANGELO, L. (1987): Management buyouts of publicly traded corporations, in: Financial Analysts Journal, Vol. 43, No. 3, pp. 38-49.

DEANGELO, H./ DEANGELO, L./ RICE, E.M. (1984): Going private, minority freezeouts and shareholder wealth, in: Journal of Law and Economics, Vol. 27, pp. 367-401.

DEANGELO, H./ DEANGELO, L./ WRUCK, K.H. (2002): Asset liquidity, debt covenants, and managerial discretion in financial distress: The collapse of L.A. Gear, in: Journal of Financial Economics, 64, pp. 3-34.

DEANGELO, H./ MASULIS, R. (1980): Optimal capital structure under corporate and personal taxation, in: Journal of Financial Economics, 8, pp. 3-29.

DEANGELO, L. (1986): Accounting numbers as market valuation substitutes: A study of management buyouts of public shareholders, in: Accounting Review, Vol. 61, No. 3, pp. 400-420.

DE JONG, A./ VELD, C. (2001): An empirical analysis of incremental capital structure decisions under managerial entrenchment, in: Journal of Banking and Finance, Vol. 25, pp. 1857-1895.

DELOITTE & TOUCHE (2003): 3. Deloitte & Touche Venture-Capital- und Private-Equity-Studie, Frankfurt a.M. 2003.

DENIS, D.J. (1994): Organizational form and the consequences of highly leveraged transactions: Kroger's recapitalization and Safeway's LBO, in: Journal of Financial Economics, Vol. 36, pp. 193-224.

DESSI, R./ ROBERTSON, D. (1999): Debt, incentives and performance: Evidence from UK panel data, in: Financial Markets Research Centre London School of Economics, Discussion Paper 344, March 2000.

DEWATRIPONT, M./ TIROLE, J. (1994): A theory of debt and equity: Diversity of securities and manager-shareholder congruence, in: Quarterly Journal of Economics, Vol. 109, pp. 1027-1057.

DHALIWAL , D./ TREZEVANT, R. / WANG, S. (1992): Taxes, investment-related tax shields and capital structure, in: Journal of the American Taxation Association, Vol. 14, pp. 1-21.

DIAMOND, D. (1991): Monitoring and Reputation: The choice between Bank Loans and Directly Placed Debt, in: Journal of Political Economy, Vol. 99, 1991, pp. 689-721.

DIAMOND, D. (1993): Seniority and maturity of debt contracts, in: Journal of Financial Economics, 33, pp. 341-368.

DIEM, A. (2005): Akquisitionsfinanzierungen – Kredite für Unternehmensfinanzierungen, C.H. Beck, München 2005.

DITTMAR, A. (2002): Capital structure in corporate spin-offs, Working Paper Kelley School of Business at Indiana University, Version 01/2002, downloaded from SSRN.

DONALDSON, G. (1961): Corporate debt capacity, Harvard University Press, Cambridge 1961.

DOWNES, J./ GOODMAN, J.E. (2003): Dictionary of finance and investment terms, Barron's Financial Guides, New York 2003.

DOWNS, T.W. (1993): Corporate leverage and non-debt tax shields: Evidence on crowding-out, in: Financial Review, Vol. 28, pp. 549-583.

DRILL, M./ BÖHMERT, S. (2003): Akquisitionsfinanzierung im Mittelstand, in: ConVent GmbH (Ed.): M&A-Jahrbuch 2003, pp. 115-118.

DRUKARCZYK, J. (1993): Theorie und Politik der Finanzierung, Verlag Franz Vahlen, München 1993

DRUKARCZYK, J. (2003): Unternehmensbewertung, Verlag Franz Vahlen, München 2003.

EASTERBROOK, F.H. (1984): Two agency-cost explanations of dividends, in: American Economic Review, Vol. 74., pp. 650-659.

EASTERWOOD, J./ SETH, A./ SINGER, R.F. (1993): Strategic redirection in large management buyouts: the evidence from post-buyout restructuring activity, in: Strategic Management Journal, Vol. 14, no. 4, pp. 251-273.

EICHNER, C.A. (2002): Management-Buy-Out Gestaltungen beim Konzern-Spin-Off, Verlag Peter Lang, Frankfurt a.M. 2002.

EINEM, C.V./ TRÄNKLE, C. (2004): Risikokompensationsklauseln und Abwicklungsfragen bei Private-Debt Strukturen, in: Achleitner, A.-K./ Einem, C.v./ Schröder, B.v. (Eds.) (2004): Private Debt – alternative Finanzierung für den Mittelstand, Schäffer-Poeschel, Stuttgart 2004, pp. 169-186.

ERNST, H. (2003): Causes and effects of a single informant bias in empirical innovation research, Working Paper No. 96, Scientific working paper series Otto Beisheim Graduate School of Management (WHU).

FABOZZI, F.J./ MODIGLIANI, F. (1996): Capital markets, institutions and instruments, Prentice Hall, Englewood Cliffs 1996.

FAHRMEIR, L./ HAMERLE, A./ TUTZ, G. (1996): Multivariate statistische Verfahren, Walter de Gruyter & Co., Berlin 1996.

FAMA, E.F. (1970): Efficient capital markets – a review of theory and empirical work, in: Journal of Finance, Vol. 25, pp. 383-417.

FAMA, E.F. (1980): Agency problems and the theory of the firm, in: Journal of Political Economy, Vol. 88, pp. 288-307.

FAMA, E.F. (1985): What's different about banks, in: Journal of Monetary Economics, Vol. 15, pp. 29-37.

FAMA, E.F./ FRENCH, K. (2002): Testing trade-off and pecking-order predictions about dividends and debt, in: Review of Financial Studies, Vol. 15, pp. 1-33.

FAMA, E.F./ FRENCH, K. (2003): Financing decisions: Who issues stock?, CRSP Working paper No. 549.

FAMA, E.F./ JENSEN, M.C. (1983): Separation of ownership and control, in: Journal of Law and Economics, Vol. 26, pp. 301-325.

FAMA, E.F./ MILLER, M. (1972): The Theory of Finance, Holt, Rinehart and Winston, New York 1972.

FAN, J./ TITMAN, S./ TWITE, G. (2003): An international comparison of capital structure and debt maturity choices, in: Working Paper, University of Texas at Austin, downloaded from SSRN.

FEESS, E. (1997): Mikroökonomie – Eine spieltheoretische und anwendungsorientierte Einführung, Metropolis, Marburg 1997.

FEINEN, K. (2001): Leasing, in: Breuer, R.-E. (Ed.) (2001): Handbuch Finanzierung, 3. Edition, Gabler-Verlag, Wiesbaden 2001.

FENN, G./ LIANG, N./ PROWSE, S. (1997): The economics of the private equity market, in Financial Markets, Institutions and Instruments, Vol. 6, No. 4, pp. 1-105.

FERRI, M./ JONES, W. (1979): Determinants of financial structure: A new methodological approach, in: Journal of Finance, Vol. 34, pp. 631-644.

FLUCK, Z. (1998): Optimal financial contracting: Debt versus outside equity, in: Review of Financial Studies, Vol. 11, No. 2, pp. 383-419.

FORST, M. (1992): Management Buy-out und Buy-in als Form der Übernahme mittelständischer Unternehmen, Diss., Schäffer-Poeschel, Stuttgart 1992.

CENTER FOR PRIVATE EQUITY AND ENTREPRENEURSHIP AT AMOS TUCK UNIVERSITY (2002): Private Equity Glossar, in: http://mba.tuck.dartmouth.edu/pecenter/resources/glossary.html, 13.12.2004

FOX, I./ MARCUS, A. (1992): The causes and consequences of leveraged management buyouts, in: Academy of Management Review, Vol. 17, No. 1, pp. 62-85.

FRANK, M./ GOYAL, V. (2003): Capital structure decisions, Working Paper, University of British Columbia and Hong Kong University of Science and Technology, downloaded from SSRN.

FRANKE, G. / HAX, H. (2003): Finanzwirtschaft des Unternehmens und Kapitalmarkt, Springer-Verlag, Heidelberg 2003.

FRANKFURTER, G.M./ GUNAY, E. (1992): Management Buyouts: The sources and sharing of wealth between Insiders and Outside Shareholders, in: Quarterly Review of Economics and Finance, Vol. 32, No. 3, pp. 82-95.

FRANKFURTER, G.M./ KOSEDAG, A. (1996): Management's perception of leveraged buyouts, in: International Review of Financial Analysis, pp. 197-221.

FRIEND, I./ HASBROUCK, J. (1988): Determinants of capital structure, in: Chen, A. (Ed.) (1988): Research in Finance, Vol. 7, JAI Press, New York 1988, pp. 1-19.

FRIEND, I./ LANG, L. (1988): An empirical test of the impact of managerial self-interest on corporate capital structure, in: Journal of Finance, Vol. 43, No. 2, pp. 271-281.

FRITZSCHE, M. (2002): Due Diligence aus rechtlicher Sicht, in: Berens, W./ Brauner, H./Strauch, J. (Eds.) (2002): Due Diligence bei Unternehmensakquisitionen, Schäffer-Poeschel, Stuttgart 2002, pp. 363-387.

FROMMAN, H. (1992): Die Finanzierung von Management-Buy-Outs, in: Lütjen, G. (Ed.) (1992): Management-Buy-Out – Firmenübernahmen durch Management und Belegschaft, Gabler-Verlag, Wiesbaden 1992.

GALE, B.T. (1972): Market share and rate of return, in: Review of Economics and Statistics, Vol. 54, No. 4, pp. 412-423.

GALE, D./ HELLWIG, M. (1985): Incentive-compatible debt contracts: The one-period problem, in: Review of Economic Studies, Vol. 52, pp. 647-669.

GANZERT, S./ KRAMER, L. (1995): Due diligence review – eine Inhaltsbestimmung, in: Wirtschaftsprüfung, Vol. 48, pp. 576-581.

GARDNER, J.C./ TRZCINKA, C.A. (1992): All-equity firms and the balancing theory of capital structure, in: Journal of Financial Research, Vol. 15, pp. 77-90.

GARVEY, G.T./ HANKA, G. (1999): Capital structure and corporate control: The effect of anti-takeover statutes on firm leverage, in: Journal of Finance, Vol. 54, pp. 519-546.

GAVISH, B./ KALAY, A. (1983): On the asset substitution problem, in: Journal of Financial and Quantitative Analysis, Vol. 18, pp. 21-30.

GERETH, B./ SCHULTE, K.W. (1992): Mezzanine-Finanzierung, Bergisch-Gladbach 1992.

GERTLER, M. (2000): The information in the high yield bond spread for the business cycle: evidence and some implications, NBER Working Paper No. W7549, National Bureau of Economic Research, Cambridge (MA).

GILBERT, F.S. (1978): Financing the leveraged buy-out through the acquired assets, in: Harvard Business Review, July/August, pp. 8-16.

GILSON, S. (1997): Transaction costs and capital structure choice: Evidence from financially distressed firms, in: Journal of Finance, Vol. 52, 161-197.

GOLLAND, F. (2003a): Der optimierte Einstiegsprozess – Lösungsansätze für einen erfolgreichen Beteiligungserwerb unter erschwerten Marktbedingungen, in: Jugel, S. (Ed.) (2003): Private Equity Investments – Praxis des Beteiligungsmanage-ments, Gabler-Verlag, pp. 173-184.

GOLLAND, F. (2003b): Erfolgsfaktoren für eine strukturierte Finanzierung im Management Buy-out, in: ConVent GmbH (Ed.): M&A-Jahrbuch 2003, pp. 84-86.

GOLLAND, F./ GEHLHAAR, L. (2003): Große Transaktionen tragen den Markt und Mezzanine Kapital gewinnt weiter an Bedeutung, in: M&A, 10/2003, pp. 447-449.

GOMPERS, P. (1995): Optimal investment, monitoring, and the staging of venture capital, in: Journal of Finance, Vol. 50, No. 5, pp. 1461-1489.

GOMPERS, P. (1998): An examination of convertible securities in venture capital investments, Working Paper, Harvard Business School 1998.

GOMPERS, P./ LERNER, J. (2000): The venture capital cycle, MIT Press, Cambridge 2000.

GOODMAN, L.S./ COHEN, A.H. (1989): Pay-in-kind debentures: An innovation, in: Journal of Portfolio Management, Winter, pp. 6-16.

GOOLD, M./ CAMPBELL, A./ MARCUS, A. (1994): Corporate-level strategy: Creating value in the multibusiness company, John Wiley & Sons, New York 1994.

GOYAL, V./ LEHN, K./ RACIC, S. (2002): Growth opportunities and corporate debt policy: The case of the US defense industry, in: Journal of Financial Economics, Vol. 61, pp. 35-59.

GRAHAM, J.R. (2000): How big are the tax benefits of debt?, in: Journal of Finance, Vol. 55, pp. 1901-1941.

GRAMMATIKOS, T. / MAKHIJA, A./ THOMPSON, H. (1988): Financing Corporate Takeovers by Individuals Seeking Control, in: Managerial and Decision Economics, 9. (1988), 227-235.

GRÄPER, M. (1993): Management Buyout – Eine empirische Analyse zur deutschen Entwicklung bis 1990, Wiss.-Verlag Vauk, Kiel 1993.

GREEN, R.C./ TALMOR, E. (1986): Asset substitution and the agency cost of debt financing, in: Journal of Banking and Finance, Vol. 10, pp. 391-399.

GREEN, S. (1992): The impact of ownership and capital structure on managerial motivation and strategy in management buyouts: A cultural analysis, in: Journal of Management Studies, Vol. 29, No. 4, pp. 513-535.

GRINBLATT, M./ TITMAN, S. (1998): Financial Markets and Corporate Strategy, McGraw-Hill, Chicago.

GROSSMAN, S./ HART, O. (1982). Corporate Financial Structure and Managerial Incentives, in: McCall, J.(Ed) (1982): The Economics of Information and Uncertainty, The University of Chicago Press, pp. 123-155.

GROSSMAN, S./ HART, O. (1986): The costs and benefits of ownership: A theory of vertical and lateral integration, in: Journal of Political Economy, Vol. 94, 691-719.

GROSSMAN, S./ HART, O. (1988): One share – one vote and the market for corporate control, in: Journal of Financial Economics, Vol. 20, pp. 175-202.

GUEDES, J./ OPLER, T. (1996): The determinants of the maturity of corporate debt issues, in: Journal of Finance, Vol. 51, No. 1, pp. 1809-1833.

GÜNTHER, T. (1997): Unternehmenswertorientiertes Controlling, Verlag Vahlen, München 1997.

GUJARATI, D. (1995): Basic Econometrics, McGraw-Hill, New York 1995.

GUL, F.A. (1999): Growth opportunities, capital structure and dividend policies in Japan, in: Journal of Corporate Finance, Vol. 5, No. 2, pp. 141-168.

GUTENBERG, E. (1987): Grundlagen der Betriebswirtschaftslehre, Band III, Die Finanzen, Springer-Verlag, Berlin 1987.

HABERMAN, S. (1978): Analysis of qualitative data, Academic Press, San Diego 1978.

HAGLE, T.M./ MITCHELL, G.E. (1992): Goodness-of-fit measures for probit and logit, in: American Journal of Political Science, Vol. 36, pp. 762-784.

HAFNER, R. (1993): Unternehmensbewertungen als Instrumente zur Durchsetzung von Verhandlungspositionen, in BfuP, Vol. 45, p. 79-89.

HALL, G./ HUTCHINSON, P./ MICHAELIS, N. (2000): Industry effects on the determinants of unquoted SME's capital structures, in: International Journal of the Economics of Business, Vol. 7, No. 3 pp. 297-312.

HARRIS, M./ RAVIV, A. (1988): Corporate governance: Voting rights and majority rules, Journal of Financial Economics, Vol. 20, pp. 231-259.

HARRIS, M./ RAVIV, A. (1989): The design of securities, Journal of Financial Economics, Vol. 21, pp. 255-287.

HARRIS, M./ RAVIV, A. (1990): Capital structure and the informationa role of debt, in: Journal of Finance, Vol. 45, No. 2, pp. 321-349.

HARRIS, M./ RAVIV, A. (1991): The theory of capital structure, in: Journal of Finance, Vol. 46, No. 1, pp. 297-355.

HARRIS, R./ SIEGEL, D.S./ WRIGHT, M. (2002): Assessing the impact of management buyouts on economic efficiency: plant-level evidence from the United Kingdom, Working Paper, October, p. 0-27.

HARRIS, T.J. (2002): Bridge over troubled waters, in: Journal of Private Equity, Winter 2002, pp. 59-63.

HART, O. (1983): The market mechanism as an incentive scheme, in: Bell Journal of Economics, Vol. 14, pp. 366-382.

HART, O. (1995): Firms, contracts and financial structure, Oxford University Press, Oxford, 1995.

HART, O. (2001): Financial contracting, Discussion Paper No. 327, Harvard Law School, Cambridge 2001.

HART, O./ MOORE, J. (1994): A theory of debt based on the inalienability of human capital, in: Quarterly Journal of Economics, 109, 842-879.

HART, O./ MOORE, J. (1995): Debt and seniority: An analysis of the role of hard claims in constraining management, in: American Economic Review, Vol. 85, No. 3. pp. 567-585.

HART, O./ MOORE, J. (1998): Default and Renegotiation: A dynamic model of debt, in: Quarterly Journal of Economics, 113, pp. 1-41.

HARTMANN-WENDELS, T. (1991): Rechnungslegung der Unternehmen und Kapitalmarkt aus informationsökonomischer Sicht, Physica-Verlag, Heidelberg 1991.

HARTUNG, J. (2002): Statistik – Lehr- und Handbuch der angewandten Statistik, Oldenbourg-Verlag, München / Wien 2002.

HARVEY, M./ LUSCH, R. (1995): Expanding the nature and scope of due diligence, in: Journal of Business Venturing, Vol. 10, pp. 5-21.

HAUGEN, R.A./ SENBET, L.W. (1978): The insignificance of bankruptcy costs, in: Journal of Finance, Vol. 33, No. 2, pp. 383-393.

HAUGEN, R.A./ SENBET, L.W. (1988): Bankruptcy and agency costs: their significance to the theory of optimal capital structure, in: Journal of Financial and Quantitative Analysis, Vol. 23, No. 1, pp. 27-38.

HAYEK, F.A. (1945): The use of knowledge in society, in: American Economic Review, Vol. 35, Nr. 4, p. 519-530.

HAYNES, M./ THOMPSON, S./ WRIGHT, M. (1999): Sources of venture capital deals: MBOs, IBOs and corporate refocusing, in: Wright, M. et al. (Eds.) (1999): Management buy-outs and venture capital, pp. 219-237.

HIROTA, S. (1999): Are corporate financing decisions different in Japan? An empirical study on capital structure, in: Journal of the Japanese and International Economies, Vol.13, pp. 201-229.

HIRSHLEIFER, J. (1970): Investment, interest and capital, Prentice-Hall, Englewood Cliffs 1970.

HITE, G.L./ VETSUYPENS, M.R. (1989): Management buyouts of divisions and shareholder wealth, in: Journal of Finance, vol. 44, No. 9, pp. 953-970.

HOCHSTÄDTER, D. (1996): Statistische Methodenlehre – Ein Lehrbuch für Wirtschafts- und Sozialwissenschaftler, Harri Deutsch Verlag, Frankfurt / Main 1996.

HÖLTERS, W. (2002): Handbuch des Unternehmens- und Beteiligungskaufs, Verlag O. Schmidt, Köln 2002.

HOFFMANN, P./ RAMKE, R. (1992): Management-Buy-Out in der Bundesrepublik, Erich Schmidt Verlag, Berlin 1992.

HOLTHAUSEN, R.W./ LARCKER, D.F. (1996): The financial performance of reverse leveraged buyouts, in: Journal of Financial Economics, Vol. 42, No. 3, pp. 293-332.

HOMAIFA, G./ ZIETZ, J./ BENKATO, O. (1994): An empirical model of capital structure: Some new evidence, in: Journal of Business Finance and Accounting, Vol. 21, pp. 1-14.

HONERT, J. (1995): Der deutsche Management Buy-Out : Bedingungen, Methodik und rechtliche Besonderheiten im Vergleich zu einem herkömmlichen Unternehmenskauf unter besonderer Berücksichtigung des GmbH-Rechts, Diss., Bremen 1995.

HOSMER, D.W./ LEMESHOW, S. (1980): A goodness-of-fit testing for multiple logistic regression analysis when the estimated probabilities are small, in: Biometrical Journal, Vol. 30, pp. 911-924.

HOSMER, D.W./ LEMESHOW, S. (2000): Applied logistic regression, John Wiley & Sons, New York 2000.

HOTCHKISS, E. (1995): Post-bankruptcy performance and management turnover, Journal of Finance, Vol. 50, pp. 3-22.

HOUBEN, E. (2002): Venture capital, double-sided adverse selection, and double-sided moral hazard, Working Paper, University of Kiel.

HOVAKIMIAN, A./ OPLER, T./ TITMAN, S. (2001): The debt-equity choice, in: Journal of Financial and Quantitative Analysis, Vol. 36, pp. 1-24.

HUG, J./ ERNST, D. (2003): Finanzierungsmodelle von Leveraged Buy-outs, in: M&A-Review, Vol. 10, pp. 441-446.

HUYDTS, H.J. (1992): Management Buyout als strategische Option zur Regelung der Nachfolge in mittelgrossen Familienunternehmen, Diss., Frankfurt a. M. 1992.

INDERST, R./ MÜLLER, H.M. (1999): Ownership concentration, monitoring, and the agency cost of debt, Working Paper, University of Mannheim, September 1999.

ISAGAWA, N. (2000): Convertible debt: An effective financial instrument to control managerial opportunism, in: Review of Financial Economics, No. 9, pp. 15-26.

JACCARD, J. (2001): Interaction effects in logistic regression, Sage University Paper Series, Thousand Oaks, CA 2001.

JAFFEE, D.M./ RUSSEL, T. (1976): Imperfect information, uncertainty, and credit rationing, in: Quarterly Journal of Economics, Vol. 90, pp. 651-666.

JAKOBY, S. (2000): Erfolgsfaktoren von Management Buyouts in Deutschland, Diss., Josef Eul Verlag, Lohmar 2000.

JARRELL, G.A./ BRICKLEY, A./ NETTER, J.M. (1988): The market for corporate control: The evidence since 1980, in: Journal of Economic Perspectives, 2, pp. 49-68.

JENSEN, G.H./ SOLBERG, D.P./ ZORN, T.S. (1992): Simultaneous determination of insider ownership, debt and dividend policies, in: Journal of Financial Quantitative Analysis, Vol. 27, pp. 247-261.

JENSEN, M.C. (1986): Agency costs of free cash flow, corporate finance and takeovers, in: American Economic Review, Papers and Proceedings, Vol. 76, pp. 323-329.

JENSEN, M.C. (1989a): Active Investors, LBO's, and the privatization of bankruptcy, in: Journal of Applied Corporate Finance, Vol. 2, No. 1, pp. 35-44.

JENSEN, M.C. (1989b): Eclipse of the public corporation, in: Harvard Business Review, Vol. 67, No. 5, pp. 61-74.

JENSEN, M.C. (1991): Corporate Control and the Politics of Finance, in: Journal of Applied Corporate Finance, No. 4, pp. 13-33.

JENSEN, M.C./ MECKLING, W.H. (1976): Managerial behaviour, agency costs and ownership structure, in: Journal of Financial Economics, Vol. 3, pp. 305-360.

JENSEN, M.C./ RUBACK, R.S. (1983): The market for corporate control: The scientific evidence, in: Journal of Finance, Vol. 38, No. 5, pp. 5-50.

JOHNSON, S.A. (1997): An empirical analysis of the determinants of corporate debt ownership structure, in: Journal of Financial and Quantitative Analysis, Vol. 32, pp. 47-69.

JORDAN, J./ LOWE, J./ TAYLOR, P. (1998): Strategy and financial policy in UK small firms, in: Journal of Business Financing and Accounting, Vol. 25, pp. 1-27.

JUNG, K./ KIM, J.C./ STULZ, R. (1996): Timing, investment opportunities, managerial discretion, and the security issue decision, in: Journal of Financial Economics, Vol. 42, pp. 159-180.

KALE, J./ NOE, T./ RAMIREZ, G. (1991): The effect of business risk on corporate capital structure: Theory and evidence, in: Journal of Finance, Vol. 46, No. 5, pp. 1693-1715.

KAPLAN, S. (1989): Sources of value in management buyouts, in: Amihud, Y. (Ed.) (1989): Leveraged management buyouts, Homewood IL, Dow Jones-Irwin, pp. 95-101.

KAPLAN, S./ STEIN, J. (1990): How risky is the debt in highly leveraged transactions? in: Journal of Financial Economics, Vol. 27, pp. 215-245.

KAPLAN, S./ STEIN, J. (1993): The evolution of buyout pricing and financial structures in the 1980s, in: Quarterly Journal of Economics, May 1993, pp. 313-357.

KAPLAN, S./ STROMBERG, P. (2001): Financial contracting meets the real world: an empirical analysis of venture capital contracts, University of Chicago Graduate School of Business, Working Paper downloaded from SSRN.

KAUFMAN, A./ ENGLANDER, E. (1993): Kohlberg, Kravis Roberts & Co. and the restructuring of American capitalism, in: Business History Review, Vol. 67, No. 1, pp. 52-97.

KESTER, C.W. (1986): Capital and ownership structure: A comparison of United States and Japanese manufacturing corporations, in: Financial Management, pp. 5-16.

KESTER, C.W./ LUEHRMANN, T.A. (1995): Rehabilitating the leveraged buyout, in: Harvard Business Review, May-June, pp. 119-130.

KIM, W.S./ SORENSON, E.H. (1986): Evidence on the impact of agency costs of debt on corporate debt policy, in: Journal of Financial and Quantitative Analysis, Vol. 21, pp. 131-144.

KLEIN, D.P./ BELT, B. (1994): Sustainable growth and choice of financing: A test of the pecking-order hypothesis, in: Review of Financial Economics, Vol. 3, pp. 143-154.

KNIGHT, F.H. (1921): Risk, uncertainty, and profit, Chicago University Press, Chicago 1921.

KOEPLIN, J./ SARIN, A./ SHAPIRO, A.C. (2000): The private company discount, in: Journal of Applied Corporate Finance, pp. 94-101.

KPMG (2003): KPMG Leveraged Finance Studie 2003 – Eine Bestandsaufnahme des deutschen Fremdkapitalmarktes für Buyout- und strukturierte Übernahme-finanzierungen, Frankfurt a. M. 2003.

KRAFFT, M. (1997): Der Ansatz der logistischen Regression, in: Zeitschrift für Betriebswirtschaft, Vol. 67, No. 5/6, pp. 636-641.

KRAFT, V. (2001): Private Equity für Turnaround-Investitionen, Campus-Verlag, Frankfurt a. M. 2001.

KRALLINGER, J. (1997): Mergers & Acquisitions, McGraw-Hill, New York.

KRAUS, A./ LITZENBERGER, R.H. (1973): A state-preference model of optimal financial leverage, in: Journal of Finance, Vol. 28, pp. 911-922.

KREBS, A. (1990): Management Buyout in der Schweiz – Rahmenbedingungen und Finanzierungskonzepte, Verlag Paul Haupt, Bern.

KREBS, A./ ECKHARDT, U. (1998): Neuere Entwicklungen in der Finanzierung von Management Buy-outs, in: Manager Bilanz, Juli 1998, pp. 16-19.

KROPP, M. (1992): Management Buyouts und die Theorie der Unternehmung, Gabler-Verlag, Wiesbaden, 1992.

KÜTING, K.H. (2000): Perspektiven der externen Rechnungslegung, in: Schweizer Treuhänder, Vol. 74, No. 3, pp. 153-168.

KUMAR, M./ STERN, L./ ANDERSON, J. (1993): Conducting interorganizational research using key informants, in: Academy of Management Journal, Vol. 36, pp. 1633-1651.

LAJOUX, A.R./ WESTON, J.F. (1999): The art of M&A financing and refinancing – a guide to sources and instruments for external growth, McGraw-Hill, New York.

LANG, L.H./ OFEK, E./ STULZ, R.M. (1996): Leverage, investment, and firm growth, in: Journal of Financial Economics, Vol. 40, pp. 3-29.

LANG, L.H./ STULZ, R.M./ WALKING, R.A. (1989): Managerial performance, Tobin's q and the gains from succesful tender offers, in: Journal of Financial Economics, Vol. 24, pp. 137-154.

LAPORTA, R./ LOPEZ-DE-SILANES, F./ SHLEIFER, A. (1999): Corporate ownership around the world, in: Journal of Finance, Vol. 54, pp. 471-517.

LASFER, A. (1995): Agency costs, taxes and debt: The UK evidence, in: European Financial Management, Vol. 1, No. 3, pp. 265-285.

LAUB, J. (1995): Management-Buy-Outs und Management-Buy-Ins in den neuen Bundes-ländern, Diss., Deutscher Universitäts-Verlag, Wiesbaden 1995.

LEE, D.S. (1992): Management buyout proposals and inside information, in: Journal of Finance, Vol. 47, No. 3, pp. 1061-1079.

LEE, H.W./ FIGLEWICZ, R.E. (1999): Characteristics of firms that issue convertible debt versus convertible preferred stock, in: Quarterly Review of Economics and Finance, Vol. 39, pp. 547-563.

LEE, H.W./ GENTRY, J.A. (1995): An empirical study of the corporate choice among common stock, convertible bonds, and straight debt: A cash flow interpretation, in: Quarterly Review Economics and Finance, Vol. 35, No. 4, pp. 397-419.

LEHN, K./ POULSEN, A. (1989): Free cash flow and stockholder gains in going private transactions, in: Journal of Finance, Vol. 44, No. 3, pp. 771-787.

LELAND, H.E. (1989): LBOs and taxes: No one to blame but ourselves?, in: California Management Review, Vol. 32, No. 1, pp. 19-29.

LELAND, H.E./ PYLE, D. (1977): Informational Asymmetries, Financial Structure, and Financial Intermediation, in: Journal of Finance, Vol. 32, No. 2, pp. 371-387.

LEMMON, M.L./ ZENDER, J.F. (2002): Debt capacity and tests of capital structure theories, in: Working Paper, University of Utah and University of Colorado at Boulder, October, downloaded from SSRN.

LESCHKE, J. (2003): Exiterfahrungen im deutschen Beteiligungsmarkt, in: Jugel, S. (Ed.) (2003): Private Equity Investments – Praxis des Beteiligungsmanagements, Gabler-Verlag, pp. 247-256, Wiebaden 2003.

LICHTENBERG, F./ SIEGEL, D. (1990): The effects of leveraged buyouts on productivity and related aspects of firm behaviour, in: Journal of Financial Economics, Vol. 27, pp. 165-194.

LIEBESKIND, J./ WIERSEMA, M./ HANSEN, G. (1992): LBOs, corporate restructuring, and the incentive-intensity hypothesis, in: Financial Management, Spring 1992, pp. 73-88.

LINK, G. (2001): Anreizkompatible Finanzierung durch Mezzanine-Kapital, Diss., Verlag Peter Lang, Frankfurt a.M. 2001.

LINS, K.V. (2003): Equity ownership and firm value in emerging markets, in: Journal of Financial and Quantitative Analysis, Vol. 38, No. 1, pp. 159-164.

LÖFFLER, A. (1998): WACC approach and nonconstant leverage ratio, Working Paper, FU Berlin, February 1998.

LÖFFLER, A. (2000): Tax shield in an LBO, Working Paper, FU Berlin, March 13, 2000.

LONG, J.S. (1997): Regression models for categorical and limited dependent variables, Sage University Paper Series, Thousand Oaks, CA 1997.

LONG, M.S./ MALITZ, E.B. (1985): Investment Patterns and Financial Leverage, in: Friedman (Ed.), Corporate Capital Structures in the US, University of Chicago Press, Chicago IL 1985, pp. 325-351.

LONG, W.F./ RAVENSCRAFT, D.J. (1993a): The financial performance of whole company LBOs, Discussion Paper, Kenan-Flagler Business School at University of North Carolina, November, Chapel Hill 1993.

LONG, W.F./ RAVENSCRAFT, D.J. (1993b): LBOs, Debate and R&D intensity, in: Strategic Management Journal, 14 (summer issue), pp. 119-135

LOWE, J./ NAUGHTON, T./ TAYLOR, P. (1994): The impact of corporate strategy on the capital structure of Australian companies, in: Managerial and Decision Economics, Vol. 15, pp. 245-257.

LOWENSTEIN, L. (1985): Management Buyouts, in: Columbia Law Review, May 1985, pp. 730-784.

LUIPPOLD, T. (1991): Management Buy-Outs – Evaluation ihrer Einsatzmöglichkeiten in Deutschland, Kilgus, E. et al. (Eds.), Verlag Paul Haupt, Bern.

MACKAY, P./ PHILLIPS, G. (2002): Is there an optimal industry financial structure?, Working Paper, Southern Methodist University, Version 11/06/2002, downloaded from SSRN.

MACKIE-MASON, J. (1990): Do taxes affect corporate financing decisions? Journal of Finance, Vol. 45, pp. 1471-1494.

MADDALA, G. (1983): Limited-dependent and qualitative variables in econometrics, Cambridge University Press, Cambridge 1983.

MADDALA, G. (1991): A perspective on the use of limited-dependent and qualitative variables models in accounting research, in : The Accounting Review, Vol. 66, pp. 788-807.

MAKSIMOVIC, V. (1995): Financial structure and product market competition, in: R.A. Jarrow et al. (Eds.) (1995): Handbooks in operations research and management science, Vol. 9: Finance, Amsterdam, pp. 887-920.

MANIGART, S./ LOCKETT, A./ MEULEMAN, M./ WRIGHT, M./ LANDSTRÖM, H./ BRUINING, H./ DESBRIERES, P./ HOMMEL, U. (2002): Why do European venture capital companies syndicate?, Working Paper, Erasmus Research Institute of Management, Rotterdam School of Management 2002.

MARAIS, L./ SCHIPPER, K./ SMITH, A. (1989): Wealth effects of going private for senior securities, in: Journal of Financial Economics, Vol. 35, 6, pp. 155-191.

MARSH, P. (1982): The choice between equity and debt: An empirical study, in: Journal of Finance, Vol. 37, pp. 121-144.

MARKIDES, C.C. (1997): Strategic innovation, in: MIT Sloan Management Review, Vol. 38, No. 3, pp. 9-23.

MAYER, H. (2004): Interview und schriftliche Befragung – Entwicklung, Durchführung und Auswertung, Oldenbourg Verlag, München 2004.

MCCONNELL, J.J./ SERVAES, H. (1995): Equity Ownership and the Two Faces of Debt, in: Journal of Financial Economics, Vol. 39, pp. 131-157.

MCFADDEN, D. (1974): Conditional logit analysis and qualitative choice behaviour, in: Frontiers in Econometrics, Zarembka, P. (Ed.) (1974), New York 1974, pp. 105-142.

MCKELVEY, R.D./ ZAVOINA, W. (1975): A statistical model for the analysis of ordinal level dependent variables, in: Journal of Mathematical Sociology, Vol. 4, pp. 103-120.

MENARD, S.W. (2000): Coefficients of determination of multiple logistic regression analysis, in: The American Statistician, Vol. 54, pp. 17-24.

MENARD, S.W. (2001): Applied logistic regression analysis, Sage University Paper Series, Thousand Oaks, CA 2001.

MERTON, R.C. (1974): On the pricing of corporate debt: The risk structure of interest rates, in: Journal of Finance, Vol. 29, 449-470.

MERTON, R.C. (1987): A simple model of capital market equilibrium with incomplete information, in: Journal of Finance 1987, Vol. 42, No. 3, pp. 483-510.

MICHAELAS, N./ CHITTENDEN, F./ POUTZIOURIS, P. (1999): Financial policy and capital structure choice in UK SMEs: Empirical evidence from company panel data, in: Small Business Economics, Vol. 12, pp. 113-130.

MICHEL, A./ SHAKED, I. (1991): RJR – A case study of a complex leveraged buyout, in: Financial Analysts Journal, Vol. 47, 5. (1991), pp. 15-27.

MICKEY, J./ GREENLAND, S. (1998): A study of the impact of confounder-selection criteria on effect estimation, in: American Journal of Epidemiology, Vol. 129, pp. 125-137.

MILDE, H. (1990): Übernahmefinanzierung und LBO-Transaktionen, in: Zeitschrift für Betriebswirtschaft, Vol. 60, No. 7, pp. 647-664.

MILES, J.A./ EZZELL, J.R. (1980): The weighted average cost of capital, perfect markets, and project life: a clarification, in: Journal of Financial and Quantitative Analysis, Vol. 15, No. 3, pp. 719-730.

MILGROM, P./ ROBERTS, J. (1992): Economics, organisation, and management, Prentice Hall, New Jersey 1992.

MILLER, M. (1977): Debt and taxes, in: Journal of Finance, Vol. 32., No. 2, pp. 261-275.

MILLER, M. (1988): The Modigliani-Miller Propositions after thirty years, in: Journal of Economic Perspectives, No. 2, pp. 99-120.

MIRA, F.S. (2003): How SME uniqueness affects capital structure, Working Paper Universidad Cardenal Herrera, downloaded from SSRN.

MITTENDORFER, R. (2001): Finanzierungsmodelle von Leveraged Buyouts, in: Stadler, W. (Ed.) (2001): Venture Capital und Private Equity – Erfolgreich wachsen mit Beteiligungskapital, Dt. Wirtschaftsdienst, Köln 2001, pp. 141-184.

MÖLLER, K. (1996): Nachrangige Verbindlichkeiten, Dt. Sparkassenverlag, Stuttgart 1996.

MODGLIANI, F./ MILLER, M. (1958): The cost of capital, corporate finance, and theory of investment, in: American Economic Review, Vol. 48, pp. 261-297.

MODGLIANI, F./ MILLER, M. (1963): Corporate income taxes and the cost of capital: A correction, in: American Economic Review, Vol. 53, pp. 433-443.

MORCK, R./ SHLEIFER, A./ VISHNY, R.W. (1990): Do managerial objectives drive bad acquisitions?, in: Journal of Finance, Vol. 45, pp. 31-48.

MÜLLER, H.P. (1996): Steuerrechtliche Fragen, in: Hölters, W. (Ed.) (1996): Handbuch der Unternehmens- und Beteiligungskaufs – Grundfragen, Bewertung, Finanzierung, Steuerrecht, Arbeitsrecht, Vertragsrecht, Kartellrecht, Vertragsbeispiele, Köln 1996, pp. 269-324.

MÜLLER-TRIMBUSCH, J. (1999): High-Yield Anleihen – Perspektiven für die Risikofinan-zierung deutscher Unternehmen, Diss., Deutscher Universitäts-Verlag, Wiesbaden 1999.

MUNRO, J.W. (1996): Convertible debt financing: An empirical analysis, in: Journal of Business Finance and Accounting, Vol. 23, pp. 319-334.

MUSCARELLA, C./ VETSUYPENS, M. (1990): Efficiency and organisational structure: A study of reverse-LBOs, in: Journal of Finance, Vol. 45, No. 5, pp. 1389-1413.

MUSIELA, M./ RUTKOWSKI, M. (1998): Martingale methods in financial modelling, Springer Verlag, Berlin / Heidelberg 1998.

MÜLLER, O. (2003a): Mezzanine Finance – Neue Perspektiven in der Unternehmensführung, Diss., Verlag Paul Haupt, Bern 2003.

MUSCARELLA, C.J./ VETSUYPENS, M.R. (1990): Efficiency and organizational structure: A study of reverse LBO's, in: Journal of Finance, Vol. 45, 5. (1990), pp. 1389-1413.

MYERS, S.C. (1977): Determinants of corporate borrowing, in: Journal of Financial Economics, Vol. 13, pp. 187-221.

MYERS, S.C. (1984): The capital structure puzzle, in: Journal of Finance, Vol. 39, No. 3, pp. 575-592.

MYERS, M.C./ MAJLUF, N.S. (1984): Corporate financing and investment decisions when firms have information that investors do not have, in: Journal of Financial Economics, Vol. 13, pp. 187-221.

NADIG, L. (1992): Spin offs mittels Management-Buyout: die Veräusserung von Unternehmensteilen durch Verkauf an das bisherige Management, Diss., Verlag Paul Haupt, Bern 1992.

NAGELKERKE, N.J.D. (1991): A note on a general definition of the coefficient of deter-mination, in: Biometrika, Vol. 78, pp. 691-692.

NATUSCH, I. (2002): Due Diligence aus Sicht einer Beteiligungsgesellschaft, in: Berens, W./ Brauner, H./Strauch, J. (Eds.) (2002): Due Diligence bei Unternehmens-akquisitionen, Schäffer-Poeschel, Stuttgart 2002, pp. 535-554.

NEUKIRCHEN, D. (1996): Steuerung von Management Buy-Out-Minderheitsbeteiligungen – Eine systematische Betrachtung aus Sicht der Finanzinvestoren, Gabler-Verlag, Wiesbaden 1996.

NEUS, W. (1989): Ökonomische Agency-Theorie und Kapitalmarktgleichgewicht, Diss., Gabler-Verlag, Wiesbaden 1989.

NEUS, W. (1995): Zur Theorie der Finanzierung kleinerer Unternehmungen, Habil., Gabler-Verlag, Wiesbaden 1995.

NEVITT, P./ FABOZZI, F. (2000): Project financing, Euromoney, London 2000.

NEWBOULD, G.D./ CHATFIELD, R.E./ ANDERSON, R.F. (1992): Leveraged buyouts and tax incentives, in: Financial Management, Spring 1992, pp. 50-57.

NUSSBAUM, P. (1995): Besicherung durch die Aktiva der Zielgesellschaft im Leveraged Buyout: Eine Untersuchung zu den fraudulent conveyance laws und den §§ 30, 31 GmbHG, Diss., München 1995.

OECD (2002): OECD Small and Medium Enterprise Outlook - 2002 Edition, Center for Entrepreneurship, SMEs and Local Development.

OFEK, E. (1994): Efficiency gains in unsuccessful managment buyouts, in: Journal of Finance, Vol. 49, No. 2, pp. 637-654.

OGNIBENE, P. (1971): Correcting nonresponse bias in mail questionnaires, in: Journal of Marketing Research, Vol. 8, pp. 233-235.

OPLER, T.C. (1992): Operating performance in leveraged buyouts: Evidence from 1985-1989, in: Financial Management, (spring) 1992, p. 50-57.

OPLER, T.C. (1993): Controlling financial distress costs in leveraged buyouts with financial innovations, in: Financial Management, (autumn) 1993, pp. 79-90.

OPLER, T.C./ TITMAN, S. (1993): The Determinants of leveraged buyout activity: Free cash flow vs. financial distress costs, in: Journal of Finance, Vol. 48, 5. (1993), pp. 1985-1999.

OZKAN, A. (2001): Determinants of capital structure and adjustments to long run target: Evidence from UK panel data, in: Journal of Business Finance and Accounting, Vol. 28, Jan/March 2001, pp. 175-198.

PALEPU, K. (1990): Consequences of leveraged buyouts, in: Journal of Financial Economics, Vol. 27, 1. (1990), pp. 247-262.

PAMPEL, C.F. (2000): Logistic Regression – A primer, Sage University Paper Series, Thousand Oaks, CA 2000.

PERILLE, R.F. (1996): Mezzanine – Efficient financing for recapitalisation or rapid growth, in: Corporate Cashflow, 17, pp. 36-38.

PERRIDON, L./ STEINER, M. (2004): Finanzwirtschaft der Unternehmung, Vahlen, München 2004.

PETERS, H.P. (1988): MBO-Finanzierungen, in: Dokumentation zum Management Buyout-Kongress in Neuss am 1.-2. März 1988, pp. 152-189.

PHAN, P.H./ HILL, C.W.L. (1995): Organizational restructuring and economic performance in leveraged buyouts: an ex-post study, in: Academy of Management Journal, vol. 38, no. 3 (June), pp. 704.739.

PHILLIPS, G.M. (1995): Increased debt and product market competition: An empirical analysis, in: Journal of Financial Economics, 37, pp. 189-238.

PILCHER, C.J. (1955): Raising capital with convertible securities, in: Michigan Business Studies, 21/2.

PINDYCK, R.S./ RUBINFELD, D.L. (1991): Econometric models and economic forecasts, McGraw-Hill, New York 1991.

POWERS, D.A./ XIE, Y. (2000): Statistical methods for categorical data analysis, Academic Press, San Diego 2000.

PRICEWATERHOUSECOOPERS / 3i (2004): Global Private Equity 2004, Survey PwC / 3i, London 2004.

RAJAN, R./ ZINGALES, L. (1995): What do we know about capital structure? Some empirical evidence from international data, in: Journal of Finance, Vol. 50, pp. 1421-1460.

REED, S./ LAJOUX, A. (1995): The Art of M&A: A merger / acquisition / buyout guide, Burr Ridge (Illinois).

REISINGER, H. (1996): Goodness-of-Fit-Maße in linearen Regressions- und Logit-Modellen – Theorie und Anwendung in der empirischen Markforschung, Diss., Verlag Peter Lang, Frankfurt / Main 1996.

REMMERS, L./ STONEHILL, A./ WRIGHT, R./ BECKHUISEN, T. (1974): Industry and size as debt ratio determinants in manufacturing internationally, in: Financial Mangement, Summer, pp. 24-32.

RICHTER, R./ FURUBOTN, E.G. (1999): Neue Institutionenökonomik: Eine Einführung und kritische Würdigung, Mohr Siebeck.

RILEY, J. (1975): Competitive Signalling, in: Journal of Economic Theory, 10, pp. 175-186.

ROBICHEK, A.A./ MYERS, S.C. (1965): Optimal financing decisions, Prentice-Hall, Englewood Cliffs 1965.

RODEN, D.M./ LEWELLEN, W.G. (1995): Corporate capital structure decisions: evidence from leveraged buyouts, in: Financial Management, Vol. 24, No. 2, pp. 76-87.

ROGGE, H.J. (1992): Marktforschung – Elemente und Methoden betrieblicher Informationsgewinnung, Carl Hanser, München / Wien 1992.

ROTHSCHILD, M./ STIGLITZ, J. (1976): Equilibrium in competitive insurance markets: An essay on the economics of imperfect information, in: Quarterly Journal of Economics, 90, pp. 629-649.

ROSS, S.A. (1977): The Determination of the Financial Structure: The Incentive-Signalling Approach, in: Bell Journal of Economics, Vol. 8, 1977, pp. 23-40.

ROSS, S.A./ WESTERFIELD, R.W./ JAFFE, J.F. (2005): Corporate Finance, McGraw-Hill, New York 2005.

RUß, O./ GEBHARDT, G. (2002): Erklärungsfaktoren für den Einsatz von Währungsderivaten bei deutschen Unternehmen – eine empirische Logit-Analyse, Working Paper No. 100, J.W. Goethe-Universität, Frankfurt a.M..

RYAN, T.R (1997): Modern regression models, Wiley & Sons, New York 1997.

SACHS, L. (1997): Angewandte Statistik – Anwendung statistischer Methoden, Springer-Verlag, Berlin / Heidelberg 1997.

SAHLMANN, W.A. (1990): The structure and governance of venture capital organisations, in: Journal of Financial Economics, Vol. 27, pp. 473-521.

SCHERR, F.C./ HULBERT, H.M. (2001): The debt maturity structure of small firms, in: Financial Management, Vol. 30, pp. 85-111.

SCHIERECK, D./ KLAB, A./ KITZMANN, J. (2004): Finanzierung von Management Buy-Outs und das Beispiel Messer Griesheim, in: WISU, 03/04, pp. 327-332.

SCHLITTGEN, R. (2000): Einführung in die Statistik. Analyse und Modellierung von Daten, München / Wien 2000.

SCHMID, H. (1994): Leveraged Management Buyout: Begriff, Gestaltungen, optimale Kapitalstruktur und ökonomische Bewertung, Diss., Verlag Peter Lang, Frankfurt a.M. 1994.

SCHMIDT, K.M. (2003): Convertible securities and venture capital finance, in: Journal of Finance, Vol. 58, No. 3, pp. 1139-1166.

SCHMIDT, R./ TERBERGER, E. (1997): Grundzüge der Investitions- und Finanzierungstheorie, Gabler-Verlag, Wiesbaden 1997.

SCHUMACHER, F. (2001): Unternehmensfinanzierung und Produktmarktwettbewerb, Diss., Duncker & Humblot, Berlin 2001.

SCHWENHOLD, F. (2001): Finanzierungsentscheidungen börsennotierter deutscher Aktiengesellschaften, Diss., Verlag Peter Lang, Frankfurt a.M. 2001.

SCHWENKEDEL, S. (1991): Management Buyout – Ein neues Geschäftsfeld für Banken, Wiesbaden 1991.

SCHWIEN, B. (1995): Das Management-Buy-Out-Konzept in der Bundesrepublik Deutsch-land – Ein Instrument zur Erhaltung und Schaffung mittelständischer Wirtschafts-strukturen, insbesondere in den neuen Bundesländern, Diss., Verlag Peter Lang, Frankfurt a. M. 1995.

SCOTT, J.H. (1977): Bankruptcy, secured debt, and optimal capital structure, in: Journal of Finance, Vol. 32, No.1, pp. 1-19.

SEBASTIAN, K.H./ NIEDERDRENK, R./ TESCH, A. (1998): Market Due Diligence: Bewertung von Unternehmen aus Sicht des Marktes, in: MAR, pp. 207-211.

SIMONOFF, J.S. (2003): Analyzing categorical data, Springer Verlag, Heidelberg / Berlin 2003.

SINGH, H. (1990): Management buyouts: distinguishing characteristics and operating changes prior to public offering, in: Strategic Management Journal, Vol. 11, special issue, p. 111.

SHAH, S./ THAKOR, A. (1987): Optimal Capital Structure and Project Financing, in: Journal of Economic Theory, 42, 209-243.

SHAPIRO, A./ TITMAN, S. (1986): An integrated approach to corporate risk management, in: Stern, J.M./ Chew, D.H. (Eds.) (1986): The revolution in corporate finance, Oxford University Press, pp. 215-229.

SHARPE, S. (1990): Asymmetric information, bank lending, and implicit contracts: a stylized model of customer relationships, in: Journal of Finance, Vol. 45, pp. 1069-1087.

SHENOY, C./ KOCH, P. (1996): The firm's leverage-cash flow relationship, in: Journal of Empirical Finance, Vol. 2, pp. 307-331.

SHLEIFER, A./ VISHNY, R. (1991): Takeovers in the 60s and 80s: evidence and implications, in: Strategic Management Journal, Vol. 12., Special edition, pp. 51-59.

SHLEIFER, A./ VISHNY, R. (1997): A survey of corporate governance, in: Journal of Finance, Vol. 52, pp. 737-783.

SHORT, H./ KEASEY, K./ DUXBURY, D. (2002): Capital structure, managment ownership and large external shareholders: A UK analysis, in: International Journal of the Economics of Business, Vol. 9, No. 3, pp. 375-399.

SHUETRIM, G./ LOWE, G./ MORLING, S. (1993): The determinants of corporate leverage: A panel data analysis, in: Research Discussion Paper 9313, Reserve Bank of Australia, downloaded from SSRN.

SHYAM-SUNDER, L./ MYERS, S.C. (1999): Testing static trade-off against pecking-order models of capital structure, in: Journal of Financial Economics, Vol. 39, pp. 219-244.

SIEMES, M. (2002): Going Private unter Beteiligung von Finanzinvestoren in Deutschland, Diss., Deutscher Universitäts-Verlag, Wiesbaden 2003.

SLOVIN, M.B./ JOHNSON, S.A./ GLASCOCK, J.L. (1992): Firm size and the information content of bank loan announcements, in: Journal of Banking and Finance, December, pp. 1057-1071.

SMITH, A. (1990): The effects of leveraged buyouts, in: Business Economics, April, pp. 19-25.

SMITH, C.W./ WARNER, J.B. (1979): On financial contracting: An analysis of bond covenants, in: Journal of Financial Economics, No. 7, pp. 117-161.

SMITH, C.W./ WATTS, R.L. (1992): The investment opportunity set and corporate financing, dividend, and compensation policies, in: Journal of Financial Economics, Vol. 32, pp. 263-292.

SOLOMON, E. (1963): The theory of financial management, New York 1963.

SPENCE, A.M. (1973): Job market signalling, in: Quarterly Journal of Economics, Vol. 87, pp. 355-374.

SUTTON, T. (2000): Corporate financial accounting and reporting, Pearson, Harlow 2000.

STEIN, J. (1992): Convertible bonds as ‚Back door' equity financing, in: Journal of Financial Economics, Vol. 32, pp. 3-21.

STIER, W. (1999): Empirische Forschungsmethoden, Springer-Verlag, Berlin / Heidelberg 1999.

STIGLITZ, J. (1969): A reexamination of the Modigliani-Miller theorem, in: American Economic Review, Vol. 59, pp. 784-793.

STIGLITZ, J. (1974): On the irrelevance of corporate financial policy, in: American Economic Review, Vol. 64, pp. 851-866.

STIGLITZ, J./ WEISS, A. (1981): Credit rationing in markets with imperfect information, in: American Economic Review, Vol. 71, 393-410.

STULZ, R. (1990): Managerial discretion and optimal financial policies, in: Journal of Financial Economics, 26, pp. 3-27.

TAGGART, R.A. (1977): A model of corporate financing decisions, in: Journal of Finance, Vol. 32, pp. 1467-1484.

TAUB, A.J. (1975): Determinants of the firm's capital structure, in: Review of Economics and Statistics, Vol. 57, pp. 410-416.

THEN BERGH, F. (1997): Leveraged Management Buyout: Konzept und agency-theoretische Analyse, Diss., Deutscher Universitäts-Verlag, Wiesbaden 1997.

THOMPSON, R.S./ WRIGHT, M./ ROBBIE, K. (1991): UK management buyouts: debt, equity, agency cost implications, in: Managerial and Decision Economics, Vol. 12, No. 1, pp. 15-26.

TICKNOR, G./ RUEDIGER, D./ KACOYANNAKIS, J. (2004): Second lien debt in LBO transactions, in: Buyouts: Vol. 17, No. 15, pp. 1-2.

TITMAN, S./ WESSELS, R. (1988): The determinants of capital structure choice, in: Journal of Finance, Vol. 43, pp. 1-19.

THIES, C.F./ KLOCK, M.S. (1992): Determinants of capital structure, in: Review of Financial Economics, Vol. 1, pp. 40-52.

TOBLER, S. (1998): Financial Engineering: Die Suche nach innovativen MBO-Finanzierungsstrukturen, in: Krebs, A./ Studer, T. (Eds.) (1998): Management Buyout - Probleme, Lösungen, Erfahrungen, Rüegger Verlag, Zürich 1998, pp. 39-57.

TOWNSEND, R. (1979): Optimal contracts and competitive markets with costly state verification, in: Journal of Economic Theory, Vol. 21, pp. 265-293.

TOY, N./ STONEHILL, A./ REMMERS, L./ WRIGHT, R./ BEEKHUISEN, T. (1974): A compara-tive international study of growth, profitability and risk as determinants of corporate debt ratios in the manufacturing sector, in: Journal of Financial and Quantitative Analysis, Vol. 9, pp. 875-886.

TUTZ, G. (2000): Die Analyse kategorialer Daten – Anwendungsorientierte Einführung in Logit-Modellierung und kategoriale Regression, Oldenbourg Verlag, München 2000.

URBAN, D. (1982): Regressionstheorie und Regressionstechnik, Teubner-Verlag, Stuttgart 1982.

URBAN, D. (1993): Logit-Analyse, Gustav Fischer, Stuttgart 1993.

VARIAN, H.R. (1994), Mikroökonomie, Oldenbourg-Verlag, München 1994.

VEALL, M.R./ ZIMMERMANN, K.F. (1996): Pseudo-R^2 measures for common limited dependent variable models, in: Journal of Economic Surveys, Vol. 10, pp. 241-260.

VEST, P. (1995): Der Verkauf von Konzernunternehmen durch Management Buyout, Diss., Gabler Verlag, Wiesbaden 1995.

VIGNOLA, L. (1974): Strategic Divestment, Amacom, New York 1974,

VOLKART, R. (1997): Finanzmanagement – Beiträge zu Theorie und Praxis (Band II), Versus, Zürich 1997.

WAGNER, K.R. (1993): Management Buy-Out. Führungskräftebeteiligung, Arbeitnehmerbeteiligung, Luchterhand, Neuwied 1993.

WALD, K. (1999): How firm characteristics affect capital structure: An international comparison, in: Journal of Financial Research, Vol. 22, No. 2, pp. 161-187.

WALL, J./ SMITH, J. (1997): Better exits, in: European Venture Capital Journal, no. 4/5, pp. 36-40.

WARNER, J. (1976): Bankruptcy costs, absolute priority and the pricing of risky debt claims, University of Chicago, July (1976).

WARWICK BUSINESS SCHOOL (1989): The performance of management buy-outs in the longer term, Coventry / London 1989.

WEITNAUER, W. (2003): Management Buy-Outs - Handbuch für Recht und Praxis, Verlag C.H. Beck, München 2003.

WELCH, I. (2002): Columbus' egg: Stock returns are the main determinants of capital structure dynamics, Working Paper, Yale.

WILLIAMSON, O.E. (1985): The economic instituition of capitalism, Free Press Publishers, New York 1985.

WILLIAMSON, O.E. (1988): Corporate finance and corporate governance, in: Journal of Finance, Vol. 43, pp. 567-591.

WILLIS, J.R./ CLARK, D.A. (1993): An introduction to mezzanine-finance, in: Chew, D.H. (Ed.) (1999): The New corporate finance: Where theory meets practice, Mc-Graw-Hill, New York 1999, pp. 243-252.

WINSHIP, C./ MARE, R.D. (1984): Regression models with ordinal variables, in: American Sociological Review, Vol. 49, pp. 512-525.

WÖHE, G. (2002): Einführung in die allgemeine Betriebswirtschaftslehre, Verlag Vahlen, München 2002.

WOHLSCHIEß, V. (1996): Unternehmensfinanzierung bei asymmetrischer Informations-verteilung, Diss., Gabler-Verlag, Wiesbaden 1996.

WOLF, B./ HILL, M./ PFAUE, M. (2003): Strukturierte Finanzierungen, Schäffer-Poeschel, Stuttgart 2003.

WRIGHT, M./ COYNE, J. (1985): Management buy-outs, Croom-Helm, London 1985.

WRIGHT, M./ HOSKISSON, R.E./ BUSENITZ, L.W. (2001): Firm rebirth: buyouts as facilitators of strategic growth and entrepreneurship, in: Academy of Management Executive, Vol. 15, 1. (February), pp. 111-125.

WRIGHT, M./ ROBBIE, K. (1996): The investor-led buyout: a new strategic option, in: Long Range Planning, vol. 29, no. 5 (October), pp. 691-702.

WRIGHT, M./ ROBBIE, K./ CHIPLIN, B./ ALBRIGHTON, M. (2000): The development of an organisational innovation: management buy-outs in the UK 1980-97, in: Business History, Vol. 42, Oct (2000), pp. 1-33.

WUJTOWICZ, R.P. (1994): Structuring acquisition financing, in: Ernst & Young (Ed.) (1994): Mergers & Acquisitions, New York, pp. 81-91.

YOGA, G. (1991): Junk bonds: How high yield securities restructured corporate America, Oxford 1991.

ZINGALES, L. (2000): In search of new foundations, in: Journal of Finance, Vol. 55, No. 4, pp. 1623-1653.

ZOMBANAKIS, A./ BALL, M. (1997): The revolution in European Funding, in: Corporate Finance, November, pp. 28-33.

ZWIEBEL, J. (1996): Dynamic capital structure under managerial entrenchment, in: American Economic Review, Vol. 86, pp. 1197-1215.

FSC
www.fsc.org
MIX
Papier | Fördert gute Waldnutzung
FSC® C083411

Kolibri 360 GmbH
Ferdinand-Jühlke-Straße 7
99095 Erfurt, Deutschland
produktsicherheit@kolibri360.de